Cameo Life Stories
Writing Guide for Everywoman

Penning Your Portrait in Words

DEBORAH HANSEN LINZER

Blue Moon Books

This book is available at special quantity discounts for bulk purchases for fund-raising and educational needs. For details, write The STORIES Center at P.O. Box 9608, Scottsdale AZ 85252-3608.

Published by Blue Moon Books

Library of Congress Cataloging-in-Publication data is available
ISBN 0-9674820-0-3

Design by Pat Kenny
Printed in the United States of America

The following people have given permission to reproduce photographs from their personal collections: Eugenia Bermudez, Janice Ballard Bond, Barbara Mark Dreyfuss, Carol Ellis, Susan Carlson Gilbert, Hazel Hansen, Donna Medoff, Gail Perry, Rev. Francine Sample, Evangeline Song

DEDICATION

To Everywoman

and to my husband, Steve Linzer,

my children, Maren Swanson, Jennie Swanson, and Scott Linzer,

and my mother, Hazel Wertz Hansen.

ACKNOWLEDGMENTS

This book and the Cameo Life Stories program have developed with the contributions of many people. I am grateful for the tradition of "Acknowledgments," which sprang from the wisdom of authors who recognized that their work was not possible without the assistance of others. I offer thanks to everyone on this list and to others unnamed, in the past and in the future, who support life story writing and women's history.

Donna Adelman, Brett Bargery, Alexandra Barnard, Jean Bateman, Betty Bergstrom, Jeanne Beckman, Eugenia Bermudez, Mary Bieberstein, Jackie Mott Brown, Rev. Linda Bunyard, Sam Campana, Betty Carlton, Michael Carman, Terrie Carter, Oscar Carter, Shaaron Cosner, Rev. Linda DeAtley, Barbara Dodge, Jan DuPlain, Barbara Mark Dreyfuss, Carol Ellis, Webb Ellis, Carole Ellison, Ann Eschinger, Laurie Eynon, Kathleen Ferraro, Gerri Fiedler, Jenny Fisher, Arlene Flecha, Doris Frace, Helen Gater, Barbara Geis, Susan Gilbert, Barbara Gledhill, Paula Goodson, Ilene Gordon, Jennie Gorrell, Lisa Graue, Donald Hansen, Hazel Wertz Hansen, Susan Hansen, Carol Harris, Eugenia Orlich Hartig, Rae Haynes, Linda Herold, Cindy Holmes, Barbara Irvine, Valerie Jackson, Carolyn Jefferson-Jenkins, Arlene Johnson, Pinna Joseph, Kathleen Kelly, Lucile Kinter, Ellie Larson, Barbara Lee, Betty Lerdall, Ken Linzer, Scott Linzer, Stephen Linzer, Ken Lucas, Leigh Lynch, Sandra Lynch, Molly MacGregor, Edith Mayo, Elaine Maimon, Meaghan McElroy, Marilyn McNeely, Joy McNulty, Mary Ann McQuinn, Joan Meacham, Donna Medoff, Stuart Medoff, Alberta Meyer, Sam Michael, Belinda Milburn, Jeanette Miller, Katherine Minott, Paul Morris, Laurie Morton, Gena Myhre, Elinor Nauen, Regina Nelms, Donna Newman, Eunice Nicks, Roselyn O'Connell, Shirley Odegaard, Carole Papalas-Sams, Marlynn Peron, Gail Perry, Annette Pomahatch, Kit Prestwood, Jan Proctor, Elizabeth Rehling, Kendra Rightsell, Trudi Rightsell, Mary Rollins, Carole Rons, Nina Sabrack, Rev. Francine Sample, Dana Campbell Saylor, Diana Schmidt, Luci Scott, Joyce Smitheran, Evangeline Song, Karen Staser, Emily Gilbert Stratford, Beth Ames Swartz, Ann Timmer, Daryl Ott Underhill, Laurie Vezineau, Laurie Voepel, Helen Walker, Juana Watson, Jay Weiss, Pat Willett, Bobbie Wold, Marsha Zandbergen, and Neil Zipkin.

Gentle Reader,

You may be asking yourself what makes this book different from all the others available on how to write your life story.

This book is part of a larger program to encourage and help you in what I consider one of the most important efforts you will ever undertake—reflecting on your life and recording your life story.

The Cameo Life Stories program (originally known as the Everywoman's Story Project) was created in 1998 *to encourage women everywhere to value their lives as important contributions to human history, to make human history more complete and more accurate by including women's life stories, and to share women's stories as invaluable sources of inspiration.*

Since then, the program has spread from mother to daughter, sister to sister and friend to friend around the United States and the world.

Welcome to a movement that is enriching women's lives, strengthening the bonds between generations, redefining the boundaries of history, enhancing society's appreciation of women's contributions and complexities, reinforcing essential respect for all individuals, and establishing a universal tradition of life story writing!

The Cameo Life Stories Program is for Everywoman

The STORIES Center (Society To Obtain and Retain International Everyone's Story) is the nonprofit organization which sponsors the Cameo Life Stories program in cooperation with the National Museum of Women's History in Washington, D.C.

Life story writing can benefit men and young people, as well as women. The STORIES Center has established a life story writing program for men. We have also created FourWords, an exciting program which encourages young people to become the authors of their life stories. That program, which includes the *Cameo Life Story Questionnaire for Young Women* and the *Life Story Questionnaire for Young Men*, is described in Chapter 10. However, our first priority is reaching women.

Those of you who need no encouragement to write your life stories might skip immediately to the practical chapters in this book which describe the effective method of life story writing I recommend. The first few chapters, though, elaborate on several very important points you might want to consider, including this cheerful warning—writing your life story can be a transformative process! Be prepared to savor all the accompanying benefits of writing your life story: greater self-respect, increased satisfaction with your life experience, a wiser perspective on the various stages of life, deeper appreciation of the aging process, and a renewed gratitude for life itself, among others.

If you are reading this book because you are having trouble writing your life story, read on. The primary purpose of the *Cameo Life Story Writing Guide for Everywoman* is to encourage you and provide you practical suggestions to help you reach your worthy goal. Your desire to write your story is wise and wonderful, whether you envision a simple essay, a meandering reminiscence, a bound pamphlet or a published book. Perhaps you have begun to translate your dream to reality, to put words on paper. Perhaps your dream is still a glimmering hope in your heart. You should write your life story, and you can. Promise yourself you won't give up.

If you know someone who doesn't think she is important enough to write her life story, please share this book with her, because its primary message is this: Every woman is important. Every woman makes history. Every woman needs to write her life story.

Create Your Own Cameo

Have you ever seen a cameo that isn't lovely? Cameos are shaped in ovals and circles, in varying sizes, in a range of materials—agate, onyx, glass, shell, silver, gold, sardonyx. They are brooches, pendants, earrings, charms. A cameo frames a woman. She may be portrayed as a profile, a bust, a full figure or in a scene, as a raised relief of carefully carved features.

Do you own a cameo? I am amazed at how many women do. When we changed the name of our life story program from Everywoman's Story to Cameo Life Stories, the news repeatedly evoked swift soft cries of delight from women. "I have a cameo my grandmother gave me when I was a little girl!" "Look, I'm wearing the cameo stickpin I got as a wedding gift." When I told my youngest daughter, Jennie, about the new name, she slipped into her bedroom and returned with the silvery black cameo my mother had just given her as her high school graduation gift.

Because it had belonged to her grandmother, Jennie's cameo was an heirloom, as so many cameos become. Tucked away in my velvet-lined jewelry box is a delicate cameo pendant in a gold filigree border, and it has hidden there for nearly forty years. One afternoon on a summer visit, when I was barely tall enough to sit up to her mahogany dining room table, Nana laid before me a few treasures she had culled from her waterfall dressing table—a rhinestone pin, a midnight blue bottle of Evening in Paris, and a small oval of a cream-skinned beauty. "It's called a cameo," my grandmother told me. That's all she said. Someday, with no other history than that—and the significance of a lifetime in my hands—it will go to my oldest daughter, Maren. Like the cameo given by my mother to Jennie, it will bear not just an image but a message from the giver, a legacy of love.

When we were struggling to find a name for our program, it was my friend Carol Ellis who first said, "Cameo," and I knew immediately it was perfect.

Cameos are for Everywoman. Your life story is a legacy, a priceless heirloom. Let it be your personal Cameo, your portrait in words. ❦

TABLE OF CONTENTS

CHAPTER ONE

How the Cameo Life Stories Program Can Help You

Are you reading this book because you have some interest in writing your life story—or because somebody who cares about you wants you to write it?

Clearly, the most important ingredient necessary for writing your memoir is the desire to do so. What other elements are necessary to successfully produce a final document that reflects all or part of your life story? Experience shows there are eight key ingredients to successful life story writing.

What we need to write our life stories

- **Motivation**
- **Self-confidence**
- **Memory**
- **Organization**
- **Time**
- **Tools and Resources**
- **Language**
- **Commitment**

No problem, right? Wrong. Unfortunately, most hopeful writers will never finish the task of writing their life story or even proceed far enough to enjoy the illuminating and edifying process of life review. It's sad. Obstacles seem to arise on every hand. Below is a partial list of the barriers people experience when facing the prospect of writing their life story. Do any of these potential obstacles ring a bell? As you read the list, check all the obstacles that apply to you.

Reasons why we don't write our life stories

☐ 1. We don't feel we are important enough.
☐ 2. We lack self-confidence in our writing skills.
☐ 3. We keep forgetting to start.
☐ 4. No one else in the family has written her life story.
☐ 5. We have too many other responsibilities.
☐ 6. We started, but it seems to be taking forever to finish.
☐ 7. We don't make time.
☐ 8. We are worried that we can't remember the past very well.
☐ 9. We don't want to think about death.
☐ 10. We're afraid our story will be boring.
☐ 11. We're reluctant to revisit unpleasant experiences in our past.
☐ 12. We don't think writing down our personal story is very important.
☐ 13. We think we are too young to begin.
☐ 14. We think it is impossible to capture a person's life story adequately in words.
☐ 15. We think that writing our life story will make us look conceited.
☐ 16. It's too much work.
☐ 17. We are disappointed in our lives.
☐ 18. We are not ready to share certain aspects of our lives with others, especially our children.
☐ 19. We have no children and think no one else will care about our life stories.
☐ 20. We compare our lives to the lives of others and think ours isn't exciting or interesting enough.
☐ 21. It seems like such a lonely undertaking.
☐ 22. We don't make a commitment to ourselves to finish.
☐ 23. We're afraid we'll go to all the trouble to write—and no one will care to read it.
☐ 24. We don't know how to use a computer.

☐ 25. We don't want to hurt our friends or members of our family.
☐ 26. Our lives are nobody else's business.
☐ 27. Our perfectionism keeps us from putting anything in writing.
☐ 28. It seems like such a big project, we're overwhelmed and don't know where to begin.

There are some obstacles over which we have no control. Illness may steal our memory or our ability to write or speak. Illiteracy may be our problem. We may be imprisoned on a desert island with no writing supplies whatsoever. (Just kidding.)

Unless you are one of those people who is unshakably convinced that writing your life story is a complete waste of time, the Cameo Life Stories project can help you. We can't write your life story for you, but we can supply the following:

- **Generous doses of encouragement to support your desire to record your story and your self-confidence to finish it.**
- **Aids and exercises to help you recall your memories.**
- **A system for organizing your story and recommendations on scheduling time.**
- **Suggestions on valuable tools and resources.**
- **Guidelines for your use of the written word.**
- **Regular exhortations about commitment!**

The first step in starting your life story is to have the desire to write it.

The second step is to read the above list of "Reasons Why We Don't Write Our life Stories" and honestly check the reasons that apply to you. Add any other reasons to the list that apply to you. Once you have identified the factors which, consciously or unconsciously, might hold you back, you can tackle and topple those obstacles.

Overcoming obstacles

The checklist above is provided to help you pinpoint problems which might prevent you from completing your life story, or from even beginning it. Recognizing hindrances at the beginning of your life story writing will save you a great deal of time and turmoil. The items you checked will indicate which of the eight key ingredients to life story writing you most need to ensure your success and which chapters in this book you will find most helpful.

1. Motivation. If you checked items 12, 14 or 26, you may lack enough desire to write your life story, which means someone may have given you this book as a gift! However, if you've read this far, please continue reading chapters 2, 3, and 4. Give us a chance to convince you that writing your life story is one of the most important goals you can achieve.

2. Self-confidence. If you checked items 1, 2, 4, 8, 10, 11, 12, 13, 15, 17, 18, 19, 20, 22, 23, 24, 25, 27 or 28, you should read chapters 1, 2, 3, 4, 6, 7 and 12. You have the desire to write your life story; you just need support and encouragement, which the Cameo Life Stories program is delighted to provide! I classify lack of self-confidence as the biggest potential pitfall you face. You will find Chapter 2, "Every Woman Is Important," and Chapter 3, "Every Woman's Life Story Is Important," most valuable to you.

I address self-confidence throughout the *Cameo Life Stories Writing Guide for Everywoman* because I find it is the issue which causes women the most concern and hesitation in writing their life stories.

3. Organization. If you checked items 3, 5, 6, 7, 13, 16, 24 or 27, you should read chapters 1, 3, 6, 7, 8 and 12. *The Cameo Life Stories Questionnaire* found in Chapter 8 will help you get started, organize your material, and complete your story in manageable increments.

Chapter 6, "Getting Ready to Write," provides details on organizing your life story. The examples of women's life stories found in Chapter 12 will give you an idea of how other women organized their memories into narrative form.

4. Memory. If you checked items 8, 9, 11 or 21, read chapters 5, 7, 9 and 12. Chapter 5 is dedicated to "Working with Your Memories."

5. Tools and Resources. If you checked items 3, 5, 6, 7, 16, 24 or 27, read chapters 1, 6, 8 and 9. The chapter primarily devoted to tools and resources is Chapter 6, "Getting Ready to Write."

6. Language. If you checked items 2, 10, 16, 27 or 28, read chapters 5, 7 and 12. Chapter 7, "Suggestions for Good Writing," deals with the use of language in your life story.

7. Commitment. If you checked items 3, 4, 5, 6, 7, 9 or 22, read chapters 6, 7, 10 and 12. Chapter 6, "Getting Ready to Write Your Life Story," is the chapter which addresses the need for commitment.

The STORIES Center sponsors Cameo Life Stories

The STORIES Center (Society To Obtain and Retain International Everyone's Story) is a nonprofit organization which was created to support the Cameo Life Stories program for women, the FourWords program for girls and boys, and a life story writing program for men.

The mission of The STORIES Center is to enhance people's self-esteem and respect for the worth of the individual by encouraging them to write and share their life stories as part of their human legacy, and to establish a universal tradition of life story writing.

STORIES refers to "everyone's" story, rather than just to "every woman's" story because The STORIES Center believes that programs similar to the Cameo Life Stories program for women should also be focused on girls, boys and men.

The primary program of The STORIES Center is Cameo Life Stories, which focuses on women in order to remedy the unfortunate omission of women from most of written history. The Cameo Life Stories program also embodies the philosophy that women and men are **equally** important contributors to human society. Many, many dedicated and enthusiastic volunteers have built Cameo Life Stories, which encourages women to write their life stories, collects women's life stories for historic archives and works with scholars and other institutions, in particular the National Museum of Women's History, to make women's life histories available for historical research.

FourWords is a program sponsored by The STORIES Center to assist young people in navigating the road to adulthood, particularly by teaching them to be the authors of their life stories. Girls are encouraged to begin writing their life stories in the *Cameo Life Stories Workbook for Young Women,* and boys are urged to start recording their life stories in the *Life Story Workbook for Young Men.* More information on these programs for youth can be found in Chapter 11.

A life story questionnaire designed specifically for men is used in the men's life story writing program.

The STORIES Center provides financial, volunteer and staff support for life story programs. Financial support of The STORIES Center comes from grants and contributions from individuals and organizations. Friends of The STORIES Center, in return for a nominal contribution, regularly receive the newsletter and additional information regarding The STORIES Center programs.

To contact The STORIES Center write to P.O. Box 9608, Scottsdale, Arizona, USA, 85252-3608, telephone 480-421-1999, facsimile 480-421-0174, or electronic mail at www.thestoriescenter.org or cameolifestories@juno.com.

Assistance offered by the Cameo Life Stories program

The Cameo Life Stories program has three primary goals:

- to encourage as many women as possible, of all ages, races, religions, nations and social and economic conditions, to recall and record their personal histories,
- to archive these individual life stories in order to provide a more complete and accurate record of the history of women, and
- to share women's stories in order to provide examples and inspiration to others to continue the work still needed to achieve dignity, freedom and safety for women and girls, so they may be full participants in creating a better world.

To achieve these goals, Cameo Life Stories provides a variety of aids which compose a coordinated system. These tools can help you write your life story.

1. *Cameo Life Stories Questionnaire*

The core of the Cameo Life Stories program is the *Cameo Life Stories Questionnaire.* Composed of 92 standardized questions, it was developed by women of all life circumstances, experiences and academic backgrounds. Although a woman may submit her life story in any written format to The STORIES Center, the *Cameo Life Stories Questionnaire* is the preferred format because it provides a guideline of questions specifically directed to women. It is also designed to gather information about women's changing roles in society, which will assist scholars researching women's issues.

Since it was first distributed at a women's award program in Phoenix, Arizona, on February 14, 1998, the *Cameo Life Stories Questionnaire* has spread throughout the United States and the world. It was originally known as the *Everywoman's Story Memory Workbook* and an explanation of the change to *Cameo Life Stories Questionnaire* is given below in the history of the Cameo Life Stories project in Chapter 11.

The *Questionnaire* was designed to reach as many women as possible, and in keeping with that commitment, the *Cameo Life Stories Questionnaire* is available as an inexpensive, independent document in English and Spanish through The STORIES Center. It is also available through computers on the Internet or World Wide Web at the website www.thestoriescenter.org.

One of the reasons the *Questionnaire* has spread so far and wide is that, as the original author, I have given permission for the text of the *Questionnaire* to be copied, as long as it is copied in its entirety. The women's committee which refined the *Questionnaire* worked hard to create questions which would include every woman's life experience, and none of us wants questions omitted which might therefore omit certain women or experiences. We welcome additions to the *Questionnaire* and encourage you to expand the existing questions as necessary to accommodate your own experience.

A critical part of the *Questionnaire* is the Cameo Release Form, which allows you to indicate what you want done with your life story and/or completed *Questionnaire* when you submit it to The STORIES Center. (The *Questionnaire* and Cameo Release Form are included in Chapter 8.)

No one is required to share her life story with anyone. We will not pressure you to provide your personal answers to the *Cameo Life Stories Questionnaire* to scholars. Even if you never answer the *Questionnaire*, though, we hope you will read through all the questions and reflect on the importance of your life and the fact that you, in your unique way, have made history.

2. *Cameo Life Stories Writing Guide for Everywoman*

This book developed out of the Cameo Life Stories program, which was created to collect and archive women's life stories in order to make human history more complete and accurate. Because the Cameo Life Stories program has reached so many women, this book reflects contributions from hundreds of women who responded to the call for their life stories.

The process of writing one's life story evokes many questions. Where do I begin? How much should I tell? Who will be reading my story? Do I need to answer all the questions in the *Cameo Life Stories Questionnaire*? Can I simply tape-record my answers? Do you want my genealogy also? What happens to my story if I submit it to The STORIES Center and the National Museum of Women's History? Can I add to my life story after I have turned it in?

I have written the *Cameo Life Stories Writing Guide for Everywoman* to answer specific questions about the Cameo Life Stories project and to answer many of the questions which arise about life story writing in general. **It is the primary handbook for the Cameo Life Stories program.** Bookstores and libraries carry other books which address life story writing, and I have included a bibliography at the back of this volume which mentions some of them.

The *Cameo Life Stories Writing Guide for Everywoman* is designed for use with all Cameo Workshops, conferences and facilitator training, as well as for individual women writing their life stories. It is also useful for women's groups, such as Cameo Circles, which are working on their life stories together. The book is intended to serve as your companion during your autobiographical adventure.

Additional copies of this book, the *Cameo Life Stories Writing Guide for Everywoman,* are available from The STORIES Center. An order form is provided at the back of the book. Books bought through The STORIES Center support efforts to collect and archive women's histories and to encourage women to write their life stories.

3. *Cameo Life Stories Workbook*

The most effective way to write your life story is to answer the questions in the *Cameo Life Stories Questionnaire* and keep your answers in a three-ring binder with all other related materials. You can create your own life story workbook, but the *Cameo Life Stories Workbook* is also available to help make your job easier. At Cameo Workshops, each participant receives a *Cameo Life Stories Workbook,* which includes the *Cameo Life Stories Questionnaire,* easy-to-understand directions on the memory road-map exercise known as "clustering," and up-to-date supporting information not found in the *Cameo Life Stories Writing Guide for Everywoman.*

4. Cameo Circles

An entire chapter of this book is devoted to Cameo Circles because they are such a valuable aspect of the Cameo Life Stories program. Cameo Circles are free and independent, and anyone can start one. These women's life story writing circles are unique to the Cameo Life Stories program. We have encouraged the formation of women's story circles from the beginning of our project. First, they provide self-discipline in working on our life stories; second, they give us the support of other women as we face the task of remembering, writing and organizing; third, the shared stories assist women in recalling their own experiences; and fourth, they offer opportunities for beginning new friendships.

Every Cameo Circle needs a facilitator, but no special training or certification is required.

Cameo Circle facilitator guidelines are included in Chapter 9 of this book. Everyone participating in a Cameo Circle is encouraged, but not required, to use the *Cameo Life Stories Writing Guide for Everywoman* and a *Cameo Life Stories Workbook*. We believe they are the most effective tools.

5. Cameo Facilitators and Facilitator Training

Cameo Facilitators are women who volunteer to facilitate their own Cameo Circles, to help start or facilitate Cameo Circles for other women or organizations, to give presentations about the Cameo Life Stories program, and to assist at Cameo Workshops or conferences.

At the request of interested volunteers, The STORIES Center has been providing facilitator training workshops which answer questions about the Cameo Life Stories program, provide guidance in organizing Cameo Circles, and give volunteers an opportunity to practice their facilitation skills. Special training is not necessary, although it is helpful. Facilitator training can be organized in any community, and Chapter 9 contains detailed guidelines for facilitators.

Women who have worked on their own life stories, who have participated in Cameo Circles, who have taught writing classes, or who are simply highly motivated might find the role of Cameo Facilitator a rewarding way to employ their experience and skills and provide a much-appreciated service to the community. There is wonderful satisfaction in helping a woman achieve a goal which is very important to her.

6. Cameo Coordinators

Serving as the primary information source in a community, state or nation is the primary role of a Cameo Coordinator. These volunteers, like Cameo Facilitators, stay well informed about the Cameo Life Stories program and assist interested individuals and organizations in using the program to write their life stories and submit them to women's history archives. Cameo Coordinators serve as designated spokeswomen for the Cameo Life Stories program.

Because the Cameo Life Stories program welcomes the participation of all women who support its goals and philosophy, it is important for Cameo Coordinators to reflect that same welcoming spirit. Cameo Coordinators seek to inform their communities as fully as possible about the desire to collect women's life stories and the need to firmly establish the life story writing tradition. They work closely with The STORIES

Center to provide news media in their areas with accurate and regular information.

One of their goals is also to help arrange Cameo Workshops and Cameo Facilitator Training as needed in their areas. Coordinators maintain regular communication with The STORIES Center and are encouraged to attend the Cameo Life Stories annual conference, which is a great way to meet other coordinators from all over the world. Cameo Coordinators are still needed in many American states and other countries. It's a very rewarding way to help make history for women!

7. Cameo Workshops

Cameo Workshops are an opportunity for women to hear the philosophy and guidelines of the Cameo Life Stories program from a trained workshop leader and to begin working on their life stories in a supportive setting. All workshop participants are provided with the *Cameo Life Stories Writing Guide for Everywoman* and the *Cameo Life Stories Workbook* by The STORIES Center. Anyone is welcome to buy the book and workbook for use in life story writing classes anywhere—colleges, church groups, senior centers, domestic violence shelters, prisons, hospice programs and so on.

Writing workshop instructors may choose to use the Cameo Life Stories program. We ask workshop leaders to use our Cameo Workshop format, which we will provide them when they contact us about running a workshop. This contact with workshop instructors is an opportunity for The STORIES Center to assess the effectiveness of the Cameo Workshops. We encourage feedback from Cameo Workshop participants to The STORIES Center.

Contact with Cameo Workshop leaders also allows The STORIES Center to help publicize upcoming Cameo Workshops through our newsletter and our national volunteer network.

8. Cameo Conferences

The first annual conference sponsored by The STORIES Center was held in Scottsdale, Arizona, in January 1999. It brought women together from around the country, inspired them to write their life stories, provided a forum for sharing, and introduced them to the tools recommended by the Cameo Life Stories program, then known as the Everywoman's Story program.

Annual conferences meet the needs of women in all stages of life story writing. Guest speakers provide motivation and detailed advice. For some, lasting friendships form in an environment which many women compare to a brief, but very BIG, Cameo Circle!

9. Newsletter

Story Times is the appropriately named newsletter for The STORIES Center. It was started by volunteer Gerri Fiedler, a retired journalism instructor. Published by The STORIES Center, *Story Times* introduces new Cameo volunteers, announces upcoming workshops and conferences, spotlights the generosity of STORIES Center donors in a "Giving Circles" column, and provides a forum for women's voices. We invite you to become a contributing writer, and we especially welcome news about Cameo Circles and the uses of the Cameo Life Stories program. Receiving letters, telephone calls and electronic mail messages from around the world is exciting, and we'd love to share the thrill with as many of you as possible.

10. Cameo Life Stories Archives

A Cameo Archives Steering Committee is charged with overseeing the archives of women's life stories collected through the Cameo Life Stories program. Representatives of The STORIES Center, the National Museum of Women's History, universities, libraries and other museums and life story repositories work together to refine the system for acknowledging life stories received, cataloguing them according to the uses permitted by their authors in the Cameo Release Forms, and sharing data with scholars. In Chapter 10, details are provided on what happens to your story when you submit it to The STORIES Center for inclusion in women's history archives.

Role of the National Museum of Women's History

From its inception, The STORIES Center has worked in cooperation with the National Museum of Women's History (NMWH). This Museum is being developed in Washington, D.C., and will be an innovative and inspirational resource for all. It will educate visitors on the roles women played in developing American society, culture, and government. NMWH will also reconstruct the past in ways that incorporate women into our nation's narrative and introduce the public to a side of the American experience usually omitted from history classes and public conversations.

NMWH has a virtual museum on the Internet, the CyberMuseum, with the first exhibit designed by Edith P. Mayo, curator emeritus of the Smithsonian Institution and curatorial consultant for NMWH. A non-profit institution, the Museum will also sponsor traveling exhibits, outreach educational programs on-site, scholarly research, educational teaching aids, and statewide lecture series throughout the country. The NMWH first vice president serves on the board of directors of The STORIES Center.

The STORIES Center has had enthusiastic support from the NMWH Board of Trustees since its inception. It is also planned that the Museum will have access to The STORIES Center's public stories for research and display in our nation's capital or perhaps in a future traveling exhibit. For further information, or to become a member of the NMWH, please contact them at their Executive Offices, 303 West Glendale Avenue, Alexandria, Virginia 22301. Visit the CyberMuseum website at www.nmwh.org or contact NMWH through electronic mail at jmeacham@nmwh.org ❦

CHAPTER TWO

Every Woman is Important

So many people hesitate to write their life stories, even though they would like to, because a nagging voice in their heads whispers very unhelpful comments. These negative messages accumulate as doubt, which leads to paralysis of the will and the wrist.

"I'm not really important enough to write my story. I haven't done anything remarkable."

"My story isn't very interesting."

"I haven't accomplished all that much in my life...."

"I am not a shining example of a good human being."

Brenda Ueland was a feisty, ebullient, creative author revered among writers for her cheerleading in the classic book *If You Want To Write*. Over and over she told her writing students of all ages that they had every right to write, that "Everybody is talented, original and has something important to say." However, in her autobiography, *Me*, she confesses that she began to write her memoirs only when asked by others. She dragged her feet when it came to writing about herself. "I find myself afraid to start," she said. "Why do I feel apologetic and hang-dog about it? I suppose it is because we are afraid of having people think we think we are important. But we are all important, I tell myself. Well, then, it is because I am afraid of making my life sound fancier, nobler, than it is. Or less so, which is just as bad."

I was raised with the notion that humility was next to godliness. My mother found it very irritating to listen to other parents brag about their children, and she made it clear to me that she had no intention of similarly irritating anyone else. She didn't brandish her kids' virtues to others, and I know she was concerned even about praising us too much directly lest we develop "a big head." I was surprised a few years ago when my friend Mary Ann Nock told me her mother had complimented her so generously when she was a child that it was a shock to grow up and discover she wasn't the world's most perfect person.

Mary Ann may be the exception in being bestowed such childhood praise and encouragement. Many of the rest of us carry around a persistent sense of inferiority or a fear of appearing too self-important. It doesn't help, either, that our society constantly bombards us with comparisons to the mythical people in advertising, who are always prettier, slimmer, smarter, richer, sexier and more popular.

Self-esteem and life story writing are related

Self-esteem is the true underlying subject of the Cameo Life Stories program and this book. Self-esteem is one of the most essential life forces we can possess. My hope is that the Cameo Life Stories program and this book will give you the encouragement to at least **begin** writing your life story–and then you will experience the next exciting encounter with self-esteem. You will find that simply the **process** of reviewing your life and examining your memories will increase your respect for the journey you have endured, the tough times you have suffered, the complicated choices you have survived, the times of happiness and contentment you were blessed with, and the wisdom you have developed in yourself.

If your self-confidence to write your life story falters, return periodically to this chapter for a dose of encouragement and a reminder that you and your story are very important. I also recommend *Revolution from Within*, by Gloria Steinem, an excellent book on the necessity of self-esteem.

Remember, **you are important because you exist. Everyone is.** Our importance is our birthright, not something we must earn. Some people may possess more money or have a higher social status or achieve greater titles than others. Some people may be born with less freedom, diminished physical capacity or fewer resources than others. But we are all important.

Each of us affects the world. Through our words, our actions, our moods and our very presence, we influence what happens around us. In addition, each of us, in a way, is the center of the universe. Only through our own senses and minds can we understand what is occurring in the external world. No one else is capable of seeing the world exactly as we do. Each of us possesses a telescope on the world which no one else has. Our view of life is unique. Our lives are important, and our individual perspectives on the world are important.

Every woman is interesting

At a gathering of women wanting to begin their life stories, Sandra Lynch mentioned that she had worked for years on her family genealogy, but it left her unsatisfied. "I have pages and pages of names and dates, but I realize they tell me absolutely nothing about the lives of my ancestors. I wish I knew more about them."

I have the same wish. Thanks to my mother's mom, Beatrice Helena Renshaw Wertz, my mother's genealogy chart is lengthy. My mother has done quite a bit of work tracking down my father's ancestry. Charts and forms preserve dates of births, deaths and marriages; places of birth, death and burial; and full names. Gathering that kind of information was a great deal of effort, but the data provides only the skimpiest skeleton on which to hang a life. Many of the bare facts provoke lingering questions which have settled in my brain like unsolved mysteries.

Why did my relatives leave Germany and Denmark in the first place? Why didn't they stay in Iowa? Why did Grandpa leave farming and become the town iceman? Why does everyone say we are related to John Hancock, but no one has traced the bloodline all the way back? I am interested in answers to the "why" questions, because those answers will reflect a string of human choices.

Each of us faces choices every day, and it is our choices that make life interesting. Making choices is the most difficult part of being human. Constantly we are looking for guidance in choosing the next step to take. We turn to books, to teachers, to friends, to God. We look to people who have had experiences similar to ours, hoping to learn from their mistakes and successes, learning to learn from their decision-making process. The most engaging fiction is that which gives us more than just a plot or a series of actions; the best novels reveal fully drawn characters, describing their feelings, foibles, finer features—**and their choices.**

Every woman's story is interesting because it is a tale of choices. Each life story is a mystery unfolding. Each personal life path is like a board game where every decision is a roll of the dice. Even when we can't fully explain "why" we have made certain choices, it is helpful to try. The "whys" are what others find most interesting.

Recognizing beauty

One more thought about being interesting. Some people equate "interesting" with beauty or personality. Many of us at some point have compared ourselves to others more attractive and found ourselves lacking. In a society saturated and dominated by visual images of attractive women and an implied standard of comparison, it's easy for most women to feel insecure about their appearance and popularity.

I've always had a love/hate relationship with my appearance. Even now, I am ambivalent about how to handle the physical signs of aging. Part of me wants to throw in the towel and let nature take its course. In the meantime, the other part of me is dying my hair and conducting an exhaustive experiment on the effects of moisturizers on crow's feet. When I worked in a corporate environment, I had to dress accordingly to be effective. I wore make-up, and I still do, because it makes me more comfortable. Foundation evens out my skin tone and a swipe of color brightens my lips and cheeks. My eyebrows and eyelashes are so fair that I look sick without eyebrow pencil or mascara. I rationalize cosmetics by agreeing with H.L. Mencken that good grooming is a courtesy to the beholder.

However, even though I am careful each morning to draw on my eyebrows so they match, I know I'm not going to win any beauty contests. Frankly, I think beauty contests should be left behind in the 20th century. Human beings will always appreciate beauty, but it is inappropriate and downright destructive to use beauty as a measure of a person's value or importance. Besides, there are so many different kinds of beauty. And who are we to judge them?

Once in the sixth grade, my Junior Girl Scout troop helped a younger Brownie troop learn camping skills, and I enjoyed the role of being older and looked up to. One of the little girls came up to me afterwards and confided, "I think Colleen Wetteland is so pretty." I was deflated. I looked over at my fellow Girl Scout (according to the Girl Scout Laws, a Girl

Scout is actually a sister to every other Girl Scout) and felt envious of Colleen. I was sort of thinking I was the prettiest girl in my troop. I tried to see her as the little Brownie had seen her. Colleen's hair was slightly darker and wispier than my thick, straw-colored hair; she was tall; she had warm brown eyes; and I noticed for the first time how her nose curved at the end.

That's when I began to look for the beauty in everyone. I realized that eyes other than the eyes in my mirror were judging attractiveness, and I didn't want to be the dolt who couldn't see what others were seeing, what others were appreciating.

LBJs—Little Brown Jobs

The point here is that beauty is interesting, and everyone is beautiful in some way. I can always count on my mother to remind me of that. I was rhapsodizing one day to her about the exciting wild birds I had recently added to my "life list," a list that many birders keep of the various species they have identified in nature. On a bird walk with the Audubon Society in Prescott, Arizona, I had spotted an Indigo Bunting, and I described to her its striking color and its rarity. Mom surprised me by saying, "Sparrows are just as important." I detected a criticism and defended myself—"But there are so many sparrows and they're all BROWN."

"Just because they're brown doesn't mean they aren't pretty," she replied. "I like brown."

Well, she was right, of course. If you aren't a birder, let me tell you that there are dozens of different kinds of sparrows (and finches of similar size and coloring), and most bird lovers on a birding excursion use the shorthand LBJ to dismiss the birds they can't identify. Since that conversation with my mother, defender of sparrows, I have faced a serious challenge trying to see those little brown birds well enough to differentiate and identify them. I've spent hours staring at my bird feeder scrutinizing crowns, wings, tails and covert parts. I have seen shades and tints and stripes and swipes of brown I had never seen before. By seeing through my mother's eyes, I learned to see beauty and interest—and importance—where I had not seen them before.

Shining the Spotlight

In my world literature class at Augustana College in Sioux Falls, South Dakota, Dr. Art Huseboe introduced me to Robert Browning's poem "Fra Lippo Lippi." Father Lippi didn't fit the role of priest very well. An orphan rescued from the streets by Catholic monks and raised for the priesthood, Fra Lippi disappointed the expectations of his calling. He was finally allowed to use his true talents as an artist. Robert Browning used the story of Fra Lippi to explain his theory of art—beauty may be in the eye of the beholder, but first the eye must behold.

Fra Lippi says,

> *We're made so that we love*
> *First when we see them painted, things we have passed*
> *Perhaps a hundred times nor cared to see;*
> *And so they are better, painted—better to us*
> *Which is the same thing. Art was given for that;*
> *God uses us to help each other so...*

He surveyed the bounty of beauty that surrounds everyone, selected one treasure, and held it up for the world to admire.

Think of your physical self. Think of your physical surroundings. How many things have you passed over a hundred times without focus or admiration? On which treasures can you shine the spotlight of your attention and your words? What beauties can you pen or paint for others to behold?

We do not have to earn our importance with work

I learned an overdue lesson from my husband a few years ago. We were spending the weekend at our small cabin in the Bradshaw Mountains north of Phoenix. Sitting on the back porch with morning coffee, we watched the food-gathering frenzy of birds and squirrels. "Reminds me of a hotel at check-out time," said Steve. With both of us relaxed and postponing other responsibilities, I decided to bring up an issue that was troubling me and affecting our relationship.

I had quit working full time "outside the home" when Steve and I married three years earlier. No longer did I bring home a paycheck or hold an executive position or dress up and go off to work every day. Instead, I had plunged into my work at home—blending our two families, remodeling our house, serving as a Brownie Girl Scout leader, getting involved in politics and other fulfilling activities. But without my former business title and paycheck, I was feeling insignificant.

Before our marriage, I was a single mom supporting my two daughters and making the mortgage payments myself, sometimes just barely. With Steve providing our entire income, I had begun to feel that I wasn't "pulling my weight," so to speak, and was silently worrying that it was unfair for me to be staying home, while Steve was carrying the burden of running his own firm and earning a living for all of us. Maybe I feared that our division of labor was unequal and that he was beginning to resent that I didn't contribute financially. Maybe I feared I was no longer the woman he married.

My coffee got cooler and cooler as I struggled with the words to explain my concern and confusion. When I finished, Steve said, "Do you really think I love you because of your title or your paycheck? I love you because you are you."

I was stunned. It's embarrassing to admit. I—who had been taught from childhood that everyone is important—had begun to forget that I was important, too, not because I earned the right to be considered important, but simply because I was a human being.

Sometimes we only feel important when we feel loved. Steve was assuring me that I was loved. Even if I were to lose his love, though, I would still be important. Love waxes and wanes in all our lives. Some of us may experience more love than others. We all know how destructive it can be for children not to have adequate doses of love. Unfortunately, not all children deprived of love in their young lives are able to discover the great essential gift they are bestowed by the universe at birth—their intrinsic worth. Even those of us with loving parents and nurturing communities may have trouble accepting, internalizing, that birthright—our natural importance.

Irons in the Fire

I come from a family with a very strong "work ethic," as it is sometimes called. The value of work and of working hard dominated our family life. With a wife and five daughters to support, my dad never missed a day's work—a remarkable feat for someone in the construction industry. He was often away from home for two weeks at a time, living in inexpensive motels in small towns that needed his crew's plastering skills. The family budget only allowed him one phone call home each week, on Wednesday nights.

My mom went back to work as a bookkeeper when my youngest sister, Jane Ann, was six years old, but for the first 20 years of her marriage, she worked at home raising five daughters. All of us were expected to do our part in managing the work load. We made our beds, cleaned our rooms, hung diapers on the outside clothesline, folded clothes, washed and dried and put away the dishes (often with much squabbling), scrubbed toilets and bathtubs, and so on. On Saturday mornings, we couldn't watch cartoons on television until our chores were done.

Mom taught us to be thorough and efficient housecleaners. We learned at an early age to keep moving, keep busy. Items to go upstairs or downstairs accumulated on the steps, and Mom would make sure we didn't go either way without carrying something. All five of us were Girl Scouts and Mom was a troop leader, so "kaper charts" with rotating chore assignments began to appear on the side of the refrigerator. Scouting taught us additional organizational skills.

Over time I acquired the unconscious belief that the more work I accomplished, the more useful I was, and the more useful I was, the more important I was. A person can get carried away with that notion. I pushed myself to do two things at once, then three. Combined with an abundance of energy, interests and idealism, my work expanded to fill my waking hours. Mom began to complain that I was never home and that I had "too many irons in the fire."

That pattern continued into my adult life. After many years at a breakneck pace, I ended up in the hospital with debilitating headaches —the ravage of stress. The message my body abruptly delivered to me was that I didn't need to be useful to be valuable. My body was valuable because it was my body. My life was valuable because it was my life. When my body—the working machine—was out of commission, no one appeared to chastise me and say, "Tsk, tsk. Your output is unacceptable. You're not doing enough to justify your existence. You are fired as a human being."

For years I have struggled to quell my drive to work all the time. Among other things, I frequently read from Ann Wilson Schaef's book *Meditations for Women Who Do Too Much.* I remind myself all the time that I don't have to prove to anyone that I am a valuable person. I am important because I live. The French philosopher Descartes expressed his philosophy as "I think, therefore I am." I prefer to say, "I am, therefore I am important."

Goodness and importance are two different things

The "bibles" of every religion and prophets of every age preach that human beings are equally important. Many of them also elaborate on the differences between people, defining what is good behavior and what is not.

Being important and being good or bad are separate issues. Of course the term "good" is relative. Often we become better people after we have been "bad." We may be good and bad in the same day. We may be a better person in different periods of our lives.

The Cameo Life Stories project was not created to collect only the stories of good people or even of people who are extraordinarily good. The stories of good people are wonderfully valuable to share with others for the inspiration they impart. However, the habit of judging ourselves and our goodness in relation to others or in relation to a particular standard is not a helpful habit to bring to the writing of your life story. The writing process may remind you of traits or actions you are not proud of, but it can also help you gain a healthy perspective on those negative features by reminding you they are an important part of your journey and, like everything else, provender for wisdom.

You make history

Every woman makes history, no matter who she is or what she does.

We make history with every choice we make. That's one of the big reasons why we are so important, and why our life stories are so important. We have been busy influencing the way the world turns. It can be intimidating to consider the repercussion our choices can have on our own lives and on the lives of generations yet unborn. At the fork in our path, do we move to Arizona or stay in our hometown? Do we accept a marriage proposal at 18 or decide to go off to college first? Do we get a mammogram we've scheduled or skip the appointment this year?

When I see the schisms and misunderstandings that have grown between women, I am saddened by how much energy we waste judging one another's life decisions. No one's decisions are easy or perfect. Complicating women's life choices on the cusp of the 21st century is the incredibly rapid change that has occurred in women's roles—in the law, in society's expectations of women, and in society's valuation of women.

Each of us is making history in her own way, and if we learn to value our individual ways of being, perhaps we can learn to mistrust faddish social judgments.

Your written life story is a celebration of your life, not a judgment of how you spent it. I find many homemakers sounding apologetic about their path, even women in their 70's who came of age when homemaking was the primary expectation of women in America. Wider options have opened for women, but no one should denigrate women who have chosen traditional women's roles.

Writing your memoirs is making history

When I give Cameo Workshops, I sometimes like to begin by taking photographs of the audience, as if it were a historic moment. Because it is. Women attending the Cameo Workshop could have spent the day caring for an ill child or meeting with their employees or planning the next space flight. They could have painted their toenails or stayed in bed watching reruns on television. Attending the workshop was a choice.

Every choice is an exercise in making history. Coming to a workshop isn't necessarily better than any other choice, but it is a change of course and often a very exciting one.

When we begin thinking of ourselves as history-makers, it becomes a little easier to write our life stories. We see that we have been shaping our personal histories, and the histories of those around us, every day, in both positive and negative ways. Some days, making history may be as simple as catching up with the laundry, sending a belated birthday card to a friend, buying a larger pair of shoes, yelling at the kids, losing our temper in traffic, spreading an unfounded rumor, or saying "thanks" to the clerk at the grocery store. Other days, making history may be as momentous as sending a large check to a worthy charity, being nominated for an Academy Award, starting graduate school, staying sober for one more day, leaving an abusive husband, taking a pregnancy test, giving your granddaughter a cameo, or beginning to write down the story of your history-making life.

Being a history-maker is an exciting job. Never a dull moment. We are the authors of our lives, writing another chapter each day. That's one of the reasons that the life review process is so highly effective in restoring a positive attitude. Reminiscence is called reminiscence **therapy** partly because it reminds us of the control we can still exert on our life circumstances.

Even the writing of our life story is one way of "making history," because it is a reflection of how we choose to use our gift of time. When we begin writing, we open a very special chapter in our book of life.

Although the Cameo Life Stories project hopes to increase significantly the number of people who write their memoirs, the current percentage of those who do is very low. That fact alone makes life story writing an accomplishment to document. And when we finish writing, we have every reason to boast about it in our autobiographies. **Don't forget to mention in your memoir that you made history by writing your life story!** ❦

CHAPTER THREE

Every Woman's Life Story is Important

"My memories and yours are unique. There is nothing like them in the world. Each set is a work of neurological art. If I owned a Picasso, I would not leave it out in the rain. The memories we carry should be treated with as much respect. We should find somewhere safe to put our memories, and the safest place is not in our own vessel, because it will inevitably break.

"The way to preserve our memories is to make gifts of them."

Richard Louv, *The Web of Life*

The Cameo Life Stories program asks every woman to record a summary of her life story and then share it with The STORIES Center archives and the National Museum of Women's History. How can a project that sounds so simple be so valuable and such a powerful influence on present and future society?

Your story is important to history

The pioneering cultural anthropologist Ruth Benedict has said, "no civilization has in it any element which in the last analysis is not the contribution of an individual."

When I say that every woman (and every man) makes history, it's true. It's just a different way of looking at history. Many of us think one has to be Eleanor Roosevelt, Florence Nightingale, Harriet Tubman or Mary Queen of Scots to make history. Some of us grew up thinking only men could make history. Unfortunately, historians of the past have had a very limited notion of which people and which events qualified for the history books.

In her book *Beyond Power,* Marilyn French makes the convincing point that most historians in the past (primarily men) have recorded the human paths of **power**—the activities of powerful tribes, nations, institutions, and individual men. In doing so, they left out the larger, more accurate picture of human life revealed in families, social life and the lives of individual men and women who didn't wield great power. Sadly, people exerting "power over" others usually succeed in directing the lives of other more peaceful, less "power hungry" people. We find ourselves in a world where power is often considered the ultimate plum, and history reflects that bias.

However, a revolution has occurred in academia over the past several decades. Historian John Clive writes about the craft of writing history, called historiography. In *Not By Fact Alone* he says, "More than ever, historians of all periods interest themselves not only in how ordinary people lived in the past, but also in how they felt and thought about the world and themselves. The latest research techniques, ranging from statistics to oral history, are used...in the service of this curiosity."

The well-known historian Barbara Tuchman writes about the increasing acceptance of biography in the field of historiography. While the purpose of modern history is to paint a broad picture of nations, ages and public life, Tuchman expresses the value of the individual life as a window on the larger world in her book, *Practicing History.*

Writing about "the new autobiography" in her book *Your Life As Story,* Tristine Rainier says, "There has been a trend toward increasing democratization of the genre through the centuries, particularly in the United States and especially since the last half of the nineteenth century....It has served as a form of revolution when seized by those whose lives and selves would otherwise be invisible...all those who feel the need to bear witness to their truth."

Sara M. Evans, in *Born for Liberty: A History of Women in America,* comments on the recent trend in historiography to include the voices of populations formerly ignored—blacks, factory workers, immigrants, and women. In an article in the *The New York Times Book Review*, April 25, 1993, Jill Johnson described this trend as "plebian autobiography."

Including Everywoman and Everyman

I prefer to use the words Everywoman and Everyman instead of "ordinary people."

The term Everyman derives from the most famous of the Morality Plays. Troupes of actors would travel from city to city and village to village providing lesson-laden entertainment to people of the Middle Ages. Everyman refers both to a representative individual and to all individuals, and the term Everywoman fulfills the same purpose.

Even the plot of the *Everyman* play, written around 1500 C.E., is appropriately related to life story writing. The main character, Everyman, receives a summons from Death, and his friends Fellowship, Kindred, Worldly Goods, Beauty, and others decline to accompany him to Death. Only Good Deeds is faithful to him, although he has so neglected Good Deeds that Knowledge and Confession must give Good Deeds renewed strength so that he can escort Everyman to his grave. Roughly translated from Old English, the subtitle of the play is "a treatise how the high father of heaven sendeth Death to summon every creature to come and give account of their lives in this world."

Everywoman seems a particularly good word to use in discussing the importance of all women, the significance of their personal "account of their lives in this world," and the necessity of including them in historical accounts of human activity.

Women's history is being explored and written as never before because courageous, patient scholars persisted in inserting the lives of women in the human record. Women's history is now being taught to an ever-increasing number of students, not just in women's studies courses but in most fields of study; not just in colleges, but in elementary, middle and high schools. It is a case of long-overdue justice, and it makes undeniable sense. The trend will continue to grow, more books will be published, and more information about women's history will be shared with the general public.

There are several aspects of women's history, however, which need the help of every woman and of the Cameo Life Stories program: 1) collecting stories from women with knowledge of a vanishing way of life; 2) collecting information on the ways individual women have transformed society to make way for themselves and other women; 3) collecting information on the ways women opened their minds and hearts to personal and social change; and 4) establishing adequate forms and forums through which women can communicate their experience.

Helping historians in the future

A great deal of history is being written and published now while some of its topics are not long past and even while its human subjects are still alive. The Cameo Life Stories project can provide information to help in writing the history of our immediate past and present.

On the other hand, many topics and human subjects of historic interest do not get serious attention until a lengthy period of time has passed, sometimes centuries. Trends in historiography may change. Society's interest in a particular issue may rise or fall. It may take time for the right interpreter, with appropriate enthusiasm and resources, to appear. That is why historians are carefully trained to research original source documents. They very often must work like detectives to uncover multiple clues which will finally create a complete picture and supply missing answers.

Historians learn to work with what they can find—letters; diaries; birth, marriage and death certificates; newspaper articles; invoices; memoirs; and so on. It can be a difficult and sometimes discouraging process. It's also a great deal of work. A historian writing a biography, for example, must assemble a variety of puzzle pieces and do quite a bit of well-educated guesswork about issues that may not be explicitly revealed in available documents. Many clues, or sources of information, are lost or destroyed over the years.

Sometimes historians, just like the rest of us, don't know what they want to know until the person they could ask is dead. Carolyn Heilbrun mentions in her book *Writing a Woman's Life* that many of us don't develop an interest in our heritage and biological roots until middle age, when many of the relatives who could enlighten us have slipped beyond our reach.

Giving your life story to The STORIES Center archives is a gift to the future. Your story is an invaluable time capsule, a glimpse into a unique woman's heart and mind. Your life story will be helpful not just as a source document to future scholars, but as a precious letter to women of the future looking for answers about what it means to be a woman and a human being.

Your story is important to relatives and friends

It is reassuring to me to know that when I entrust my story to The STORIES Center archives, it will be catalogued and preserved for future generations of my own family. Although I plan to pass my life story on to my daughters, with instructions to pass it on to the next generation, I cannot ensure against fire, loss, theft, neglect, or bulldozers. I've heard too many horror stories of grandchildren dumping their deceased relative's personal effects by the truckload. My dear friend Shirley Odegaard lost all her personal records of the 1970s Arizona struggle for the Equal Rights Amendment in a house fire.

A bulldozer almost took the last tangible reminder of my great, great, great, great grandmother. In August 1978, I accompanied my dad and my mom and her two sisters, Joyce Brugman and Mary Lou Kelly, to a family reunion in Henry, Illinois. The Wertz family was gathering, and I was going to meet a branch of kin I was completely unfamiliar with. My mom and Aunt Joyce and Aunt Mary Lou have acquired their mother's interest in genealogy, so they were excited about the trip for several reasons—they could visit the Aunt Gladys they remembered with affection from their childhood, they could meet distant relatives who might provide them with genealogical tidbits, and they could visit for the first time the graves of Illinois relations.

So many American families have been separated by great distances that the tradition of visiting family graves has declined, but it remains an important ritual in my family—and to me. Maybe that 1978 trip made a lasting impression on me.

Between visits to Aunt Gladys and huge potluck meals at a local church, our South Dakota delegation drove the uncrowded back roads north of Peoria searching for tiny, yet carefully mowed, cemeteries. Sometimes we were lucky to arrive when the caretaker was there, perhaps a nearby retired farmer with a tractor and a mower, who could point us toward the headstone we sought. Otherwise, we wandered through the orderly rows, careful not to step on the grass in front of each headstone, searching for the names that appeared on the genealogy sheets we clutched.

When we found the patiently waiting relative, we checked the gravestone to make sure our records were accurate, drew a sketch of the gravestone's location in the cemetery, then took a picture of the inscription, usually with one of us kneeling beside it. We said no prayers, but our visit alone held a certain reverence. My elders explained to me how the person was related and what they knew of him or her, and they fussed over the plot if any weeds had crept in. It was the way they paid their respects.

Mom had vivid memories of playing on the nearby family farm as a little girl and of her Uncle Keith showing her a tiny family burial ground. She was determined to see it again, but relatives at the reunion seemed hazy about its location, saying "Now that you mention it, I know it's out there somewhere in the woods." Through Mom's persistence, we finally found a young girl on a neighboring farm to show us where it was. "I'm afraid there may be some poison ivy up there," she warned us.

The six of us squeezed into the blue Oldsmobile and followed directions slowly down a gravel road. The road was under construction, and we all felt a stab of dismay when the little girl pointed at our destination. The hill we needed to climb loomed on our right, thick with ancient oaks and underbrush, but the hillside before us had been carved and laid bare by a bulldozer. We hiked as fast as we could, Mom trying to retrieve as much as she could from her memory. "I think there are three graves, all by themselves. Maybe a fence around them."

I wondered, why weren't they in a regular cemetery? Did they allow people to be buried on their own property back then? How far back **was** "back then"? How did my relatives end up with a farm in such beautiful country, high on a rolling bluff, with the Illinois River carved on the horizon? Why had the rest of "us" left for Iowa, then South Dakota? Did anybody ever visit these graves? What if the bulldozer had destroyed the tiny plot of sacred ground? Could poison ivy penetrate cotton slacks?

Message in the poison ivy

We caught our breath at the breast of the hill, then waded into the glossy green leaves. There they were—two headstones, one fallen and one slumped but standing. In the weathered sandstone grave marker on the right was incised "Maria Conarro, beloved wife of Charles. Died April 1841."

I couldn't believe it. I couldn't quite grasp that I was related to anyone who had died so long ago. The Civil War had ended in 1865. Ancient history. And the name Maria. Where did that come from? It sounded Italian, not German or Scandinavian. As a newlywed, I was touched by the words "beloved wife." I'd seen the words on many graves, but they seemed to hover, almost spoken, between the two of them there, all alone, together.

As we peered over the edge of the towering hill, which plunged in exposed mustard clay and rock to the road, we fretted among us about the construction work. We wondered about moving the headstones out of harm's way. The hidden graveyard had been protected for more than 100 years, but I was worried. We couldn't weed the ivy, but we took pictures. Afterwards, we stopped at the old family farmhouse and told the unrelated family living there to warn the heavy equipment operators.

My two daughters have heard my story of "meeting" great, great, great, great grandmother Maria. What I can't explain to them is the unique sadness of knowing nothing more about her than the few words surviving in a stand of oak. Among the hundreds of descendants she helped create, there must be at least a daguerreotype of her. Or is there? Old letters in a trunk? A wrinkled wedding certificate in some antique mall?

I cannot know her, or touch her, nor she me. What's the use of wanting to know about someone gone so very long ago? The stone marker introduced me to Maria and left me caring about her. It also left me caring about my other grandpas and grandmas and relatives still alive. On the long car trip home, my mother and my aunts reminisced about their lives together and apart, and I copied their words in a hand-sized spiral notebook. I need to write up my notes and send them to The STORIES Center archives, so the great, great, great, great grandchildren can get to know the ladies who paid respect to Maria Conarro.

The mother's voice: What are we telling our daughters and our sons?

One evening I was home from my first year in college and a rare opportunity presented itself—my mom, the night owl, sat at the dining room table with a cup of coffee resting on the red terry tablecloth, wearing a nightgown faded from a thousand washings.

My mom and I seldom had any time alone together. She was raising five girls and working full time as a bookkeeper. I'd been a typical teenager, wrapped up in myself, my friends, and my activities. In fact, one of our few occasions to talk alone had been about five years earlier, when Mom celebrated Mother's Day by having a special visit with each one of us individually in her bedroom.

Maybe it was the memory of her earlier invitation to speak openly with her in private that gave me the courage to broach a subject I'd wanted to ask her about. At some point in the past year I had finally taken a closer look at my birth date—then at my parent's wedding date. June 6 to January 10. Seven months. Not nine.

I went ahead and asked, "Mom, I know I weighed only five pounds when I was born, but was it because I was premature?"

She started to cry. I'd never seen her do that. She was always the stoic one.

"When your dad and I got married everyone in the family knew I was pregnant. It was humiliating. But over the years I searched through the family genealogies and counted the days between the marriage dates and birth dates of the first born children, and I realized I wasn't the only one."

That incident transformed my relationship with my mom. For the first time, she became a human being to me. It was so liberating to realize she wasn't perfect, because if she wasn't perfect and was still so strong and responsible and respected, then I could be imperfect, too, and still be OK.

In her book *The Mother's Voice*, Kathy Weingarten makes the very important point that women become so accustomed to shaping the version of themselves they present to their children, they sometimes leave out vitally valuable information.

We all have to "edit" ourselves. Because it is too risky to reveal our vulnerabilities in the workplace, we prepare an employee version of ourselves for the job that is responsible, competent and appropriately dressed. When we are meeting our boyfriend's parents for the first time, we carefully compose ourselves inside and outside for the presentation. Good mothers and fathers put great thought and effort into their roles as models for their children. In all this self-editing, we often forget that we need to add rather than subtract; we forget there are things we need to say instead of avoid saying.

Human beings yearn for information about other human beings and how they handle the difficulties they face. Mothers know they must provide information about life to their children when they are best able to use that information. Let's not forget that our children need to learn about us, as well—that we are human beings, capable of mistakes and equally capable of learning from them. Let's not wait too long to begin sharing with our daughters, granddaughters, sons and grandsons what it means to be a woman and a maturing person.

Share Your Story With Friends

Cameo Life Stories has brought wonderful new friends into my life. In a program that encourages sharing, making friends comes naturally. In my discussion of Cameo Circles in Chapter 9, I mention that Cameo Circle members usually make friends of one another. That's because your life story is a gift. The simple giving of that gift evokes appreciation. Your story is a source of knowledge, understanding and connection. The more we share, the better we get to know each other.

Two of the women who have become active as volunteers, Gerri Fiedler and Vangie Song, have been friends for nearly 20 years. When Gerri read Vangie's life story, she says she was shocked at how much she learned about her long-time friend. Vangie agrees that sharing her life story was a pivotal event in their relationship. "It added a whole new dynamic to our friendship. In all these years we have never really talked about our pasts, and yet my past is a big part of who I am." Now she is pushing Gerri to get her life story written!

Your story is important to contemporary society

Anita Hill was a keynote speaker at the 1999 national training conference of Federally Employed Women (FEW), which attracts thousands of the one million women who work for the federal government. Anita Hill made history in 1991 when she challenged the suitability of Clarence Thomas for the United States Supreme Court, contending that he had engaged in sexual harassment. Her recent book *Speaking Truth to Power* is a memoir of that pivotal episode in American history.

Anita Hill's actions exemplify the power of women speaking out about their lives. "I found my voice, and I won't lose it again," she said in her FEW address. "I wasn't the only one who found her voice. Thousands of other women found their voices, too. Silence is not our protection. Society will only learn and heal if our voices are heard," she said.

"Let everyone hear you. Let them know who you are. You must be willing to share your stories."

Women's Stories Inspire Other Women

One of the most popular literary genres at present is the memoir, and a spate of women's autobiographical stories is being published and read. Reading in general is experiencing a resurgence in the United States, and book clubs, composed primarily of women, are springing up everywhere. Women are the largest segment of the book-buying public, and many women are demonstrating their fascination with the stories of women's lives.

An inspiring collection of short, true stories from women's lives is *Every Woman Has a Story* by Daryl Ott Underhill. Check the Suggested Reading List at the back of this book.

Sharing our life stories with other women is a helpful and satisfying process, as many of us have learned in Cameo Circles. At every Cameo Workshop there are women shocked to discover that others are sincerely curious about why they married or didn't, why they had children or didn't, why they returned to school or didn't and so on. Relating tales from our lives in Cameo Circles or Workshops helps jog our own memories, but also reassures many women that they are not alone, that others have suffered and overcome similar adversities.

Luminaries—Women Who Light the Way

And what about the stories of women who have pushed for change? People increasingly look at women's history and ask, "How have women's lives changed so drastically?" The answers to that question lie in the life stories of the women who worked on behalf of women and their communities. Who started day care centers for children of working mothers? Who sued to end sex-segregated Help Wanted ads in the newspapers? Who quit putting up with sexual harassment on the job? Who helped raise money for women political candidates? Who objected to the lack of sports teams for girls? Who fought to end discrimination against women by insurance companies? Who started shelters for battered women and programs to stop child abuse?

We find inspiration, not just in the biographies of famous women, but in the actions of "ordinary" women who demonstrate compassion, courage and perseverance in their activism. The goal of the Cameo Life Stories program is to collect the stories of these contemporary activists now, before it is too late. Many of the women working for change are so busy making the world a better place that they don't take the time to write the story of their part in social change. It never occurs to some of them to write down what they have accomplished.

Women who work for change are luminaries in the full sense of the word. They shed light on a path for other women to follow; they lift the shroud from the dark corners of inequality. Their accomplishments, no matter how small, are stellar. They are shining examples of the power of women sharing their experiences and using their voices to shape a better world.

The *Cameo Life Stories Questionnaire* specifically encourages women to record the efforts they have made to improve their own lives, the lives of other women and girls, and the larger community. Please use these questions as an opportunity to reflect on your own contributions to a better world.

No one will judge the relative importance of your contributions. What seems insignificant to one woman may be a tremendous act of courage for another. Gloria Steinem, one of the most influential women activists of the 20th century, refers to women's efforts at change as "outrageous acts and everyday rebellions." Steinem, who has concentrated her efforts primarily on helping women, says progress may be as simple as "telling him to pick up his own socks."

Think about your own moments of epiphany, courage, strength and action. An activist is "a person who favors intensified activities" and the word is not a pejorative term but a self-description to be proud of. However, if you prefer, think of yourself as a luminary or as a "luminaria." In the Southwest we have adopted the Mexican holiday custom of lining our walkways with luminarias, small brown-paper bags lit from within by a candle nestled in sand.

Buddha said, "Make of yourself a light." When have you shed light on another's dark path? Illuminated an injustice? Opened a window in your own mind and heart?

The questions in Chapter 8 will help you think in more specific terms about your personal examples of luminosity. Did you persevere against the odds to send your daughters, not just your sons, to college? Have you ever taken a stand at a parent-teacher association meeting? When did you object to demeaning banter about women in the office? When did you finally tell the emergency room doctor that you didn't get your black eye from bumping into a door?

At the end of the *Cameo Life Stories Questionnaire* in Chapter 8 there is a checklist titled "I Can Make History." It provides a place for you to record the progress you make in writing your life story. It also suggests additional steps you can take to improve the world by sharing your story and women's history in general. Just carrying out any of the suggestions on the checklist makes you a luminary!

Women's Organizations Change the World

Women also find inspiration in the work of women's organizations—groups composed of women or dedicated to women's concerns. All of them have made significant contributions to society, as well as to individual women and girls. Society needs to be reminded of their invaluable role, too.

The Cameo Life Stories program is urging these organizations to provide women's history archives with a record of their efforts. We can all find motivation in the example of such groups as the General Federation of Women's Clubs, Business and Professional Women, The League of Women Voters, the American Association of University Women, Girl Scouts, Camp Fire Boys and Girls, United Methodist Women, Church Women United, National Council of Jewish Women, the National Organization for Women, the Parent Teacher Organization, the Parent Teacher Association, and many, many others.

The STORIES Center and the National Museum of Women's History are eager to preserve the activist history of women's organizations, on the local, state and national level. Individual women writing their life stories should remember to record their involvement in organizations. As Nina Sabrack, president of the League of Women Voters of Metropolitan Phoenix, explains it to League members, "When you write your story, you are writing the story of League." Many women's organizations are organizing Cameo Circles and are challenging their members to write their life stories to preserve the history of their members and of their organization.

Women's Stories Inspire Social Changes

Do you remember when there were no rape crisis centers—anywhere? Do you remember when there was no such thing as "battered women's shelters," safe houses for victims of domestic violence? Were those the good old days, when problems of rape and wife beating didn't exist? Of course not. Those problems existed in the old days. They were probably worse because women had no where to turn for help. Because abuses were ignored and kept under wraps, society did not work to check the abuses and public opinion did not exert pressure on men to change their behavior toward women.

In the old days, it was dangerous for women to discuss their victimization because they had few protections from violence or from the judgments of society. Society does not like to be bothered with troublemakers, and historically it responds by blaming victims themselves for their troubles. In the case of women, to whom did they make their appeals for help? To other women with the power to help them? Not in the old days. There **were** no women in power. Almost everyone in authority was a man—legislators who could change laws, mayors who could use the bully pulpit to influence public opinion, police who could arrest violators, ministers who could preach to their congregations.

It took incredible courage for women to begin to speak up and tell their stories, but it was the only way they could change their lives, and the lives of other women, for the better. For 72 years they spoke out just to acquire the right to vote.

The Cameo Life Stories program asks you to write your story and submit it to the archives. It doesn't ask you to proclaim your story from the housetops.

However, our shared stories can often help educate others about the present as well as the past, and they can suggest ways that society might improve its ability to respond to the problems of women and children. In some communities, the Cameo Life Stories program has generated publicity which resulted in local newspapers running stories on women's lives. Newspaper articles have helped spark interest in life story writing, but they have also helped communities focus on human needs which require attention.

Your Story Can Enlighten Men

Our stories, when shared, can be the catalyst to enlighten men who might otherwise remain in the dark about women's needs in general—and our personal needs in particular. Being honest with the men in our lives about who we are shows respect for ourselves—and for them. Many men are raised without sisters. Many never get to know their mothers as people. All men are exposed to conflicting images of womanhood in contemporary life. They will never learn the truth about real women in general and about the women in their lives unless we tell them the truth.

Since boys grow up to be men, it is also important that boys learn to respect women and to see their capabilities realistically. Unless we tell them the truth about what it means to be a woman, they will receive a steady diet of misinformation and confusing messages from other sources, especially the media. Our society is pervaded by advertising, which continues to sexualize and stereotype women. Pornography, which treats women as objects and simply sexual beings, is still rampant in most cultures.

Molly MacGregor, executive director of the National Women's History Project, provides a startling example of the need to educate boys. In a survey a few years ago American boys were asked, " Do you think it's bad to treat females as less important than males?" They replied, "Only for girls."

Of course, it's not just bad for girls, it is bad for the boys and the men they will become. Boys, as well as men, need to hear from women themselves that women are just as important as men, and that any other notion is just a bad habit that society is finally smart enough to abolish.

Your story is important to you

Writing our life stories is good for us! It is therapeutic, it is transformative, and it offers the well-earned pride of accomplishment.

Life Review Therapy for Seniors

First of all, writing life stories is actually therapeutic. It was my friend Dr. Georgia Hall, a specialist in gerontology, who first called my attention to the benefits of life story writing for the elderly. She referred to it as "reminiscence therapy" or "life review therapy" and directed me to the work of Robert Butler. In his book *Aging and Mental Health*, Butler cites a long list of studies which confirm the therapeutic benefits and satisfaction for the older person of life story writing. As he says himself, "A summation of one's life work by some means is useful. The goals and consequences of these steps include a re-examination of one's life that may result in expiation of guilt, the resolution of intrapsychic conflicts, the reconciliation of family relationships, the transmission of knowledge and values to those who follow, and the renewal of ideals of citizenship and the responsibility for creating a meaningful life."

Rose Riesgraf is a registered nurse who works with the elderly and teaches at the community college in Red Wing, Minnesota. As she says, "Many times when older people come to the nursing home, it's because of an acute illness, and they are thrown from their normal situation into a completely different one with no opportunity to plan or process the abrupt change. Reviewing their memories is one way they can reclaim some sense of control over their lives, focus on their self-worth, and do some inner healing."

Fear of Facing A Difficult Past

When we review our lives, we cannot completely silence our inner judge, and yet the distance of age makes us wiser and kinder to ourselves. Trusting our own kindness gives us courage to look boldly at what we have done.

It is a very human tendency to slink away in shame from some of our actions, to avoid facing mistakes we have made or humiliations we have suffered. But from the safe distance of time, we can take a closer look, hopefully with greater wisdom and objectivity.

Women in Cameo Workshops have mentioned their reluctance to write about certain memories or periods of their lives because they are afraid of reliving them. Ceah Ure is head of the mentoring program for Fresh Start, a nonprofit organization for women getting back on their feet. As she puts it, "Many women don't want to explore their past because it is too frightening. They have felt pain too terrible to feel, and they don't want to feel it again."

Like many counselors, however, Ceah has found that women who confront and write about a difficult past can experience healing. Recent studies reported in the *Journal of the American Medical Association* show that writing about traumatic personal experiences measurably improved the health of some patients suffering from chronic asthma or rheumatoid arthritis.

In her book *Writing as a Way of Healing*, Louise DeSalvo discusses how writing has alleviated physical and emotional pain for herself and others.

There is a dark corner in everyone's life. I believe in shining the light on those dark corners for our own sake.

Transformative Memoir

Not only does writing your life story capture your self-portrait in words, it can actually transform you.

Professionals in the field of public opinion research have long known that the very process of asking people questions can influence their answers. As Mike O'Neil, president of the polling firm O'Neil and Associates in Phoenix, Arizona, points out, the wording of questions in opinion polls is such a careful science because the wording can skew a person's interpretation of a question and thus skew the resulting answer. Pollsters must take into account the inevitable fact that the process of asking and answering questions is transformative.

Beth Ames Swartz is a friend and an internationally known artist. Her passion to create a better world infuses her work, which she refers to as "transformative art." I borrow from her concept when I refer to "transformative memoir."

The process of reviewing our life path stretches us, opens us.

As we remember our journey and try to record it faithfully, we are inevitably drawn to examine it. We may be writing along, reliving an experience and transferring it to the page, when we pause–and 15 minutes later we discover that time has stood still as we rolled the memory around in our minds like a snow globe in our hands, peering in through the swirling drift, striving for a better look.

The *Cameo Life Stories Questionnaire* encourages self-examination, helping you explain your life to others by helping you to understand it first. It is transformative to think about the ways we "edit" the information we share with others. When we tell any story, we pick and choose what to pass along and in what order. We may add humor or a punch line. We might dramatize a simple occurrence or play down a major crisis. Sometimes we may spend painful hours or even days figuring out how to explain something—for example, telling our parents why we received a "D" on our math exam or telling our spouse how we scratched the car. We consider whom we're talking to, how much we're going to say, what light it puts us in, when we're going to tell the story, who else is going to find out, and what the consequences will be.

As Mandy Aftel points out in her book *The Story of Your Life: Becoming the Author of Your Experience*, we frequently tell stories in a way that is consistent with the way we see ourselves. If you think of yourself in terms of "nothing phases me" or "I'm an easy-going person," you may leave your angry feelings out of your stories. If you see yourself as a religious person who sets an example of faith for others, you may leave out mention of your occasional doubts or confusions.

Many of us edit our stories depending on our audience and how they perceive us. If our spouse expects us to be always upbeat, we have a tendency to satisfy that expectation. If we have a boss who suspects we are incompetent, we probably avoid telling her much of anything, for fear of saying the wrong thing.

The same tendencies may accompany us to the desk as we begin to write about our lives. However, the *Cameo Life Stories Questionnaire* provides us with a tool to help us examine those tendencies and even bring them into the story. Think about how you shape your life story to portray yourself to others. This process is part of the transformative nature of creating your own Cameo. Thinking about the ways you edit yourself may change your mind about what you decide to include in your life story. And remember that you may choose to prepare several versions of your story—one for yourself and one for your family.

Pride of Accomplishment

What a source of pride it is to realize how much we have done, how much we have learned, and how much we have grown. Writing about ourselves reminds us of our own personal progress and underscores our sense of accomplishment.

Sharing our life stories also involves this pride. Most of us know the pride of ownership—"This is *my* life." Add to that the pride of survival—"I made it"—and the group experience of sharing our survival pride—"We made it!" War veterans understand this bond among those who have survived a similar, trying ordeal. Life makes veterans of us all, and it can feel good to share our war stories with others who have survived the life journey at the same time we have.

The decision to share your story is a personal one. The special release form at the end of the *Cameo Life Stories Questionnaire* allows you to specify what you want done with your written story once you entrust it to The STORIES Center archives.

You may want to consider preparing several versions of your story, one for the records and one for sharing.

"I Just Want Someone to Know"

For several years, I was executive director of the Center Against Sexual Assault (CASA) in Phoenix. I was hired for my skills in management and fundraising, not in counseling or social services. At first I was shocked at the number of children we served who were incest victims and by the number of rape victims in the city. I also learned that a sizeable percentage of our adult clients had been sexual-abuse victims as children and were trying to heal. Sharing their stories of abuse with trained counselors was part of the healing process, but each woman (and man) decided whether or not to share with anyone else.

As head of the agency, I worked hard in the community to raise CASA's visibility and to raise money to keep it viable and growing. In that role, I found myself in many one-on-one situations with women volunteers—homemakers, retired women and those working full time outside the home. Time after time a woman would pause in our conversation and relate to me her own experience of sexual abuse—a date rape or childhood molestation by a neighbor or whatever it was.

"I've never told anyone," they would sometimes say. Or they would tell me they thought it might be helpful to me in understanding their strong desire to help our cause. But even the women who clearly kept their secret to themselves wanted someone to know. They didn't want the story of their abuse to disappear entirely, because it was too important. It had happened, it was real, and it had changed their lives in some way.

For some women, The STORIES Center archives may be the one place they choose to store away a secret they do not feel comfortable sharing with anyone else. The process of writing about their experience may help them heal. They may use their own abuse as motivation to help improve the chances of healing for someone else, but not through the telling of their own story. They want it on record, though, so someone knows the truth. ❦

CHAPTER FOUR

How the Cameo Life Stories Program is Valuable to History

One of the most human of all impulses is to reflect on our personal experiences. We look to our personal past to help understand what's happening to us in the present. From information about the past, we learn about our families, our jobs, our religion, our community, our nation and our universe. We need history—our past—to function. Luckily, each of us has been given the physical ability to utilize history; we have a memory.

On a very primitive level, we use our memory to ensure our safety. We learn not to touch a red-hot stove—again. Remembering that if we hit our brother we will be consigned to "time-out" or worse, we learn not to hit. We use history to learn from our mistakes.

The past also gives us inspiration. Before recorded history, poets were the people who taught generation after generation about its heroes and heroines and their mighty deeds. Books were one of the most significant of human inventions because they allowed more stories—more history—to be remembered by a greater number of people.

From our earliest childhood, history influences us.

History shapes us; we shape the future.

Making history more accurate

What if history is an imperfect art and the history books need adjusting?

Imagine reading about geography before someone discovered that Earth was a round planet. Imagine society before it realized that babies result from intercourse. Imagine living in a world where it was considered quite natural to buy and sell other human beings and where all the history books reflected that belief.

Consider how our ability to shape the future is influenced by what we know and what we are led to believe.

History is not a god, it is not a set of commandments, and it is not set in stone.

While some "facts" may not change, our understanding of them may. I went to the store yesterday. That is a fact. **Why** did I go to the store? To buy bread, to take a break from writing, to exchange a sweater, to run away from home?

The more accurate history is, the more helpful it is. Cameo Life Stories helps supply many of the missing details about women's lives, which answer many of the "whys" about human society and make history more complete and more accurate.

Clearly, the women who choose to answer the *Cameo Life Stories Questionnaire* and submit their answers or an alternate life story narrative to The STORIES Center are self-selecting. Great effort is being made to reach every population of women. The more stories that accumulate in the archives, the richer will be the reservoir of data about women's lives.

Supplying the bricks of history

Our past—our history—is a collection of memories and stories about societies and individuals. Historian Jacques Barzun likens biographies to the bricks of which history is made. How accurate is a history which generally omits 51 percent of the human race? How helpful is a history which reflects a primitive bias? How inspiring is a history which has no heroines?

Unfortunately, history has left out women. Less than two percent of American history textbooks deals with women, according to the National Museum of Women's History.

Luckily, history can be fixed. It is our good fortune to have increasing numbers of trained historians–many of them women—who are devoted to setting history straight.

Luckiest of all, every woman can help. If biographies are the bricks of history, let's give history bricks. Instead of throwing bricks at the imperfect history we inherited, let's build a newer, smarter, fuller Human History.

> We are the new Human History bricks!
> What are we building, what will we fix?
> A castle, a fortress, an ivory tower?
> A Pentagon, White House, or tribute to power?
> No, we are building a circle of stories,
> A home for our memories, lessons and glories,
> An archive of truth for both women and men,
> To turn to for wisdom, again and again.

We are the bricks of history because we are the people making history. We are the ones on the front line of experience. We are each the center of a universe. We act and we remember. We must value our stories and we must share them. We must write ourselves into history.

Visualize the planet Earth as a one-dimensional circle rather than as a globe. In the center of the human race milling about on this huge circular plain, picture an inner circle of the individuals who have traditionally controlled not only the course of "great" events, but the description of those events as well. The number of people represented by the inner circle is tiny in comparison to the number of people outside the circle, and yet, historically, it has been incredibly difficult for individuals outside the inner circle to wield a similar power—in particular, the power of inner circle historians to define the human experience by describing it in their own terms.

Should those of us outside the inner circle keep trying to penetrate the inner circle in order to achieve change? Once inside the inner circle, should we do battle with its defenders in order to gain more control of our destiny?

I suggest we simply walk away from the inner circle, walk out into the fascinating, complex human race and draw an entirely new line around us all. We need to ignore the boundaries that keep us out of human history and draw a new circle that embraces every woman, every girl, every man and every boy.

In sixth grade confirmation class I memorized a quatrain by Edwin Markham which I've always liked, and it seems appropriate here:

He drew a circle that shut me out,
Heretic, rebel, a thing to flout,
But love and I had the wit to win,
We drew a circle that took him in.

With the Cameo Life Stories program, women lovingly draw a new, larger circle that embraces everyone in the arms of history.

Urging society to treat women as important

During the 1998 elections, my home state of Arizona had an unusual number of women on the ballot. It suddenly struck me one day that we might end up with every one of our top state offices filled by a woman—governor, secretary of state, attorney general, treasurer, superintendent of public instruction, president of the Senate. When I mentioned this possibility to a friend, his first reaction was "That's bizarre!"

I looked at him with a disbelief that matched his. "Think about that," I said. "Imagine how bizarre it has been to live in a world where everyone with any authority at all is a man."

The 1998 fall elections provided Arizona with an executive slate that **was** all women. The good news is that society is finally recognizing what women in their hearts have known all along—as human beings, women and men are a little different from one another, but they are equally capable at working to make the world a better place.

However, our school books, newspapers, museums, statues, churches, universities, legislatures, courtrooms and relationships do not yet reflect the equal importance of women in the human race.

Treating women as inferior human beings is a very **bad habit** that reflects poorly on us human beings. It's a bad habit that has been around long enough to cause a great deal of harm, not just to women, but to society as a whole, and it's time to kick the habit. Without repeating all the arguments that others have stated so well, let me just mention a few good reasons why all of us must stop thinking of women as second-class humans.

◆ **It is unkind.** Every major religion on the planet was created to express a doctrine of love and respect for our "fellow" human beings—for good reason. Treating others as lesser beings is the greatest possible affront we can commit.

◆ **It is destructive.** When we think of other people as inferior—and treat them that way—we damage ourselves and we damage them. In ourselves, we shrink our capacity for wisdom and understanding, and we cripple our ability to love and to build a better world. When we, consciously or unconsciously, treat others as less important or less valuable, we damage their ability to be full, healthy and confident participants in making the world a better place. We damage and sometimes destroy their ability to stand on their own two feet and take good care of themselves and their families. When that happens, who is left to take care of them?

◆ **It perpetuates a vicious cycle.** As the tree is bent, so shall it grow. Psychologists consistently confirm what all of us know from personal experience—that it is not always our innate abilities and interests that determine who we become; we are significantly shaped by the ideas and expectations of others. Some of us will flourish with sun and water. Others will inch into maturity pruned like a bonsai tree. Others of us are imprisoned from childhood in arid darkness. Anyone who is a victim of child abuse knows exactly what that means.

Being crippled by ideas can be as damaging as being crippled by physical abuse. Thinking of other people as inferior is abusive. Abusive ideas are often perpetuated from generation to generation. Plato, the revered philosopher, uses an example of people raised in a cave, unable to see out. The only world they know—and the only world they **think** exists—is a cave. Do we want to raise our daughters, or our sons, in a cave? We live among too many "cave men" already.

The Cameo Life Stories program is spreading the message to women and to the world that women's lives are important and that we must treat ourselves and each other with the respect deserved by every human being.

Focusing on how history shapes women's lives

When we strive for understanding of another person or an issue, it is helpful to consider the conditions that have shaped that person or issue. When we are writing our personal stories, it helps to look at those factors which have affected our development.

For example, a child whose parents read to her often is more likely to develop a love of reading than a child who has had little exposure to books. Statistics have shown that children raised in a violent home are more likely to use violence themselves. Stereotypes about various ethnic groups are dangerous, but it is clear that traditions and ways of thinking are passed from generation to generation within cultures.

History can also have a strong influence on who we become. Think of the effect of such significant inventions as the automobile and the telephone and of such social changes as compulsory education and the invention of mass media. The ups and downs of the national economy can seriously affect millions. For example, a depression can force families to move great distances in search of employment, or a period of low interest rates may allow more people to purchase a home. There are many people who can speak with firsthand experience of the upheaval war has caused in their family.

Every woman is a unique individual. One thing all women have in common, however, is the law that governs the society they live in. In America and around the world, women have been treated much the same by the law–it has put greater limits on them. Women also have in common the social boundaries of the society they live in. Again, women throughout the world have had their ability to develop their personal talents and interests restricted by society. This is not to say that women did not find fulfillment or make invaluable contributions to their families and society in the cultures and eras where their roles were restricted. But the fact remains that women have had their life options severely restricted for centuries, and their self-fulfillment was limited to a narrow range of possible roles.

As you reflect on your life as a woman while writing your life story, you might find it helpful to look at the history of women in the United States and how it affects us now. For example, let's look back to the position of women not that many generations ago.

Women in America in 1848

Consider the status of women in the United States in 1848:

- Women were not allowed to vote.
- Women were forced to follow laws created only by men, since they could not serve in any legislative body.
- Married women legally ceased to exist as separate individuals; they couldn't write wills, sign contracts, get credit, and so on.
- Women had no rights to their own money, earned or inherited.
- The law allowed husbands to imprison, beat, rape and in some cases, murder their wives without punishment.

- Divorce laws favored men, and women almost never received custody of their children in a divorce.
- Most occupations were closed to women; those open to them paid very little.
- Not one college in the United States admitted women.
- Women, supposedly honored as keepers of morality, were restricted to a subordinate position in the church.

Five Women Called for Change in 1848

The struggle against slavery inspired women to unprecedented public activity during the 1830s and 1840s, although many men resented women's participation. Elizabeth Cady Stanton and Lucretia Mott traveled with their husbands all the way to London to report on their many efforts at an international anti-slavery convention. Not only were they forbidden to speak at the convention, they were banished to an upper balcony. Because they were women.

Elizabeth and Lucretia realized that women would not be able to contribute all they were capable of contributing to society until they had the freedom to use their individual skills, talents and natural human rights.

Elizabeth was busy raising six children and Lucretia dedicated her life to freeing the slaves of America, but in 1848 they resolved to take action to improve the deplorable status of women. They met over tea at the home of Jane Hunt and were joined by two other Quaker friends, Mary Ann M'Clintock and Martha Wright. The five women decided to use their anti-slavery organizing experience to work for improved conditions for women. They scheduled a convention for ten days later, and Elizabeth began to write the Declaration of Sentiments, a statement modeled on the Declaration of Independence which spelled out the inequities women were suffering.

On July 19 and 20, 300 people, including 40 men, showed up for the convention to discuss women's rights at the Wesleyan Methodist Chapel in Seneca Falls, New York. They adopted the Declaration of Sentiments, but only after much arguing over the most "radical" issue—the idea that women should be allowed to vote. They finally agreed to ask for "woman suffrage," which women did not achieve for yet another 72 years.

Susan B. Anthony joined efforts to improve the lives of women about a year after the first Seneca Falls Convention, and she and Elizabeth became best friends and the pre-eminent leaders of the 19th century women's rights movement.

Women's Rights National Historical Park

The Seneca Falls Convention is significant because it was the first formal assembly to discuss women's rights. Considered the first women's rights convention in the world, the Seneca Falls Convention initiated a widespread movement for greater justice and opportunity for women and girls, and it continues to have a major impact on human society.

In commemoration of the extraordinary significance of the Seneca Falls Convention, the U.S. Women's Rights National Historical Park has been established in Seneca Falls in western New York state near the Finger Lakes. The park was created by Congress in 1980 to protect and preserve the significant historical resources associated with the origins of the women's rights movement in the United States.

Administered by the National Park Service, the Park includes many sites—the partially preserved Wesleyan Methodist Chapel; a sophisticated Visitor Center containing several floors of statues, interpretative exhibits and interactive sites; the Declaration of Sentiments Waterwall, a monument featuring the text and names of the signers of the Declaration of Sentiments embedded in steel letters on a slate wall bathed in a continuous waterfall; the original home of Elizabeth Cady Stanton; and the M'Clintock House, where the Declaration of Sentiments was first drafted.

Providing women with a model for life story writing

Cameo Life Stories is a valuable contribution to women's history because it provides a model for women to use in writing about their lives. Carolyn Heilbrun in *Writing a Woman's Life* and Jill Ker Conway in *When Memory Speaks: Reflections on Autobiography* both lament the absence of precedent for women in telling their stories. Tales of male adventure and achievement abound, from the earliest epics to contemporary biographies and memoirs. Traditional narrative forms for men, particularly the "quest" plot exemplified in *The Odyssey*, emphasize a man's personal power to achieve a special destiny.

Heilbrun and Conway observe that women, on the other hand, even strong and accomplished women, demonstrate discomfort in claiming "agency." That is, they have a tendency to suggest that they reached their position of power or distinction or influence through means other than their own drive and ambition. They may explain that fate intervened, or that they had the help of God, or that other people empowered them.

And women writing about themselves up to now have found few female autobiographies to use as models for their own. As Heilbrun puts it, "We can only retell and live by the stories we have read or heard. We live our lives through texts. They may be read, or chanted, or experienced electronically, or come to us, like the murmurings of our mothers, telling us what conventions demand. Whatever their form or medium, these stories have formed us all; they are what we must use to make new fictions, new narratives."

There are five primary ways that Cameo Life Stories provides a model for women's life story writing.

◆ **Establishes a tradition of writing women's life stories.** The most important contribution is simply establishing the example of women's life story writing. The mission of Cameo Life Stories is to solidify women's life story writing as a universal tradition. Being able to participate in an existing tradition erases much of the self-consciousness that accompanies any activity women perform for the first time or in small numbers. Women embarking on their memoir journey hear the echoes of admonitions directed at them since childhood—"don't get a big head," "be humble," and "don't brag." However, if life story writing is standard practice for women, then writing about ourselves is no longer in itself a suspect, conceited activity which we need to defend.

◆ ***Cameo Life Stories Questionnaire* provides a model.** Another contribution of Cameo Life Stories is the *Cameo Life Stories Questionnaire*, which provides a model or format for women to follow in writing about themselves. Many life story books provide a set of guiding questions, but the *Cameo Life Stories Questionnaire* is distinct because its questions are designed specifically to capture life experiences unique to women. Because the *Questionnaire* targets women, it has, by its nature, attracted women's participation and widespread support.

The *Cameo Life Stories Questionnaire* is a model for women because it encourages a woman to focus on issues especially pertinent to her as a woman. Every effort has been made to be as inclusive of women's varied lives as possible, although women from countries other than the United States may need to add information which the *Questionnaire* doesn't adequately solicit. Would it be better to construct a model which didn't focus on gender issues? In any life story, gender issues are impossible to avoid. Men's traditional narratives are a good example of how gender experience not only permeates but shapes the life story.

The questions about women's experience are in addition to, not a replacement of, many other questions about life experiences. In this way, women are encouraged to explore a variety of areas of influence and development in their lives, including the ways that being "born female" may have had an impact.

◆ **Encourages self-examination.** *The Cameo Life Stories Questionnaire* provides a third contribution to women's history in encouraging women to focus their life story writing on self-examination. This underscores the message which many women need to hear, that writing about themselves is unselfish, not only because it is a gift to one's family and to women's history, but also because it is a means of personal growth. The emphasis on explanation in addition to bare facts enriches the historic record, as well as the woman writer.

◆ **Question-by-question approach.** Cameo Life Stories also provides a life story writing model by offering a question-by-question or story-by-story method of explaining one's life. Women's life stories have been variously described as "quilts" and "tapestries," as opposed to the male life story metaphors such as the quest. Whatever fabric, textile or garment metaphor finally results when all the questions are answered, the *Cameo Life Stories Questionnaire* is a "piecework" approach to life story writing. This model would probably be helpful to men in recording their life stories because it helps avoid the tendency to follow only one thread or theme through one's life, as well as the tendency to oversimplify explanations.

◆ **Recognizes women's own efforts.** Finally, the *Cameo Life Stories Questionnaire* is a model that asks women to consider the issue of "agency." A woman must ask herself to what extent she has been the captain of her own ship and to what extent her choices have been shaped by other influences. The male narrative model, which positions the central character as the supreme agent, is not necessarily an accurate model, as most women know. Women know full well that many a male achievement was bought with the aid of others, often women. By tradition, a woman describing her achievements shares credit with others. She is wise to acknowledge the variety of people who have influenced her life journey, thanking those who have helped along the way. If she is wise enough to recognize that everyone has assistance, and that all victories and failures are shared, she is also wise enough to identify which impulses, ambitions, ideas, energies, and triumphs are her own.

Establishing a new tradition of life story writing

Some people write their life stories. Most don't. Some institutions promote life story writing, but most do not.

The Church of Jesus Christ of Latter-day Saints (LDS) has established a strong tradition of genealogy. The LDS genealogy center in Salt Lake City is famous as one of the largest repositories of genealogical data in the world. Genealogy societies exist in most communities, and tracing family roots has become a popular American pastime, so at least some families are making an effort to research their connection to past generations.

While genealogy and life story writing have some elements in common, genealogy focuses more on names and dates. Life stories put meat on the bones of bare facts, and they bring a person alive on the page.

A primary goal of The STORIES Center and Cameo Life Stories is to establish life story writing as a universal tradition, beginning with women. Although life story writing may seem daunting to many people, once it becomes an expected aspect of the culture, resistance to the idea will decrease. Also, in the manner of traditions, creative and efficient ways of doing it will develop. Imagine how much easier it will be to write our life stories when we are introduced to the idea as young people and we can begin at an early age to record our experiences and reflect on the influences at work in our lives.

Encouraging the preservation of life stories

Our Inherited History, so to speak, is dominated by the stories of "great" institutions, events, and individuals—governments, nations, movements, inventions, wars, wars and more wars, kings, generals, presidents, dictators. This is extremely important information, which I hasten to say to those who might be uncomfortable with the idea that Everywoman and Everyman belong in history. Yes, if we collect the life histories of every woman and every man on the planet, we will have ourselves a very large circle of stories indeed.

Worried about a repository large enough for everybody's story? We can learn to deal with greater quantities of historical information, just as we have learned to handle the information explosion in all areas of life. That's what computers are for.

Of course, someone still has to sort, categorize and interpret the data, which is a great deal of work, but maybe we'll just need more historians, including volunteer historians like us, to help with that work. Increasing our respect for history and training more historians would be a good thing for humanity.

In addition to changing the way the history profession deals with history, we need to encourage people to preserve life stories within their own families. Certainly, in our consumer society with its over-emphasis on "stuff," we can each find a safe place to store one more thing, especially when that item comes to be considered a prized possession. We should record our personal histories and treat the resulting documents as the treasures they are, handling them with the same care as legal papers and cherished heirlooms.

Adding the stories of Everyman to history

We need to start with a drive to collect women's stories, because they are so glaringly absent from the human record. But The STORIES Center will also collect the equally valuable bricks of Human History from men.

The *Life Story Questionnaire for Men* is designed to help men tell the stories of their lives in a mode different from the standard male plot line, and it is directed to all men, not just those who are famous or powerful.

Many men have chosen nontraditional lives, and these stories need to be added to the record. The life stories of famous people, and of men in particular, often omit areas of their experience, which gives us a truncated view of these people. Very few men, for example, live their lives completely devoid of nurturing relationships. Relationships are a vital part of every human life and are as important to a life story as the details of a career. The *Life Story Questionnaire for Men* asks men to provide history with more truthful, more complete descriptions of their lives and to examine what influences shaped their development.

How are Cameo Life Stories different from traditional ways of telling life stories?

Cameo Life Stories encourages each woman to reflect on significant influences, decisions and activities that have affected her role as a woman and her role as an influence on others throughout her life.

Many of the books available to guide women and men in writing their life stories provide questions and suggestions, but the Cameo Life Stories program emphasizes self-examination. Women's lives are changing rapidly and dramatically. Why? We must often turn to historians to explain to us the "bigger picture" which influences our individual lives, such as economic depressions, international hostilities, scientific discoveries, and so on, but historians must often turn to us to see how broad social influences translate into our everyday lives.

For example, the percentage of women working outside the home increased steadily throughout the 20th century. Why? And how does that shift in women's roles affect family life? What is the impact on traditional homemakers and on the functions homemakers have traditionally performed? What is the impact on child care and on education? How does the change affect men, their career choices, the number of hours they work, their attitudes, their stress levels, and so on? How do working women adjust in a culture trying to keep up with their increasing participation in all areas of human endeavor? Is women's health being affected? Are laws being influenced?

All these factors impinge on our personal lives. They influence who we are, who we become, and how we influence our children and other adults.

Don't let all this talk about social trends discourage you from tackling your own story. You do not have to be a trained historian to write about your life. You aren't expected to psychoanalyze your life, just reflect on your experience and write what you remember. *The Cameo Life Stories Questionnaire* will ask questions that are related to larger social issues, but the greatest value of your answers lies in your own experience.

Coordinating access to women's life stories archives

Completed *Cameo Life Stories Questionnaires* are housed in the The STORIES Center archives in cooperation with the National Museum of Women's History and the Fletcher Library at Arizona State University West in Phoenix. Written life stories in formats other than the *Cameo Life Stories Questionnaire* answers will be archived as well. In addition, we welcome into the archives any women's life stories collected previously or gathered in future research studies or volunteer projects.

The three organizations above are committed to making women's life stories available to scholars in all disciplines, while protecting the wishes of the individual women who have provided information about themselves. Computer technology will aid access to life stories archived by The STORIES Center and, in the future, link life story archives at other locations.

Inquiries about using the archives for women's history research should be directed to the executive director of The STORIES Center in Phoenix, Arizona, or to the National Museum of Women's History in Washington, D.C. ❦

HOBO DAY

CHAPTER FIVE

Working With Your Memories

On the great wide sea of Memory
Where dream ships come and go,
Skimming tides of friendship,
That know neither ebb nor flow;
Where winds of Love blow softly,
O'er waves of azure blue
That wash the sands of Arcady;
There—I oft-times cross to you.
J. B. Downie, "The Sea of Memory"

Museums of memory

"We make and remake ourselves through memory," says Rebecca Rupp, author of *Committed to Memory: How We Remember and Why We Forget.* "Memory, built up over years and decades, is one of the few human creations that is entirely and inimitably one's own. Like fingerprints...no two human memories are the same. Each is...a personal museum."

I like the concept of the mind as a museum, maybe because my first impression of museums was based on one of the quirkiest and most intriguing ones I've ever seen. The Pettigrew Museum in Sioux Falls, South Dakota, is so named because it is literally housed in the three-story Victorian former residence of the illustrious Senator R.F. Pettigrew. Thoroughly modernized now, in the 1950s it possessed the combined essence of a haunted house, an antique store and a private collection. Ask anyone of my era who visited the place as a child, and you can bet they will remember at least two unforgettable items—a yellowed skeleton reclining on a dusty upper shelf, and an authentic Lakota tepee towering past a second-floor balcony in the center of the house.

Many of the fine contemporary museums and interpretive centers do a much better job of organizing facts and artifacts, guiding visitors along a narrative path designed to clarify a few key themes. But the old Pettigrew museum strikes me as much more analogous to our minds —warehouses of stored odds and ends, some obviously having received more attention than others. In one corner of our mental repository is an arrowhead collection lovingly labeled, in another corner a neglected doll.

If someone were to dump out the contents of our memories, as I yearly turn my purse upside down and shake out every last penny and crumpled tissue, we would find a unique assortment, as unique as the contents of women's purses. Sharing the contents of my purse isn't something I've ever done. I'm fairly confident, though, that each purse contains a different match book, a different key chain, different bills, and different letters to be mailed.

Because of our varied experiences and interests, our minds collect different souvenirs of our walk through life. *The Book of Knowledge,* my childhood encyclopedia, answers a childlike question about memory with this explanation: "You and your brother go walking in the country, past a field in which there are two white horses. You are fond of horses, so you notice this scene and remember it for a long time, but your brother soon forgets it. It made no impression on him. He loves flowers, and he remembers that on the walk you passed a pond full of yellow and white pond lilies."

Our minds are collectors, constantly gathering recollections of our life and storing them away. I remember in high school when we studied the poem "Ulysses" by Alfred, Lord Tennyson, I was struck by the line "I am a part of all that I have met." Even then it seemed to me more appropriate to say, "All that I have met is part of me," although I suppose both ideas are true. As we traverse through time we save bits and pieces of experience which accumulate as a storehouse of memory.

We are what we remember

The word "museum," by the way, derives from the word "muse," which refers to any of the nine sisters of Greek mythology who inspire the arts. Our memories—our personal museums of art, science and what-have-you—are generally available for us to visit when we feel like it. Most of us don't take the time, and many of us find even our own past a bit boring when compared to all the interesting activities crowding the present, but the museum is **our** private residence. We have the key, but the key fits only **our** memory museum, and no one else can enter.

When we first fall in love and when we are making a new friend, we often pay a visit to our private memory museums, gather up exhibits which interpret who we are, and spread them out for the other person to see.

In a way, that's what writing your life story is like. You select the memories that mean the most to you, or that best describe you, and you carefully label them and set them out for someone else to see and read and, you hope, understand.

Admittedly, show-and-tell is sometimes easier. When Steve and I were first married, we visited, in our first year, his hometown, first home, grade school, high school, skating rink and favorite pizza parlor; his undergraduate college, the gymnasium where his lacrosse record still stands, his ragged fraternity house and his favorite beer parlor; his law school, bus route, summer job location and Chicago relatives. We did the same routine with my life. We were trying to make up for our missing "shared history," and it worked well. We had a synchronicity of intense interest in each other. We shared so much because we were marriage partners, but most of us never share that much of ourselves with our children or grandchildren.

It would be wonderfully convenient if we could hold an open house of our memory museum (keeping a few inner doors locked, perhaps), but we can't. Our most plausible method of revealing ourselves to others is through a written record of our memories.

Laura Ingalls Wilder's beloved memories

Are you familiar with Laura Ingalls Wilder? Laura was born in 1867 near Pepin, in the Big Woods of western Wisconsin. Her only daughter, Rose Wilder, grew up to become a widely published journalist who encouraged her mother to record her experiences in a rapidly vanishing period of American life. Laura eventually produced a series of eight books geared to young people, and her "Little House" stories are beloved by people all over the world.

For several years, Laura and her parents and sisters lived near DeSmet in Dakota Territory, and Ma and Pa settled there while Laura and her husband Almanzo moved to the Ozarks. I was able to visit Laura's family homes in eastern South Dakota with my own family, and it made us feel close to a woman whose prairie life so closely matched that of our own ancestors. In fact, most of the locations where Laura lived have been restored or recreated and opened to a curious and adoring public, so in addition to Laura Wilder's books, we can physically see many of the mementoes that bring her world to life. In the Surveyor's House in DeSmet, for example, we saw on the kitchen wall the china shepherdess the Ingalls family had carefully carted from their log cabin near the Mississippi River. Underneath the shepherdess a card read, "Laura felt a house wasn't home until the china shepherdess was unpacked and displayed."

Laura Ingalls Wilder began writing her books when she was 65, and they are feats of memory for which millions are grateful. Laura was the first to admit that she had to flesh out some of her memories with imagination because she couldn't remember everything exactly, but the books stand as an honest reflection of an American pioneer girlhood. As Rebecca Rupp puts it, "We are what we remember." The Laura Ingalls Wilder we know today is the Laura that Laura recollected.

Our china shepherdess

Because her books have won her so many devoted fans, Laura has a legacy that includes several biographies, a television series and numerous museums throughout the Midwestern United States. Most of us will never achieve her level of recognition, but I remember thinking, when I saw the china shepherdess, "Wouldn't it be interesting to know what one item other people would put in a museum?" What would be the one item which best represents them, or the one item without which home wasn't home?

I daydreamed of a "People's Museum," which would accept one item and an explanatory card from every American. Perhaps we could create a People's Museum on the Internet.

Clearly, memory is composed of much more than physical objects, and yet a particular object often serves as the touchstone of memory.

Think of the china shepherdess: "Her little china shoes, her tight china bodice and her golden hair were as bright as they had been so long ago in the Big Woods. Her china skirts were as wide and white; her cheeks as pink and her blue eyes as sweet as ever. And the bracket that Pa had carved for Ma's Christmas present so long ago was still without a scratch, and even more glossily polished than when it was new." Gazing on the precious emblem of home, Laura remembers another home, another Christmas.

When I try to pinpoint only one object to describe, I feel the panic of a collector! I have so many things, not necessarily of monetary worth, but important to me. Mentally I start sorting through my memorabilia box. My eyes scan my bookshelves and the interior of the curio cabinet. I also wonder if there is there anything I have lost or given away that I would retrieve if I could?

Daniel L. Schacter is professor of psychology at Harvard University. In his book, *Searching for Memory*, he discusses the three functions that allow us to remember: 1) the encoding of information into memory, 2) the memory trace created in our brains, and 3) the retrieval of memory. "Engram" is the word he borrows from earlier researchers to describe step two, the imprinting on our nervous system which preserves the effects of our experience. The key to tapping into our engrams or memories is the use of retrieval cues, stimuli which activate our memories.

"Because our understanding of ourselves is so dependent on what we can remember of the past, it is troubling to realize the successful recall depends heavily on the availability of appropriate retrieval cues. Such dependence implies that we may be oblivious to parts of our pasts because we fail to encounter hints or cues that trigger dormant memories. This may be one reason why encountering acquaintances we have not seem for years is often such an affecting experience: our old friends provide us with cues and reminders that are difficult to generate on our own, and that allow us to recollect incidents we would ordinarily fail to remember."

Some of the things which lead us to memory are mementos—knick-knacks from the World's Fair, pine boxes from Yellowstone Park, match-books from a romantic restaurant. My mother cherishes a small clear pharmacy bottle filled with sand. Grandma Wertz (Mom's mother) and her best friend collected the fine river sand on an all-day hike that stood out among all the days of their friendship.

Ornaments of memory

My parents' annual Christmas tree has become a veritable museum, a collection of memories represented by an amazing variety of ornaments acquired through the years. One of the most treasured is a black, shiny wooden cat named Oswald. Dad says Oswald was a popular cartoon figure of his 1930s childhood. Christmas isn't Christmas without Oswald. Every year Mom hauls out all the decorative paraphernalia, much of it dating from my childhood. When she is finished decorating, the house serves up a feast of memory, which is half the fun of Christmas to me.

My friend Carol Ellis maintains a tradition established in her family years ago. Every year she pulls out of storage the "mushy memory tree," a rather battered, small artificial green Christmas tree on which she hangs mementoes of departed family members—a framed photograph, a tie, and an old card, for example. For those of you who might want to imitate this tradition, Carol's family pronounces mushy to rhyme with pushy.

While working on this book, I took myself on a field trip to a place as fascinating to me as a museum. I visited a local antique and collectibles mall. In aisle after aisle dealers have arranged their wares, which all have one thing in common—they all belonged at one time to someone else.

I frequently shop at antique or collectibles shops because I like searching for reminders of my own past, and I love to give gifts that restore a bit of precious memory to friends and family. When I'm walking the aisles, I frequently hear other patrons remarking, "Oh, look! We had one of these when I was a girl." Or, "Can you believe I sold one of these at a garage sale for a dollar?" Many of them are indulging, as I am also, in strolling through a memory lane. The sight of objects from our past conjures immediate recollections. We pause by battered coffee grinders, high-riding canvas baby buggies, Limoge hand-painted china like Nana's, faded prints that hung in our bedrooms, Roy Rogers paraphernalia, dog-eared books. Even those of us under 50 can expect to find artifacts from our youth appearing as valuable collectibles.

Clothes speak of the past

Clothing in general doesn't bear up well over time, but intact treasures can still be found in trunks and those coveted Lane cedar chests. My mother still has some of her favorite outfits from high school stored in round metal Pepsi drums. A yellow knitted sweater with three-quarter-length butterfly sleeves that look more like bat wings when you raise your arms. A white dotted swiss (navy blue fuzzy dots on snowy white fabric) off-the-shoulder drawstring top with a matching full-circle skirt. She let me wear the dotted swiss to a dance when I was in high school, but I had more fun in it twirling around the living room and suddenly dropping on the carpet so the skirt would settle in a perfect circle around me. Imagine my chagrin when my daughter asked to borrow one of my 1980s suit jackets because the bulky shoulder pads qualified it as retro!

For the 150th anniversary celebration of the 1848 first women's rights convention, a group of us in Phoenix wanted to do a historic fashion show. Connie Mulholland did the research and lined up 22 women to represent key figures in the historic progress of women. Thanks to my friend Rénée Wilkie at the Antique Centre, I came up with a white muslin lawn dress from 1910, when the suffragists were working so hard to win the ballot for women. Rénée also produced an intricate, pale yellow muslin wedding ensemble which, judging from the unique sleeves, was handmade between 1885 and 1889, the year the first International Woman's Suffrage Association was formed.

We took dozens of pictures at our historic fashion show. My daughter Maren dressed as Alice Paul, the young woman who, inspired by the militant British suffragists, stepped up pressure for the vote in America and was among the White House picketers who were "jailed for freedom." I had an 1848 pattern made up in Wedgwood blue moire, and I felt like the woman I portrayed, the Rev. Antoinette Blackwell, who was the first ordained minister in America. There was something about touching old muslin and slipping into heavy, broadcloth petticoats that transported us in time, allowing us to step into the shoes of the women who bequeathed us our political freedom.

Dressing up can have that effect. When my dear friend Marilyn McNeely announced her daughter Gail was getting married, I offered to host a wedding shower. As we talked about the wedding plans, Marilyn reminisced about her own wedding in 1950, and the lovely shower her friends gave her, surprising her with an album depicting her married future with artwork from women's magazines.

It gave me an idea. We concocted a bridal shower for Gail with a '50s theme. Marilyn dug out her album and brought it, and several of us dressed to match its illustrations. Leslie Watkins and her daughter went shopping together at a vintage clothing shop and came wearing slim, belted wool dresses hemmed just below the knee and pillbox hats with veils. I found a blue cotton v-neck dress studded with rhinestones, the skirt flaring out from a self-belted waist. I whipped up a Sandra Dee hairstyle and unearthed a pair of black patent-leather flats. To top it off, I planned some really "keen" vintage shower games, and we served coffee and cookies on clear glass snack sets from the same era.

As I watched Gail unwrap her gifts, I drifted back in memory to the first bridal shower I ever attended—my cousin Sandy Shawd's. I felt so grown-up just to be invited, and yet so young, going with my mother and not quite understanding the significance of the occasion. Wearing the blue dress, I revisited Sandy's shower for a few moments as a woman. Looking across the party at my daughters, I wondered what they would remember of this timeless female tradition.

Charm bracelets

Remember charm bracelets? Growing up in the 1950s, I had a lovely silver bracelet, and from it dangled a bevy of "charms" I received as gifts. Each charm—a tiny metal figure—represented an interest of mine. I confess I cherished my charm bracelet so much that I kept it safely stored most of the time in my jewelry box, and it has safely followed me through the years.

I think it may be time to restore charm bracelets to fashion, especially for those of us engaged in reflecting on our lives. Besides being a good conversation piece, they are a joyfully jingling reminder that we are complex compositions of many interests—they can serve as a "mindfulness" bell to draw our attention back to who we really are. Do you have a charm bracelet buried in your jewelry box? Find it, lay it out and examine each charm. Put it on and wear it for a day. Ask your friends if they still have their charm bracelets. If you are involved in a Cameo Circle, designate a session where everyone brings her charm bracelet or another piece of jewelry which is personally meaningful. Write about the jewelry and include your written piece in your *Cameo Life Stories Workbook* as part of your answer to Question 14. (See the *Cameo Life Stories Questionnaire* in Chapter 8.)

When I was trying to think of a way to describe the charms on a charm bracelet for those who've never seen one, the word "icon" came to mind, an icon being an image or representation. Ironically, the icons which adorn our computer screens may be our modern version of the charm bracelet. Many computer software programs display tiny pictures to represent various files. One can also create a special computer file of favorite sites to visit, so it is possible to bring up on our computer screens a string or bracelet, if you will, of miniature pictures which reflect our interests.

Of course, not all of our memories are associated with objects, but objects can be the "genie lamp" we can rub to conjure up the memories we want to appear. My husband collects something we are **required** to rub periodically—with silver polish. When his grandfather came to America from Russia, he brought a set of ceremonial Jewish wine cups which he passed on to his grandsons. Steve collects these small kiddush cups of Russian silver. They are a physical and emotional link to his religious and cultural heritage.

There are other keys to memory you can use in the same way: high school and college yearbooks; programs from recitals or public events; ticket stubs from movies, musicals, plays and concerts; love letters; old postcards; old newspapers and magazines; and any journals or diaries you've kept.

Ephemera

In the antique business, paper items which survive the ravages of time are known as "ephemera." Ephemeral things are those which have a short life—May flies and sunsets, for example. Luckily, collectors have learned to value cultural artifacts made of paper, an easily destructible material, and have developed specialized methods of preserving them. Through antique trade publications available at libraries, bookstores or collectibles shops, you can find dealers who specialize in certain aspects of ephemera, such as postcards. These publications also provide the dates and locations where these dealers gather to sell their materials at trade shows.

Antiquarian book dealers can be another source of ephemera. Some people get a thrill from being able to see, hold or own a relic of the past, even if it as simple and apparently as unrevealing as an autograph, which is another area of specialized collecting. I admit to being one of those who finds it easier to touch history by leafing carefully through a 1912 issue of *Scribner's Magazine* or copies of *House Beautiful* from 1908 with an illustrated ad for McCrary iceboxes.

My mother has a pair of old ice tongs displayed at home. Although I've seen them used in country kitchens as paper towel holders, in our family they are the emblem of my Grandpa Wertz. When my mom tells someone her dad was the iceman for Mitchell, South Dakota, she says it with as much pride as if he had been the mayor. It's very probable that he was just as well known and esteemed as a politician, because he was the reliable purveyor of an essential commodity.

Arthur Wertz's job was to deliver blocks of ice, custom-carved for his customers' oak, metal-lined iceboxes. What made the iceman popular to the town youngsters were the remnant ice shavings trailing from the ice truck, Midwestern manna on a scorching summer day. According to Mom, kids would flock around Grandpa as he obliged their clamors for a cold treat.

I didn't know my Grandpa until later, after his iceman days, when he read Zane Grey novels, brought home trinkets he won at Bingo, and tried to convince me I didn't like ice cream. Through my mother's eyes, though, I see in the ice tongs my Grandpa's teasing smile, his strong arms lifting the ice over his shoulder, his responsible rising in the dark early mornings, his whistling while he worked.

Memorabilia—songs, colors, poems

Mom doesn't need the ice tongs to recall her father, but they are a ready reminder. If there ever were any "ephemera" that spoke of that father-daughter relationship, not much remains. There were no letters and maybe only a few cards.

The same is true of my relationship with my own father. Only a few paper items survive, largely because there were so few to begin with. I left home about the time long-distance phone calls stopped being exorbitantly expensive, so we've never exchanged many letters. I have two or three he sent me when he was working out of state for weeks at a time, and I think somewhere at the bottom of a memorabilia box there may be a handwritten note from "Santa Claus" thanking me for the milk and peanut butter sandwich, which is what we were led to believe Santa preferred.

There are other nonphysical things, however, which never fail to call my dad to mind. Songs. He has a beautiful voice, a mellow, baritone vibrato. On the two-hour drives to and from our grandparents' homes, he would sing "The Tennessee Waltz," the Davy Crockett song, "Moon River" and countless others that came on the radio.

The color green. On the first day of first grade, Miss Morris walked down the aisles between our desks passing out colored paper, allowing us to choose our favorite. I hadn't thought about my favorite color until that moment. I quickly picked green because I knew it was my dad's favorite, and green has been mine ever since. Every time I am asked my favorite color, I answer "Green, because it was my dad's."

The poem "Li'l Orphant Annie" by James Whitcomb Riley. When I was six years old, my mother sat me down at the blonde oak kitchen table and proceeded to help me memorize the long, four-stanza poem written in Riley's characteristic Hoosier dialect. Mom told me Dad had learned it when he was six, and now it was my turn. When I close my eyes, I can still retrieve "all us other children, when the supper things is done,/ We set around the kitchen fire an' has the mostest fun/ A-listenin' to the witch-tales 'at Annie tells about...."

I was jubilant the day I stumbled on a 1953 set of the *Book of Knowledge* at a Savers thrift store. It was identical to our childhood volumes and had the "Li'l Orphant Annie" page I remembered so well—poem, picture and paper. I was ready the day my youngest came home from third grade and announced, "We're studying poetry and I need to learn a poem for Poetry Day when the parents come." Aha! Now all three of us can recite it together, and I think I may have recruited my nephew, Myles Morton, into our ranks.

Suggestions for working with your memories

Following are some exercises you may find helpful in jogging your memory.

1. People's Museum

If the imaginary People's Museum asked you to donate one object which would represent your life, what would it be? Do several things come to mind? Make a list. Describe one of your chosen objects as fully as you can, and explain why it is the object of your affection, or why it is important to you. Write a description assuming it will accompany your item in the museum. Read Laura Ingalls Wilder's description of the china shepherdess if you need an example. Does the item you describe evoke additional memories? Describe one of the memories in as much detail as you can remember. Half the fun of writing about our memories is savoring the sweetest ones, and savoring involves as many senses as possible. In addition, detailed description is good practice for writer. This exercise may help you answer Question 14 in the *Cameo Life Stories Questionnaire* Chapter 8.

2. Tree of Life

Visualize your favorite tree. Keep in mind that trees are miniature ecosystems and are home to many other creatures and nature's debris. Trees host birds, bird nests, bird feeders, kite remains, bugs, butterflies, airborne seeds, dried leaves, blossoms, fruit, seedpods, snow, ice and so on. Draw your chosen tree on a blank piece of paper. It may be an evergreen (a Christmas tree, if you prefer), a deciduous tree (with or without its leaves) or a large bush. Draw onto the tree some of the objects which have been significant to you in different periods of your life. If you prefer, you might decorate your Christmas tree with meaningful objects.

Another version of this exercise is to find a bush or tree branch with many small but sturdy limbs. Stand it upright in floral foam secured to a plate or bowl with floral clay. From the branch hang small representations of your favorite hobbies, talents, causes, and memories. When I was young we would use lilac branches, paint them white and hang Easter eggs from them.

3. Collectibles Shop

Technically, an antique is an item more than 100 years old. We may not have had many real antiques in our lives, but we can always find collectibles. Search a collectibles shop or mall (usually a shop with multiple dealers and therefore greater variety) for familiar artifacts from your life or examples of objects you may have used, made or envied. You might even get lucky and find something you have been searching to replace. Study the items you find and mentally practice writing a brief description. Bring a notepad and make notes of the memories these objects evoke. Later practice describing one object in detail, using all the five senses if possible. Above all, indulge in a bit of reverie. The objects are not the end in themselves but a door to the memories that compose your life story.

4. "Dress-up"

Have you every played "dress-up" as a grown-up? Compile an outfit you might have worn as a teenager or a young woman. If you don't still own the clothes yourself, or can't fit into them, you can find similar ones at vintage clothing stores and thrift stores, many of which now have special sections devoted to "retro" clothing and furnishings. For years I've kept a big box of dress-up clothes for my girls—first for their little girl play and later for special dress-up and dress-down days at school. Dress yourself up in a period outfit. How does it feel? What memories come to mind? Write down your reactions and include them as part of your answer to Question 11 in the *Cameo Life Stories Questionnaire,* Chapter 8.

5. Custom Cookbook

For Christmas one year, my sister Laurie Morton and I took a shoe box full of our grandmother's favorite recipes and created a simple booklet featuring the foods best loved by her family. Nana's grandchildren created a charming cover and assembled the recipe books as a gift of memories for all the children, grandchildren and great-grandchildren who had gathered in her home and savored her watermelon pickles, peach jam and other delicacies.

Food is a big part of our lives and can stir many memories with its flavors, aromas, ingredients and associations. When you are reaching into the past for clearer memories, try sifting through an old cookbook or actually preparing some of the dishes you remember serving and enjoying. Charlotte Bleh Juarez of Peoria, Arizona, created a book of recipes and memories reflecting her Scottish heritage. *The Four Midwestern Sisters Christmas Book* by Holly J. Burkhalter does a great job of blending childhood holiday memories and recipes for the foods that accompanied them.

6. Music

Songs, especially the "golden oldies" of our youth, frequently bring memories flooding back. Sort through your old phonograph albums and tapes. If you don't own your favorite records anymore, tune in to a local nostalgia radio station, one that plays your favorite songs or music from the period when you formed your musical taste.

My painter, Bob Lagrander, grew up painting alongside his French-Canadian grandfather and says he learned to endure music from the 1930s and 1940s all day long. Even his wife, Maria, and daughter, Tiffany, now use Bob's description of it—"pepére music." ❦

CHAPTER SIX

Getting Ready to Write Your Life Story

Tiger, tiger, burning bright,
In the darkness of the night,
What immortal hand or eye
Could frame thy fearful symmetry?
William Blake, "The Tiger"

You can write your own life story.

You are a tiger burning bright, a special person lit with the fire of life.

What hand could possibly record in words, what eye could possibly visualize, an adequate portrait of your "fearful symmetry," your precious self?

Your hand and **your eye**. You can frame your own life story, and you will do it beautifully. You do not need to be a professional writer or have extensive writing instruction.

Writing about your own life is easier than you might think.

"Is writing the only way to tell my story?"

Scrapbooks have become a very popular pastime in the United States. People are creating masterpieces of memorabilia with attractively arranged and decorated displays of photographs and mementos. These albums reflect great care, and the families of the scrapbook artist are very lucky to receive such heirlooms as legacies. Each scrapbook tells a story in pictures, artifacts and occasional narrative.

Scrapbooks without words or narrative will be difficult for future generations to decipher. Chronological photographs tell the visual story of our external changes in appearance, but they don't necessarily answer the questions others may have about our lives. Supplementing scrapbooks or photograph albums with your life story—or answers to the *Cameo Life Stories Questionnaire*—would provide the best of both worlds.

When it comes time to archive your life story with the National Museum of Women's History, a scrapbook will be difficult to duplicate, ship and store. What many women have effectively done is provide a few representative photographs of themselves. Black and white photos, color photos or very clear photocopies of photographs are fine.

Another popular form people have begun using to capture their life stories is a videotape or audiotape oral history. There are companies which provide oral history services for a fee, or you may look for someone from a local school, college, museum, or library to assist you in preparing an oral history of your life. In addition, there are several good books to guide you in recording your life story through the use of your spoken words, rather than written words.

One drawback to stories on videotape or audio cassette is that they require transcription, which can be time-consuming and expensive. A written life story can be more easily read and reproduced. In addition, through new technology, it can be scanned onto computer, stored in an infinitesimally small space, and easily retrieved.

If you are uncomfortable writing, you might consider beginning with an audio or video version of your story, then using your words to create your own written story. You could transcribe what you have said verbatim, or use the process of writing to amend your story, adding or subtracting as you wish. A good friend was interviewed on videotape for Kit Prestwood's college course "Chronicling Women's Lives." Half a dozen times she has bemoaned, "Oh, I wish I could do it over!" She had forgotten to make certain points, or clarify others. One of the beauties of writing—especially on computer—is that it's easy to add or delete.

In defense of videotape, it is a wonderful way to communicate your personality to your descendants, but even then, the visual record is limited to one point in time, unless you splice in videotape of yourself from different periods in your life.

Keep in mind that **the *Cameo Life Stories Questionnaire* was designed to make writing your life story as easy as possible**, while still capturing important information and enough details to make it valuable to history. The primary purpose of this book about the Cameo Life Stories program is to help you overcome any obstacles—including any aversion to writing—that would keep you from telling your story in words.

Give yourself permission to write

I agree with Dorothea Brande in her book *Becoming a Writer* that the biggest stumbling blocks for writers are not matters of technique but of nerve.

We can't write if we don't believe we should be writing.

Believing is the key.

For many years I was so busy with my career and my family that I felt luxuriously lucky to find a quiet weekend morning when I could write in my journal. It took me years to fill one notebook, because the entries were sometimes a year apart.

When I remarried, my brief hiatus from full-time employment stretched into years as I filled my days with remodeling projects, a Brownie Girl Scout troop, and a myriad of volunteer activities which both my husband and I supported. I told myself I had no excuse, then, not to start writing, if that's what I really wanted to do. Hadn't I told myself for years that I wanted to write?

With both daughters in school and Steve at his office, I would sit at my desk. Then the questions began. What should I write? What do I want to say? Who is going to read it? Why would they want to? Who am I? What if I am terrible? What if I embarrass myself because my ideas are unoriginal and shallow to boot? What if I am behind on the latest techniques?

After awhile, I would get up from my desk, depressed, and delve into my other activities, where I didn't have to face such debilitating self-doubts. I had no idea where to begin. In all the years I spent learning about great authors, I never learned about the work a writer must do just to begin writing. I assumed that great writers were born and that the writing poured from them as naturally as song from a bird.

My best friend in high school, Elinor Nauen, ran off to the East Coast by way of Michigan State and a converted school bus and ended up writing poetry in a rent-controlled apartment on the Lower East Side of New York. She made literary friends, attended poetry readings at St. Mark's, started her own poetry magazine and furnished her one-room home with neighbors' rejects deposited on the sidewalk three floors below. Eventually, Elinor became the travel and fiction editor for *Woman's World* magazine and later for *First* magazine. She has compiled a book of women's writing about automobiles called *Ladies, Start Your Engines* and a book of women's writing about baseball called *Diamonds Are A Girl's Best Friend.* Elinor is also an occasional speaker to writing groups around the country, and I finally turned to her for advice. She reminded me that writing is a craft, not just a gift, and suggested I take a writing class.

Of course. How embarrassing not to have thought of that. I had assumed I possessed the skills I needed to write, but obviously something was missing. Just as I would need to take classes in interior design to improve my home decorating skills, I needed a creative writing class. So I signed up. Repeatedly.

My writing classes were terrific. I had great instructors, met other earnest adults and young people wanting to write, and actually produced a variety of written pieces.

However, when the classes ended, so did my writing. Being enrolled in a course disciplined me to attend class and complete my writing assignments by the prescribed deadline. I had acquired a clearer idea of what I wanted to say and how to go about finding a publishing venue for my work, but I had not yet learned how to apply my bottom to a chair and write without someone **telling** me to. I practically begged my husband to give me assignments, then I wouldn't take him seriously. My wonderfully supportive writing teacher, Paul Morris, would call me out of the blue and ask, "How's the writing going?"

"Not well at all," I would lament. "I clean all morning and get all my other responsibilities done, then the kids come home, and next thing I know, it's dinner time, and after that I'm exhausted."

Paul, ever even-tempered and never one to take advantage of a tempting irony, would respond, "Why don't you do your writing first?"

Why, indeed! I knew I had the basic skill, the desire, and the time to write. If only I could **make myself make time.**

What I realized—and was embarrassed to explain to Paul Morris on the phone—was that, in my heart, I didn't really **believe** I had the right to sit down and write. Writing, when I examined it, seemed an entirely too self-indulgent pastime, compounded in its undeservedness by the equally unacceptably bad habit of sitting still. What gave me the right to do something I really loved doing when my children were working hard in school and my husband was working all day to support the family?

I struggled with this issue for years. I found myself drawn to every book and article which defended the contributions of homemakers as equal in value to paid work. I tried to convince myself that my long days of housework and volunteer work earned me the right to take time off for a "hobby."

I even went so far as to tell myself that the writing was **work**. Nothing doing. I wasn't able to convince myself that writing was work—good ol' valuable, highly respected work—because I secretly believed that nobody else, including my family, would buy that argument. And I was more concerned about what **they** thought than what **I** thought.

Breakthrough came again from Elinor. At the end of a chatty long-distance telephone visit, she added, "Deb, I just have to tell you about this great book. It has made such a difference for me. I know I may sound a little preachy about this, but I can't emphasize enough how much it has helped me with my writing." I copied down the title and author—*The Artist's Way*, Julia Cameron—as Elinor went on to describe how she and several friends met weekly and followed Cameron's suggestions.

I slipped off to my favorite bookstore that afternoon and carried home the book as if it were the Holy Grail. After skimming through the 222-page paperback, I decided to take the plunge and commit myself to the 12-week self-directed course Cameron outlines as a system for unblocking one's creativity—as a writer, painter, sculptor, dancer, musician, crafter or dabbler in any field.

If her book sounds promising to you, I encourage you to try her prescriptions because they had an extraordinary effect on me. What impact did *The Artist's Way* have on me?

It helped me begin believing I should go ahead and write. Cameron has published several related books, including *The Vein of Gold* and *The Right to Write*, and all of them offer a trove of tips to motivate people to explore their creativity. The message with the biggest impact on me was that creativity is the gift of a higher power and is meant to be exercised. It gave me a sense of permission, in expressing that the desire to create is a very natural desire that most people experience and act on somehow. I began to feel that I was not alone in feeling a need to express myself, and I began to believe it wasn't selfish to take time to write, but rather it was unfair to myself **not** to.

In case you're wondering what I wanted to write, it wasn't the Great American Novel. I wanted to write about my life. My journal-writing, when I found time for it, was very satisfying, because it helped me think more clearly. As I wrote about my experiences and my reactions, I began to see patterns and answers. Writing helped me understand myself and others better, which gave me a greater sense of wisdom and stronger feeling of peace. That was worth writing for.

Organize the tools you need

Your primary goal should be to make the experience of writing as easy and as pleasant as possible for yourself so you will be motivated to continue.

A Place to Write

You need a place to write. Preferably, you need a place where you won't be interrupted. Naturalist and author Ann Zwinger, one of my favorites, writes that most women don't know what it's like not to be interrupted. Natalie Goldberg is a well-known writing teacher and author of several excellent writing books, including *Wild Mind* and *Writing Down the Bones*. She is a fervent advocate of writing in cafes and public places. However, recalling memory and recording detail require concentration, and if you are the kind of person, like I am, who is easily distracted by the very interesting world around you, you might be better off sequestering yourself with some privacy.

Some people like to write in bed. Before rising for her afternoon obligations, Edith Wharton put in a full morning's work on her novels in bed, at her palatial home, The Mount, where she also had maids to bring her breakfast, no less.

I know several people who like to work on their dining room tables. They don't like being isolated, and the larger table gives them plenty of room to spread out. Susan Goldsmith and I spent an entire day hunting antique stores for the perfect writing surface for her new office. She finally settled on a 1920s oak dining table with end leaves that slide out of sight when necessary.

Now that so many of us work on computers, you may want to work at your computer desk. You can even take the laptop to bed with you.

I am partial to desks. Desks, plural, is accurate. I think desks are such wonderfully utilitarian inventions, and they come in so many shapes and sizes. In my home, several secondhand wood desks serve as attractive furniture and sturdy workhorses as well. A tall, deep red, secretary holds my note cards and family addresses in the hallway. In a corner of our bedroom, a kidney-shaped mahogany kneehole desk stores my financial records in its petite but plentiful drawers. Where I most long to sit over my journal, though, is at a dark, rectangular desk with a broad surface where I keep a small book rack to prop photos and letters against. Two matching lamps shed plenty of light on my pages, and I have room for a teacup and saucer without worrying it will spill when I shift positions.

Virginia Woolf advocated that every woman have a room of her own. I advocate, at the least, that every woman have a desk. It can be an island of calm, a bastion of self-preservation. Make your work area as alluring as possible! Don't go overboard to the point of distracting yourself from the task at hand, but create a visual tableau that will draw you. Put a fresh flower on your desk. Remove unrelated clutter. Dust. I like to light a candle when I begin to write and blow it out when I stop, not so much for the aroma therapy as for inspiration when I am tempted to bolt. The candle burns steady, and the steady flame communicates it steadiness to me.

Wherever you feel most comfortable working, stake your claim and lay in supplies.

A Three-ring Binder is Essential for Your *Cameo Life Stories Workbook*

As you begin to write, you will find that one memory leads to another. You will be in the middle of describing your childhood home and realize that you also want to write about your school, your mother, your best friend, your favorite dress, your pet hamster and the day you got lost after school. You will feel like a mother hen with a brood of little chicks scurrying about. How do you organize everything and move ahead?

You need a three-ring binder, page dividers, and a copy of the *Cameo Life Stories Questionnaire.* From The STORIES Center you can order the *Cameo Life Stories Workbook,* but with a little extra effort you can create your own. The workbook you will receive from The STORIES Center is a packet of page dividers, imprinted with the 92 questions in the *Cameo Life Stories Questionnaire.* You can create a similar set of dividers by yourself. It helps to use the dividers with tabs that extend to the right of the pages you'll be writing on. On each divider type or print one of the questions and number the tab to the right accordingly.

Next, adopt a three-ring binder as the "hard cover" for your *Cameo Life Stories Workbook* and insert the dividers. Binders with a clear vinyl sheet over the cover allow you to slip paper behind the protective vinyl so you can create a cover for your book. Remember the silhouettes our teachers drew of us in grade school? Since you are creating a written Cameo, consider making your personal cameo or silhouette your book cover. Sit as close as possible against a plain, light-colored wall with a bright light shining on you and casting your distinct shadow onto a piece of white paper or poster board taped to the wall. Have someone trace your outline on the paper, then cut out your silhouette, lay it on a piece of black paper, trace your white paper silhouette and cut it out of black paper. You may have to splice on an extra piece of black paper to attach your nose or the back of your head!

Be creative with your cover. Jackie Mott Brown, an artist and author with a story in Chapter 12, encourages women to make artistic collages as workbook covers. You might enlarge a favorite photograph on a copy machine and use that as a cover.

The beauty of a three-ring binder is that it allows you to add, subtract and rearrange your pages of writing at will. If you make a mistake, you can throw the page away and slip in a new one. You may write ten different pieces in response to one question, store them randomly but safely in your workbook, then sort them later into the order you prefer.

Over the years my desire to write my life story has led me to buy every pretty preprinted life story journal I saw, ones with expensive covers and illustrations and high-grade paper. I've bought blank journals of handmade paper with marbled boards and hardcover books from major publishers. I've never written a word in any of them, largely because I didn't want to mess them up. In the bound books with printed questions, I could tell right away that some questions would require much more space than allowed, and I could never figure out how to insert an addendum attractively. My daughters will probably inherit a nice cache of blank journals and a rather beat-up but bulging *Cameo Life Stories Workbook* from me. Guess which they will cherish.

Computer, Typewriter or Hand

If you are working on computer, the simplest word-processing software will serve. If the technology is new to you, practice a bit first, so if you experience any frustration you won't blame it on the writing process itself. You want the writing to be as positive and enjoyable as possible. Take a computer class if you need to. Keep an easy-to-read manual about your software program handy. It always helps to identify a human being who is familiar with your program and can get you out of a jam, often over the phone.

Stories which are written on typewriter or computer are infinitely easier for others to read than longhand. If you cannot type, don't let that stop you from writing your story. Just try to write as legibly as possible. I always write in my journals in longhand, because I enjoy the leisurely pace and the feel of a good pen in my hand. If I want to cover a great deal of ground quickly, I move to the computer. (My old electric typewriter languishes in the garage because I couldn't stand its annoying hum when I couldn't think of anything to say.) If you prepare your story in longhand, consider finding a typist to transcribe it for you. Transcribing will give you an opportunity to review your words and make any revisions, and it will produce a clean, clear copy for your family, your heirs or future historians. Many Cameo Life Stories—those for which we have permission—will be scanned and entered into a computer database, and typed copy will be much easier to read.

However, I want to stress that The STORIES Center will accept handwritten stories. Older women are our priority, and many of them have not had the opportunity or inclination to learn to type or work on a computer. Lack of "computer literacy" should not stop anyone from writing her life story or submitting it to women's history archives!

Notepad

In all cases, you will need a notepad and a pen or pencil beside you as you compose, so you can make notes as you go along. Once you are in a writing frame of mind, many ideas and memories may begin to emerge, and you won't want to lose track of them. Take time to make intelligible notes and keep your notes with your story-in-progress.

In your notepad, also be prepared to remind yourself of related personal assignments: "Call Mom for a copy of the family history," "Ask Steve if he remembers where those old World War II ration books are," or "Find my grade school diary."

Working on Computer

If you are working on computer, my computer-savvy friends plead that you "save" what you have entered every 15 minutes or so to avoid the tragedies wrought by power outages. Also, they recommend you save your document to a disc at the end of every writing session. A further fail-safe practice is to keep an updated copy of your work somewhere else, either on a computer disc or as a printed hard copy.

You may decide to answer all the questions in the *Cameo Life Stories Questionnaire* on one computer document or file, but if you are loquacious and you don't want to scroll through a lengthy document on your computer monitor each time you begin writing, try creating a separate computer file or document for each numbered question and answer. When you are done, you can print each file or answer separately and assemble the hard copies in chronological order in your three-ring binder. Keep a master list of all the computer files you create, with a brief clue about the content of each, in case the file name alone is not descriptive enough.

Keep extra paper on hand, as well as extra ink cartridges for your printer.

Reference Books

Unless you have a computer software program that provides you with a dictionary and a thesaurus, keep those two "bibles" handy, also. However, if you are sailing along with your narrative and get snagged on a particular word, underline a blank space and come back to the space later. You may lose a train of thought more precious than one word if you linger too long searching for just the right synonym or a correct spelling.

If you need to consult a book about punctuation or grammar, do so after you have already finished writing and are ready to go back and edit. Most writing instructors recommend that you let your initial work sit for awhile before you begin to edit or polish or "clean it up." The wait gives you some distance from what you've written, allowing you to read it more objectively. You will be more likely to spot gaps in chronology or sentences where, in your haste, you didn't explain something clearly enough.

You may need to turn to an encyclopedia or history books for background information related to your stories. Many people don't even buy a set of encyclopedias anymore because they are available on computer. However, I remain a loyal fan of the printed book, one I can hold in my hand, underline, mark pages in, and leave spread open. Historical subjects in encyclopedias don't change that much, so you don't have to worry about having an old set. I prefer them. They can be found at thrift stores and garage sales, and I don't feel guilty about marking them up.

If you are trying to recall a particular year in your life—for example, the year you got married or had your first baby, I suggest you turn to the "annuals" produced each year by the encyclopedia companies. These collect by the dozens at the Goodwill and Salvation Army thrift stores and usually cost no more than a dollar. They are a great "slice of life" look at life in America and around the world that year, discussing top news stories, key people, timely issues, and the arts and cultural phenomena, like clothing and television programs.

Your Writer's Toolbox

"You'd lose your head if it weren't attached!" my mother used to sigh in exasperation as I dashed around the house looking for things. I hate to think how many years of my life I have wasted searching for stuff that would hide from me when I needed it most.

When you are ready to write, you don't want to squander time preparing. Keep a writer's toolbox handy, a container devoted to a few essential writing aids. Tuck into it a copy of this book, a writing manual like *Write Right*, an easy-to-handle dictionary if you don't have an automatic spelling checking system on your computer, an extra copy of your signed "My Commitment" pledge, several bookmarks, inspiring photographs or pictures, pens and pencils, and a small notepad for jotting ideas as you compose.

For those of you who suffer from the proclivity to lose things, one more hint. When you head off to your Cameo Circle with your *Cameo Life Stories Workbook*, carry it each time in the same cloth bag or briefcase. Always return it to the same location near your desk. If you misplace your *Workbook*, it'll be easier to find in its dedicated carrying case. If it eludes you too long when you are ready to write, simply turn to the *Questionnaire* in the *Cameo Life Stories Writing Guide for Everywoman*, start fresh and add the new pages to your *Workbook* when it reappears, like a smug little puppy, from its capricious holiday.

Maintain your momentum—complete your Cameo

Use the "My Commitment" form at the end of this chapter to help you successfully finish your Cameo. After you have signed your commitment form, make a copy of it and keep it handy. For example, you may tape it above your computer, or tape it to the inside of the three-ring binder you are using as your life story workbook. You may want to post it by the kitchen sink or your bathroom mirror where you are sure to see it daily. You may want to reduce it to the right size to fit in an attractive frame on your desk.

The point of having your commitment form ever present is to remind you constantly of your best intentions, so you maintain a regular schedule which becomes habit.

Carolyn Warner is a well-known speaker and the author of the *Treasury of Women's Quotations.* When she ran for governor of Arizona a few years back, she shared one of her grandmother's favorite sayings in her speeches: "Sow a thought and reap a deed; sow a deed and reap a habit; sow a habit and reap a character; sow a character and reap a destiny."

Making your time spent on your life story a **habit** is your best chance of completing it.

Invoke Your Personal Muse

Another technique to help you persevere is to invoke your personal muse!

Many writers speak of needing their "muses" to give them the inspiration to write. The Muses are nine Greek deities who, according to ancient mythology, were the daughters of Zeus, king of the Greek gods, and Mnemosyne, the goddess of memory. The home of these sister nymphs was claimed by the Greeks to be Mt. Helicon, and by the Romans to be Mt. Parnassus.

Over the centuries, each Muse has become identified as the patron of a particular branch of the liberal arts and sciences. Clio, the Muse of history, is usually depicted reading a book or with a heroic trumpet or water clock; Calliope, the Muse of epic poetry and eloquence, is shown as a stately young woman; Erato, the Muse of love poetry, is crowned with roses; Euterpe, the Muse of lyric poetry, is credited with inventing the flute and is always found carrying it; Melpomene, the Muse of tragedy, wields a sword; Terpsichore is the lively young Muse of dance;

Thalia, the Muse of comedy, holds a mask; Polyhymnia, the Muse of the hymn, wears a solemn mood; Urania, Muse of astronomy, bears a globe. Pegasus, the winged horse, belonged to the Muses.

Does it inspire you to imagine yourself the beautiful Calliope, giving wings to her words, soaring through the heavens on the back of her loyal Pegasus? Does it help to think of Mnemosyne, embodiment of memory, mothering you along? I like to think of Clio keeping me company with her nose in a book, as opposed to Terpsichore out kicking up her heels, while I am huddled over my keyboard.

Give yourself a Muse. For centuries writers have often considered their lovers or spouses as their muse. You can always invent your own Muse and install her (or him) in the pantheon of minor deities. Find a reproduction of a painting of your chosen Muse, or a photograph, or a physical emblem that gives you inspiration, and install it on your desk or your designated writing space. Let it help you give wings to your words.

Cameo Life Stories Writing Workshops and Retreats

Even those of us unable to devote the time to a regular Cameo Circle meeting may need the encouragement, discipline and interaction with others provided in a group setting. Workshops provide an introduction to Cameo Life Stories, get you started on your *Cameo Life Stories Questionnaire*, and help you establish a personal system for completing your life story. Intensive retreats are designed for women with limited time who would like to devote a long weekend to the completion of their life story, in the company of other women.

For more information on how you can participate in a Cameo Life Stories Workshop or Intensive Retreat, call The STORIES Center in Phoenix, Arizona, USA at 1-480-421-1999.

Make a commitment

Here are some ideas to consider before you pledge to write your life story.

1. How soon would you like to finish?

Every story has a beginning and an end. Visualize a date for finishing your story that has some special significance for you. The calendar's announcement of a new millennium provoked a million inventive ways to celebrate—with parties at the Taj Mahal, at the top of the Empire State Building, and on ships straddling the International Date Line in mid-Pacific. Celebrate by writing your story! You'll have a great deal more to show for your effort at the end.

Are you expecting a child, a grandchild, or a niece or nephew? Awaiting a blessed event can be nerve-wracking or the equivalent of a watched kettle. One of the most precious gifts you can give your kin is the story of your life. Why not pace your work on the *Cameo Life Stories Questionnaire* according to the due date? (Or a week sooner, in case you are recruited to help with the newborn prematurely.)

Maybe you have "all the time in the world." You are retired or your nest has just emptied, and you are looking for a significant project. You could legitimately work on your story for years to come. Especially if you are working with a Cameo Circle, you could linger over some questions for weeks at a time, allowing everyone to write, share, reflect and write, share and reflect again. Cameo Circles which meet weekly could easily plan a two-year cycle, with time off for holidays.

Setting a goal more distant than two years away, however, is inviting the temptation to put off the project indefinitely. I hope your goal is to get it done. Once you have completed the questions, you may want to take time to go back through your workbook and make additions or create a second version of your story for a different audience—for example, extracting anecdotes for a newspaper or magazine article.

When I realized I needed and wanted to write a book to encourage women to write their life stories, the months ahead seemed jammed as ever with commitments. One discretionary period presented itself, however—December, the month I usually devote to the holidays. Most other women I know do the same thing, whether they work inside or outside the home, and they try to limit their outside commitments so they can spend any free time with their families and preparing for celebration.

Since December seemed like the best time to take a break from my community obligations, I made arrangements to sacrifice the month to the book. I warned my friends and co-workers (co-volunteers) that I would be incommunicado throughout the holidays. My teenage daughters weren't too happy and complained that I was the "Grinch Who Stole Christmas," but I promised to decorate our tree with them right after Thanksgiving and hold the family gift exchange—for Christmas **and** Chanukuh—on New Year's Day.

Once I made the commitment to write and told everyone I was going to do it, they respected my decision. It put extra burdens on my husband, but he was not only a trooper, he was my greatest ally. "You can celebrate the holidays every year," he said. "Write the book." It was only when I retreated into a closet to write that he shook his head.

Remember that there is no deadline for submitting your story to the archives of The STORIES Center and the National Museum of Women's History. However, it will help you to set a specific goal for completion of your life story.

2. What regular time period is the best time for you to write?

Decide what time of day and which days of the week are best for you to carve out for your project. Chapter 9 on Cameo Circles will discuss the particulars of organizing a group of women to work together. Identify some "windows" in your schedule. You may have to create a window. I would never encourage someone to over-commit herself to the point where she feels stressed and cannot manage her responsibilities. On the other hand, I've found that if I say "yes" to something I really want to do, it frequently replaces an activity that may have lost its appeal to me anyway.

Julia Cameron suggests that people developing their creativity produce three "Morning Pages" each day, three pages of random writing that gets your hand moving on the page before the rest of your day begins. Getting up earlier may appeal to you, or you may decide to turn off the television set an hour earlier at night. If you work full time outside the home, you might consider finding a quiet corner during your lunch hour. Maybe you can arrange for a few hours every Sunday afternoon. Make a date with yourself and keep it. If the time you choose has too many demands on it, pick another regular time period and stick to it. If you respect your appointment with yourself, others will respect it also.

How much time should you set aside? It depends, of course, on when your deadline is and how much you want to write. You can always come back to a question later. Also, not every question will apply to you. In general, however, try to set aside close to an hour because it sometimes takes a few minutes for you to relax and focus and begin remembering.

If you figure an average of one hour per question in the *Cameo Life Stories Questionnaire* (working on your own), it would take you just a little more than two weeks of full-time work to complete your story! An hour each day, five days a week, would allow you to finish roughly 90 questions in 18 weeks—just four and a half months. Completing the questions at the rate of one per week would take you less than two years.

3. Designate someone to finish your story if you cannot

There is one person I suggest you discuss your life story project with, and you will know best who that is. You may be unable to complete your story because of illness, disability or death. None of us wants to imagine any of those things could happen, but they are part of life and another good reason to begin your story now. Who do you know who would be able to tie up loose ends for you and make sure your story gets submitted to The STORIES Center? Make sure you discuss your project with someone you trust. Show her this book or the *Cameo Life Stories Questionnaire*, tell her where your completed answers are stored (on computer or in a notebook), keep your other source materials stored with your *Questionnaire*, and make sure she has the Cameo Release Form to send to The STORIES Center.

When your story is submitted to The STORIES Center archives, it will be assigned a number, and unless you submit it anonymously, an acknowledgment letter will be sent to you indicating the number your story was assigned. You, your designee or your heirs should keep this acknowledgment letter from The STORIES Center with your valuable family papers. If you permit access to your papers in your Cameo Release Form, your heirs may at any time in the future find your story in the archives. Utilizing your story's designated number will help, since there may be more than one woman with your name in the archives and future family members may not recall your name correctly. (In their hypothetical defense, you may have divorced and dropped your married name, which they might be unaware of, for example.)

Beyond that, should you tell anyone else about your personal commitment to completing your Cameo Life Story? What works best for you? Are you good at making excuses—if you've been telling everyone for ten years that you're writing your memoirs? Maybe you need other people asking you periodically, "How are you coming with your autobiography?" Maybe you don't want other people's expectations hovering over you. Don't plan to share what you are doing if your friends and family will tease you or undermine your dedication. If they give you a hard time, tell them you're putting them in your story, and see what they say.

4. When should you begin?

Begin NOW. Begin in the IMMEDIATE FUTURE—perhaps today! People serious about committing to a goal are exhorted to avoid two key words: "tomorrow" and "try." If you find yourself avoiding action by promising to do it "tomorrow," stop using the word. If using the word "try" allows you to weasel out of taking action, stop saying, "I'm going to **try** to get started tomorrow," or "I'll try to work on my Cameo." Think of these "t" words as the "terrible two" and expunge them from your vocabulary if they trip you up.

Now, indulge in a brief exercise. You'll need paper and a writing instruments. Draw a horizontal line from one side of the paper to the other. On the left end of the line, place a zero. Take a moment to contemplate your estimated longevity. At the far right end of the line, put down the age you think you'll live to be. You have just created your own simple time line.

When I was first asked to do this exercise, I was about 29 years old and attending a time management seminar. Our Time Systems speaker asked us to liken ourselves to a car we want to keep for many, many years. "To keep a car in good running condition you need to change the oil and filters on a regular basis, do periodic tune-ups, and replace a few parts." He pointed out, "You need to take the same care with your life if you want to keep operating for a long time." What he didn't mention was the possibility of totaling your car in an unforeseen accident.

How optimistic were you in establishing your upper age limit? I remember a silly superstition occurring to me during the exercise. My first reaction was to say I'd live to 100, but I backed off, worried that 100 would seem greedy to "the gods." I settled on age 92. For those of us with relatively good health and happiness, it's human nature for us to want to live a very long time. We focus on life and deal with death only when forced. We all know, though, that we never know when death will come.

There's a story I want to share with you, and I could do so in another section of this book, but I'm sharing it **now**, as you are poised to make a commitment to yourself.

On a mild Phoenix day a few years ago, I was standing in line waiting to get my car from the valet at a restaurant where the Arizona Center for the Book held its monthly Feast for the Mind luncheons.

"What a beautiful day," I remarked.

A woman ahead of me turned slightly and said, "Yes, but it won't last. Before you know it, it'll be horribly hot again."

The line for cars was long enough to allow us to chat, and it turned out that Marn Peron was still a relative newcomer to the city and not enamored with it. She and her husband had sold their successful business in the Midwest, and he had taken early retirement in the Valley of the Sun. Her two youngest sons were in high school, but she had been uprooted from a cherished home, her friends and her family, and was still trying to find her place in this huge community.

The Center for the Book was encouraging people to belong to book groups and she was starting one. Would I like to join? I told her I'd think about it. Then she mentioned she was writing her memoirs. We exchanged phone numbers as her car appeared, a long, spotless Mercedes, which seemed appropriate, because Marn herself was sleek and flawless, her ash blonde bob with every strand of hair in place, her clothes expensive, subdued and classic, her skin tone even, her nails precisely done.

At the time I was trying to develop a motivational book for women like myself who were working for change and getting tired in the process. I was also engaged in *The Artist's Way* regimen and was ready to join a "creative cluster," a group of artists who support each other.

Maybe it would be easier to share my uncertainties and derelictions with a stranger, especially one who seemed to need a friend, I thought. A few days later, I called Marn and she was enthusiastic. We agreed to meet mid-afternoon Friday in the upstairs coffee shop of Borders bookstore. There she was, prim, prompt and primed. We spent the first day getting better acquainted and discussing our individual goals.

Once a week for nearly two years after that, we convened at 2:30, Friday afternoons, with our week's progress in hand. I looked forward to Marn's installments like the Americans who waited on the docks for ships' news of Dickens' little Nell. Her life was not extraordinary, in the sense that she had not discovered continents or invented the airplane, but she raised it out of the ordinary with her wry humor, crisp writing style and loving memory. She told her life in stories and told them so well I could see the folks in her childhood church, her dad striking a tent, her friend Melanie shocking the neighbors at a party.

As 1998 neared, I told Marn I wanted to mark the 150th anniversary of the first women's rights convention in some especially significant way for myself and, I hoped, for others. I galloped into the Spirit of Seneca Falls, a committee of women eager to heighten public awareness of women's history. I drafted the *Everywoman's Story Memory Workbook* and shared it with Marn, my writing cohort. Knowing most women would need prodding to write their life stories, I designed women's writing circles on the model of Methodist women's circles and the "conscious-raising group" of my 20s. Again I turned to Marn for help because she had been a reading teacher. With Shaaron Cosner, a high school English teacher, author and historian, we developed a simple protocol for women's groups to work on the *Everywoman's Story Memory Workbooks* together. Marn led the first Everywoman's Story Circle session, a dedicated meeting of our shared book group.

By May 1998 we were holding facilitator training sessions and the program was spreading all over the United States. Shaaron, Marn and I had a meeting scheduled with Kit Prestwood at the Arizona State University West Campus Women's Resource Center, but Marn called to say she was going to the doctor that afternoon. "I just got a clean bill of health during my annual physical, but I'm having some tests done because of a terrible pain in my side," she said with no fuss. A week later, an ultrasound showed spots on her liver.

Her husband canceled the annual family trip to Lake Michigan, and Marn dropped out of everything. When one of her stories was published in the *Arizona Republic* newspaper, she sent me an extra copy with a note, "I just cannot talk out loud. Gregg handles all my phone calls and takes me to the doctor like a car to the auto mechanic. I just cry."

When she went into the hospital, a team of specialists stood by. Everyone hoped the cancer had spared enough of her live, so that the cancerous section could be removed and the rest would regenerate. Marn's e-mail messages before her surgery were optimistic. She was a Christian Scientist and fervently believed in the power of mind over body.

On her second day after surgery, she lay frail and her smile was weak. The surgery had come too late; her body was riddled with cancer. She didn't moan or wail or complain; maybe she'd done all that in private. But I was angry—furious, helpless and incredulous—that my beautiful, kind friend, a blessing to everyone who knew her, was going to die. I had no idea what she needed me to say or do. Be cheerful and stoic? Be positive and confident of a miracle? I wanted to scoop her up in my arms and hold her close and transfer my own good health and strength into her body. But there were wires and tubes and she was exhausted, and all I could do was cry and confess my anger. "I know," she said. "I was angry, too. I had plans...."

She went home and began to prepare for chemotherapy. I left for Seneca Falls, New York, for Celebrate '98 festivities with my youngest daughter. When I returned, Marn was stationed in her living room on the sofa, in a pretty nightgown and on the 300-thread-count sheets she had recommended so highly to me. Gregg was trying to defrost the refrigerator. I gave her bits of my news, and she told me her older sons were flying in. She seemed in good spirits, but she was probably trying to think about what I needed. I blathered on, and even suggested I bring over a tape recorder so she could work on her memoirs some more.

"Oh, I couldn't do that," she said slowly.

It stunned me when I realized she meant that literally. I told her I was leaving town for a trip to see my parents and would be driving home through Colorado to see my sister Jane Ann and her new baby. I would hurry back.

As I was leaving, our friend Donna Newman arrived, and we spoke softly at the door. "Marn has decided against the chemo," she said. "It won't make her well, and she doesn't want the sickness that goes with it."

On August 11, my husband called me long distance after supper to say that Marn had passed away the night before. She was only 56. I missed the memorial service, though Steve went and told me later how strong her family had been, how confident that she was in a better place. I woke up in the middle of the night in my parents' upstairs double bed, sobbing, and remembered why. I cried for 1,600 miles.

Marn is both a palpable absence and presence in my life. I constantly have things I want to tell her and questions I want to ask. But I think of her often, and in my memories she is showing me a new knitting book, assessing a recent novel, gleefully displaying her granddaughter's pictures.

I still have Marn, because I have my memories. I also have her stories. How glad her sons must be, as well, to have her memoirs, a written Cameo of their beautiful mother.

5. Sign your name to your commitment

This is when you really get serious. When you sign your name on your personal commitment to write your story, you are pledging yourself to a goal that will give you great pride. You should be proud of beginning your story; you should be proud of yourself every time you add a paragraph. And think how proud you will be of yourself when you finish! Not only that, think of the inspiration you will provide to other women who would like to write their stories, but just haven't done it yet.

Remember the Chinese proverb, "A journey of a thousand miles begins with a single step." Making a commitment is the first step. ❦

MY COMMITMENT

Recognizing that I have helped make history, and recognizing that the Cameo Life Stories program is requesting my life story in order to create a more accurate and complete human history, I am committed to preparing and submitting a summary of my life story to The STORIES Center archives in cooperation with the National Museum of Women's History.

I will also encourage other women, young and old, to acknowledge the vital importance of women's lives in shaping history and encourage them to complete the *Cameo Life Stories Questionnaire* for themselves, for their families and for history.

I plan to complete my life story by: ______________________________

(date)

______________________________ ______________________________

(Full Name) (Signed this date)

CHAPTER SEVEN

Suggestions for Good Writing

How do you eat an elephant? One bite at a time.

How do you write your life story? My suggestion is to use the *Cameo Life Stories Questionnaire* and answer one question at a time. In her book *Bird by Bird*, writer Anne Lamott explains her advice to other writers with a story about her younger brother. Despairing one night over the term paper on birds due the next day, he asked his dad how he was ever going to finish the unwritten paper in time. His father's gentle but direct advice was that he write the paper "bird by bird."

Assembling your life story in small increments makes it seem so much easier. It gives you more flexibility with your time because you can write in short time segments, tackling only one story, event or question at a time.

Write your story piece by piece, question by question

Several writers have suggested that women's life stories are like tapestries or quilts, textiles that are created most often by a woman's hand, slowly, thoughtfully and lovingly. I like the quilt metaphor. My former neighbor in Minneapolis, Gladys Epple, first introduced me to the beauty of quilts and the satisfaction of the quilting process. She gave me a gorgeous pink and black quilt in the fan pattern when I moved to Phoenix. On a visit one spring, she brought along a sewing basket laden with cotton scraps of color and flower and as we chatted, she stitched together the small geometric shapes of fabric into a "Log Cabin" design in 8-inch squares. The squares would be the building blocks of a bedspread for my daughter Maren, whose life Gladys had held in her capable hands when I first returned to work as a new mother.

"Crazy" quilts, those assembled from whatever remnants of material come the quilter's way, are a good metaphor for women's lives and life stories. We compose a vibrant, queen-size comforter from a seeming hodgepodge of free-form fabrics, colors and patterns. And we stitch it together in our hands, unhurried, **piece by piece.**

Think of writing your life story as creating a quilt. If you're not familiar with the plethora of patterns quilters have established over the centuries, page through a book with colored pictures. What kind of quilt are you? Maybe you won't know until it's done. Maybe we should call our life stories Cameo quilts. Focus on the fun of reaching into your sewing basket and lifting out one by one your lovely pieces of material. After all, where would a writer be without "material"?

Think of each question in the *Cameo Life Stories Questionnaire* as a piece of quilting material and savor the process of stitching them together. Before you tackle the questions, however, think about your overall goal—the finished quilt. While I have stressed the benefits you'll enjoy in the process of writing your story, it is especially valuable to finish the job. For most of us, it helps to be specific about our goal, set a deadline, and then work backwards on a calendar, establishing intermediate deadlines.

Begin writing with a road map—clustering

"Clustering" is the best method I can recommend for preparing yourself to begin writing. This simple and effective technique goes by other names, as well, and is described in books about writing. It is very simple and very effective. In our life story writing workshops, we take four to five minutes to cluster a topic before we begin writing about it. Clustering helps you capture your thoughts quickly on paper, and it provides a record of your thoughts and memories to follow when you begin to write.

When sketched out, a cluster looks like the Sun with planets revolving around it.

To cluster, select a subject or a question from the *Cameo Life Stories Questionnaire*, such as Question 14: "Were there any pets, toys, imaginary playmates, books, dolls or games that were especially important to you as a child? Describe them. What influence did they have on you?"

I always use the example of books in our workshops because books have had such an extraordinary influence on my life, and I know they have influenced other women, often more than they realize.

To begin, write the word "books" in the middle of a blank, preferably unlined, sheet of paper and circle that theme, which becomes the hub of further thoughts. Concentrate on the subject and the specific question. Visualize books in your life. What images and recollections begin popping up like popcorn? Capture them in short descriptions as quickly as they arise, summarizing your thoughts in distinct groups around the circumference of the hub theme. Circle those word clusters. Draw lines to connect the circles of ideas that relate to one another. For example, link your hub topic with surrounding circled clusters.

You are going to end up with a drawing that looks like a sputnik or an exotic cheese ball with satellites. Sorry about mixing my metaphors, but this becomes your road map for writing.

What images, ideas and memories came to your mind as you brainstormed about books? When I do this exercise, I am reminded of my grade school trips to the bookmobile, my excitement at discovering the potential of "chapter books" with longer stories, my junior high school love affair with Nancy Drew mysteries, the role of the Bible in my religious training, the book groups I have enjoyed, my pleasure in browsing through bookstores, and so on.

When you finish your clustering exercise, you are ready to write. Start with one of the satellite thoughts, the one most appealing to you. Write about it for at least 15 minutes. If you need to stop writing for any reason, file what you have already put on paper in your *Cameo Life Stories Workbook* (your three-ring binder) under Question 14. File both your clustering exercise and your prose.

The next time you return to address Question 14, you will have your road map waiting for you. You won't have to wonder what to write about. You will already have tapped into your memories. When you start writing the next time, if you remember new things, just add them to your existing cluster. It's reassuring to know that, when you have a limited period of time available to write, you can turn immediately to your clustering exercises with some of your necessary homework already done.

Another suggestion. As I mentioned in Chapter 5 on memory, our brains need retrieval cues to help us remember. Studies have shown that people tend to access their memories first on a general level, especially on a "life period" level. Cameo Life Stories questions are retrieval cues for different subject areas. If you have trouble remembering at first, try concentrating on one of your life periods—for example, grade school, high school, early married life or retirement. Then apply the specific Cameo Life Story question to that life period. That may open the door to general-event memories and then lead you on to more specific recollections.

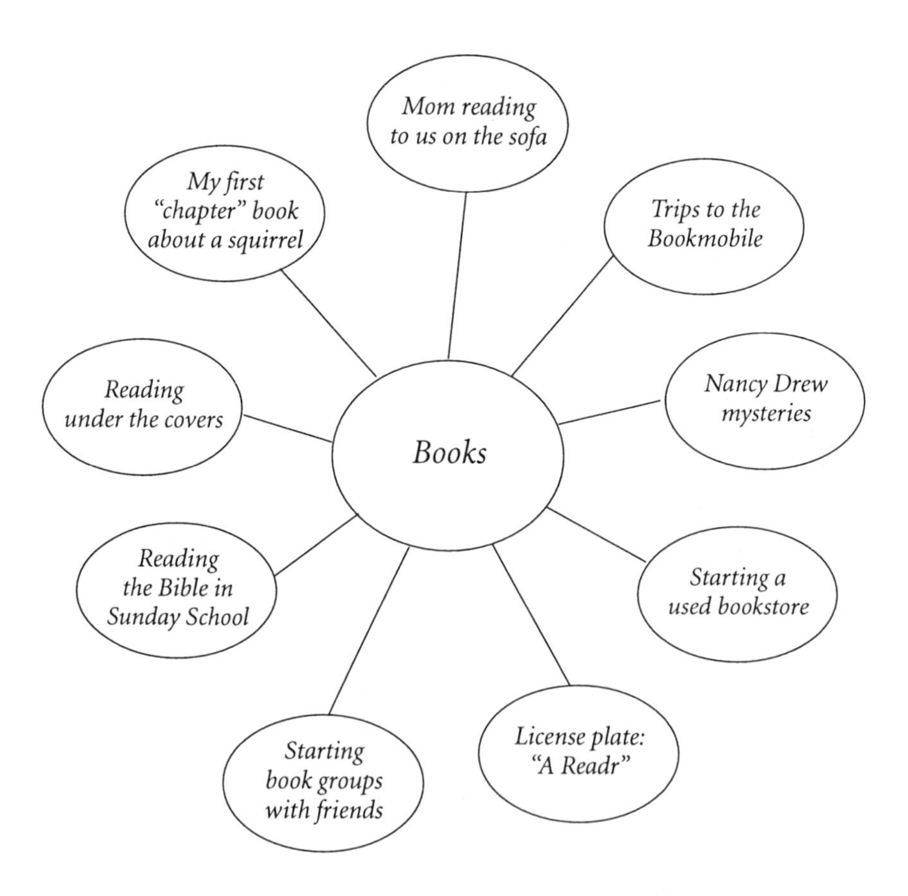

"I'm not a very good writer"

People can mean different things when they say they're not very good at writing. They may mean they are embarrassed by their poor grammar skills or that they are uncomfortable expressing themselves on paper. Perhaps they are recalling a bad grade on a high school essay. The reason for considering yourself a poor writer doesn't matter.

No one is going to grade your efforts. Nor are you submitting your story directly to a literary agent or a publisher as a potential bestseller. If that becomes your goal, there are excellent books to consult which will advise you about publishing opportunities and processes.

You are writing about yourself, and your writing style reflects who you are.

When I lived for a year in the Ponderosa pine forest just outside of Prescott, Arizona, I started a small newspaper for the village of Groom Creek. One of my dearest friends and best contributors was Robert "Sully" Sullins, a retired American Airlines maintenance supervisor who served as our unofficial mayor. Sully provided a regular column called "Old Timer's Tips" and was always dropping off suggestions and information on the clean, white backs of cut-up Pall Mall cigarette cartons.

Sully has the worst spelling of anyone I've ever met in my life—and I used to teach remedial English to college freshman football players. Even Sully said he was the worst speller he knew. His writing was easy to understand, though, because it was always phonetic, and his words looked the way they sounded.

His former employer used to give Sully a hard time about the memoranda he would post on the job, but as he pointed out to his boss, "My employees read every word in my memos because they get a kick out of my spelling!" One of Sully's creations has already been immortalized—literally put on the map. He didn't like the spelling of "Maripai," our main road off the highway, because it didn't look the way it sounded, so he convinced the highway department to replace the old sign with "Marapai" and print the new spelling on official maps.

The way Sully writes is a big part of who he is, so when he writes his life story for The STORIES Center, I hope he submits it in his own penciled hand. Unfortunately, the pieces of cigarette cartons might be a bit awkward to file in the archives.

If you are terribly self-conscious about your use of punctuation or grammar, ask a friend to proofread and make suggestions to you. Good grammar does make reading easier, but I just want to emphasize that it's not a requirement. Unless you are submitting your work for publication, technical accuracy in your writing is a low priority.

My editors for this book, Gerri Fiedler and Nina Sabrack, have used *The Associated Press Stylebook and Libel Manual* and *The Chicago Manual of Style* as guides.

Gerri and I are in recovery from literary perfectionism and stress that a goal of perfection in your life story is an unnecessary burden. Strive to write fluidly. If you choose to tidy up your grammar, style and spelling, do so after you are finished composing. Editing as you go interrupts your natural voice and your train of thought. Constant editing can be a hard habit for some of us to break.

Gerri tells me she was sitting in church recently when she noticed "The Lords' Prayer" printed in the order of service. "Probably nobody noticed but me, but putting the apostrophe after the 's' implies we have more than one Lord, so I felt I had to say something to the church secretary. She didn't seem to mind my scrutiny of the bulletin, but I did feel bad about bringing it up."

According to Gerri, writers are allowed to use only two exclamation points a year. She has granted me special dispensation because she knows I think and speak in exclamation points. She is also of the firm opinion that quotation marks and parentheses are hurdles the reader must jump and should be avoided.

"I'm no Shakespeare"

Shakespeare is acknowledged as the most talented handler of language the world has known. He was one of a kind, so none of us needs worry about trying to follow in his footsteps.

It took me a long time to figure that out. As a child, I was a voracious reader, and I got the notion back then that I would like to be a writer. Maybe I played too many games of "Authors," the cards with pictures of famous American authors and their four best-known works. Maybe it was the way literature was taught, but I became convinced that I couldn't write after all because most everything had already been written. Not only that, but I couldn't risk writing anything that wasn't the caliber of a Shakespeare, Emerson or Dickinson.

A woman novelist once told me that there are only a few key themes in human life, but it takes many voices to express them. When I considered how few people actually read Shakespeare, I knew she was right.

My book group brought this idea home also. Even in our well-read, well-educated group, we don't agree on what is a good book or an interesting book. We each appreciate different authors—for their varied plots, settings and styles.

In the workshops I have given, I have heard hundreds of women read aloud the spur-of-the-moment stories they have produced in timed writing exercises. I am consistently delighted at the quality of the written work. So are the women themselves. Even short pieces with no editing whatsoever are personal, lively and interesting. One of the secrets of this good writing is that the writers don't have time to cook up long-winded, stilted, book-sounding verbiage or worry about impressing anyone.

Use your own voice

Your life story will be most valuable and most appreciated if you write in your own style and your own natural voice.

The best advocate I know for this point of view is Brenda Ueland, author of the 1934 book *If You Want to Write.* She says, "...if you speak or write from **yourself** you cannot help being original." She also warns that you must write from your true self, however, and not from the self you think you should be.

One way to help yourself maintain a natural tone in your writing is to pretend you are writing a letter to your best friend. You'll want to include all pertinent details, but you won't feel constrained by the pressure of anticipated criticism. Many of us keep journals, and our journals reflect a natural flow of thought. However, journals are very different from autobiography or Cameos because they tend to emphasize our feelings of the moment. I often use my journals to vent or to explore options in making a decision, so I can fill page after page with my thoughts. This is not the stuff of which life stories are made, although you might need to refer to your journals to refresh your memory of events and your reactions to them. You might even consider passing on your journals to someone in your family or to a historical society, but the journals themselves would not usually constitute your life story.

When you write naturally, in the same manner in which you speak, you make your writing uniquely yours. There are additional ways to add your personal touch to your life story. Supplement your narrative with other expressions of your personality. For example, if you are artistic you might want to illustrate your life story or insert photos of your artwork. If you enjoy cooking or are praised for your baked goods, include some of your favorite recipes. Are you a poet? Weave in your poems. Are you a collector? Describe your collection and why it is important to you, then include photos if possible. Consider incorporating letters.

Although I never met my dad's father, Guy Hansen, and he never wrote his life story, he wrote his older brother often from the battlefields of World War I. When Great Uncle Harry died and his children were sorting through papers, they found a packet of letters from Guy dated 1918 and 1919 and sent them to my dad. Mom had all the letters copied, and together they give us grandchildren a glimpse of a man we would love to have known, who touched us with his boyish yearning for home, his eager inquiries about his prized Rhode Island Red chickens and his shyness with the French girls who could speak no English.

One of the women in my workshops told us about her daughter-in-law, a young mother who developed cancer in her 30s. When this young woman learned she was going to die, she began writing letters to God. These letters are part of her legacy, and they have been an inestimable comfort to her family, as they will be to her children when they are older.

Bring your story alive with detail

You are the center of your universe. You are the reporter on the scene. How can you most effectively convey your experience to someone else?

Remember to Use Your Senses

While you are remembering, remember with your five senses–touch, smell, taste, sight and sound. When you rode a horse for the first time, how did the horse hair feel? If you rode in the desert, how did it smell? Do you recall the taste of trail dust? How loud was the thunder that spooked your mount? Describe the look on your guide's face as you galloped past.

As you are writing, collect these sensory impressions from your memory and transfer them to paper so that your reader can see, smell, touch, taste and hear as you have.

Colorize Your Memory Movies

Add color whenever you can. Color is one of the easiest visual clues for your reader to connect with. The color names on paint chips are too esoteric to mean much of anything to someone else, but most everybody will know what you mean by red, crimson, scarlet, vermillion or barn red. Be as specific as possible about the green you remember. Was it sage, heather, sea foam, teal, emerald or spring green? What color was your house, your best dress, your "black eye," your first car?

Who, What, When, Where, Why and How

The "five W's" were drilled into us in journalism school. Unfortunately, we were required to cram as many of them as possible into the first paragraph of every news story. This constitutes a writing method known as the inverted pyramid. A top-heavy article allows editors to lop off final paragraphs of an article without sacrificing key information.

Having spent years under the tutelage of English literature teachers, the kind of writing I was taught in "J-school" came as an abrupt shock to my system. I understood the value of "Just the facts, Ma'am," but I had trouble adjusting to the brevity. Later my journalism training served me well in the business environment when I needed to communicate quickly and accurately.

Your life story is not a news article, so you don't have to worry about keeping it short. On the other hand, you'll want to communicate clearly and accurately by providing the answers to Who? What? When? Where? Why? How?

Tell tales and create scenes

If you start writing with a summary in mind, you risk ending up with a eulogy instead of a life story. Sometimes the religious figure officiating at a funeral knows very little about the deceased, and the result is an expression of general platitudes about death and the person no longer with us. "She was a good mother." "She never met a stranger."

One of our workshop exercises is to write for 15 minutes about our mothers or someone else important to us. This gives us another perspective on writing about ourselves, and it makes us reach for explicit examples and stories that portray the person. It takes two seconds to sum someone up as "a good mother," but in 15 minutes you can write about the time your mother scolded you and you slammed out the front door and told your friend that you hated your mother, and the next thing you knew she had flown out of the house, grabbed you by your collar and sent you off to your room with a swat. You can also tell about the time she took you to buy your first bra or sat down and talked to you about your period or came to stay with you when you had your first baby.

When you write about yourself, remember that stories will reveal who you are just as well as, if not better than, a summarized description.

Painting a scene is also important. When my mother describes "playing house" on the farm as a little girl, it helps to know if I should be visualizing the Ponderosa or Little House on the Prairie. Details about her surroundings answer my questions. For example, her parents rented a farm outside of Mitchell, South Dakota, where they still didn't have electricity in the mid 1930s, and they used the "root cellar," a hole dug in the dirt beneath the basement floor, to store vegetables. The only trees in sight were the rows of Chinese elms planted in the "shelter belt" to protect the two-story white clapboard farmhouse.

You may find that many of your memories are preserved as stories and scenes. Recreate them. If, for historical purposes, you want to leave a record of the chronology of your life, try preparing a separate time line to accompany your life story. This can be especially helpful to you in pinpointing dates and remembering where certain incidents occurred. Keeping your calendars from year to year will help you keep track of dates. By providing a succinct time line with your life story, you can avoid the need to write a narrative life story that proceeds strictly in chronological order.

Feel free to explore issues and themes, such as those in the *Cameo Life Stories Questionnaire.* For example, how has your spiritual life changed over time? How has your ethnic background affected your life choices? How has being female influenced your path? Even in addressing issues which involve self-examination and assessment, however, try to avoid writing an essay or a premature eulogy for yourself.

Turn over a new leaf—in a book

Growing up in Sioux Falls, South Dakota, I received an outstanding education in English and literature from Janie Mae Johnson, Vera Sadler, Lorraine Norman, Anne Kleinsasser, Marian Pfaff, and Muriel Nuffer in the public schools; and later from Don and Lucy Fryxell, William Geyer, Arthur Huseboe, Ted Hong, and Sandra Looney at Augustana College. As a result, I believe in phonics and diagraming, and I believe that **reading is the best way to learn to write**.

At the back of this book is a Suggested Reading List that recommends books in several categories: writing, history, women's history, self-esteem and memoir. If you are interested in expanding your reading regimen to include both classic and contemporary first-rate writing, here are several suggestions.

◆ Consult the book *Good Reading: A Guide for Serious Readers* by Olga S. Weber at your public library.

◆ Take literature classes at your community college. Although I am the former director of public relations and marketing for the Maricopa Community College District, it is from my experience as an adult student at two MCCD community colleges that I can recommend community college education. The classes are small, the schools are better prepared for adult students returning to higher education, and your chances of getting an instructor with a doctorate for introductory courses are probably higher than at a four-year school.

◆ Check with your local library for suggested reading lists in your interest area. Most librarians will be thrilled at your interest in expanding your reading horizons. In addition, many libraries provide meeting space for book groups, including Great Books discussion groups which are coordinated out of the University of Chicago.

◆ Contact The Center for the Book in your state through the National Center for the Book at the Library of Congress. (101 Independence Ave., SE, Washington, D.C., 20540-4920. Telephone: 202-707-5221 or electronic mail at cfbook@loc.gov). Each of the 36 Centers for the Book share a common mission, "to stimulate public interest in books, reading, libraries and literacy," and many of them support book groups and provide suggested reading lists.

◆ Join or start a book group. Books are available to guide you in organizing a book group and selecting good books to read. Perhaps you can convince your group to focus on memoirs.

Most important, **read**. Read up. Read something a little more challenging or difficult than you normally would. Read out. Try reading books outside your current interest areas; stretch yourself to learn something new.

Reading memoirs and autobiographies will show you how other people portray themselves in words, but there is also great value in reading good **fiction**—short stories, novels, plays (such as Shakespeare's), mysteries, even romance novels. In the past few years, the techniques of good fiction writers have crept into nonfiction, producing great interest in a new genre known as "creative nonfiction." The term refers to a stylistic embellishment of the truth. When you read a well-written novel, you are most likely unaware of the writer's craft, but the novelist has labored to manipulate, for maximum benefit to you, plot, characterization, setting and other building blocks of a good story.

When you read, look for the techniques each writer employs, and think about how you might use those techniques in your own writing. Reading is also the best way to expand and freshen your vocabulary. Keep a dictionary handy when you are reading, and look up unfamiliar words right away. If you own the book you are reading, circle the new words and new techniques you identify and make a note in the margin of the page, then mark the page with a bookmark or small Post-It note on which you can scribble a note to yourself.

Learn from experienced writers

Many women attracted to life story writing are already proficient and published writers. Cameo Workshops have become excellent venues for meeting committed writers, both professional and nonprofessional. Those with published books have found workshop participants interested in reading their work.

Even accomplished writers know that their writing skills must stay honed and fresh. Above all, they perfect their writing skills through practice. That means writing. Writing. And more writing.

In addition, they turn to other professional writers for example and inspiration. They attend workshops and conferences and they read books which give detailed advice on how to be a better writer. There are many such books available, so it is not necessary for me to repeat the same kind of information in this book. I have tried to provide a simple summary of helpful techniques for the nonprofessional writer.

However, there are several books on writing which life story writers might find useful to consult. *Write Right* by Jan Venolia is "a desk drawer digest to punctuation, grammar and style." *Writing Life Stories,* by writing instructor and author Bill Roorbach, is a good guide to creative nonfiction techniques. ❦

M L KING JR SCHOOL
PHOENIX ARIZONA
MRS. MILLER
GRADE 5
1977

CHAPTER EIGHT

The Cameo Life Stories Questionnaire

Dear Everywoman,

Welcome to your autobiographical adventure!

Following is the *Cameo Life Stories Questionnaire.* It is designed to 1) guide you in writing about your life and 2) provide a standard set of 92 questions specifically geared to women's life experiences.

Consider the following questions as tools to help you remember significant influences, events, decisions and activities in your life. You may attach a résumé if you like when you submit your completed *Questionnaire* to The STORIES Center, but our emphasis is more on information that résumés don't reflect—memories, ideas, feelings, environment and so on.

Please don't be discouraged by the number of questions. All the questions may not apply to you; answer only those you wish. Not all questions require lengthy answers. On the other hand, write as much as you like. You may find the question-answering process very similar to journal writing, which often has the wonderful benefit of revealing to ourselves information we were not conscious of having. You can always add more to your story later and submit an updated version at any time.

The *Cameo Life Stories Questionnaire* was developed with the input of a wide variety of women—historians, educators, writers, homemakers, executives, older women, young women, mothers, single women and women of a wide range of religious affiliations and ethnic backgrounds. If you find your personal life experience is not represented in these questions, please feel free to add whatever information you feel is important. We don't want any woman to feel excluded from the Cameo Life Stories program. It was created to include every woman.

We suggest you write your answers to questions on separate pieces of paper, not on the *Questionnaire.* Number your answers to correspond to the questions. It's helpful to keep all your papers, including notes and photographs, in a three-ring binder or a notebook of your choice. Many people are recording their stories on computer.

The Cameo Life Stories program is a not-for-profit program affiliated with the National Museum of Women's History. Our goal is to encourage as many women as possible to write their life stories, preferably using the *Cameo Life Stories Questionnaire,* and to submit their stories to the women's life stories archives of The STORIES Center.

The format of this *Questionnaire* is simple to encourage ease in copying. If copied in its entirety, the *Cameo Life Stories Questionnaire* and this introductory letter may be reproduced to facilitate widespread distribution.

Since the first *Cameo Life Stories Questionnaires* were given out at an Arizona women's event on February 14, 1998, the Cameo Life Stories project has spread throughout the United States and the world, passing from mother to daughter, sister to sister and friend to friend. Cameo Circles are forming among friends and family members and in such settings as libraries, churches, synagogues, senior centers, hospice programs, domestic violence shelters, and women's organizations.

You are important. You make history. Your life makes a difference in the world. Write your life story to share with your family and with the future.

When you complete your *Questionnaire,* complete and sign the Cameo Release Form at the back of the *Questionnaire.* Make a copy of your answers and the completed Cameo Release Form for your own use. Send a clear copy of your *Questionnaire* answers and Cameo Release Form to The STORIES Center. You may submit to the archives a narrative life story instead or in addition to *Questionnaire* answers.

Spanish and e-mail versions of the *Cameo Life Stories Questionnaire* are available. For more information, contact the Cameo Life Stories program of The STORIES Center at 480-421-1999 in Phoenix, Arizona, or the National Museum of Women's History in Washington, D.C.

Your life story is important. Please start answering the *Cameo Life Stories Questionnaire* as soon as possible.

Sincerely,

Deborah Hansen Linzer

Deborah Hansen Linzer
President and Founder
The STORIES Center

Cameo Life Stories Questionnaire

Life's Beginnings

1. Where were you born? (town, state, country) How many people lived in your childhood hometown or city?
2. What is your birth date? Do you tell others your age?
3. Describe your natural parents, stepparents, adoptive parents or foster parents.
4. Describe the landscape of your hometown, your neighborhood or the rural area where you grew up.
5. Describe the first home you remember living in.

Being a Girl

6. How did your parents feel about your being a girl?
7. When did you first realize boy and girls were different?
8. How many sisters or brothers did you have? Were they older or younger than you? How did you get along with each other?
9. Were boys and girls treated differently in your family? How?

Your Interests and Appearance

10. What were your typical and favorite childhood activities?
11. Describe your appearance as a child, as a teen, as a young woman, as an older woman. How have your feelings about your appearance changed over time? How did you feel about your hair? Your body? What are your attitudes about clothing? Are there articles of clothing you once wore which women no longer wear? Has a cameo ever played a role in your life?

Religious or Spiritual life

12. What was your family's religious affiliation when you were a child? How religious was your family? How religious were you? Have your feelings about your religion or spirituality changed over time? What has been your source of spiritual support throughout your life?

Childhood Education

13. What kind of school did you attend as a child? How many students attended the same school? What subjects did you like best or excel in? What subjects did you dislike?

Childhood Influences

14. Were there any pets, toys, imaginary playmates, books, dolls or games that were especially important to you as a child? Describe them. What influence did they have on your development?
15. What individuals most influenced you as a child? Parents? Grandparents or other relatives? Teacher? Religious figure? A neighbor?
16. Did you belong to any youth groups? Which ones? What influence do you think they played in your development? (for example, Girl Scouts, Camp Fire, 4-H, church or temple youth group)
17. What influence do you think race or ethnicity played in your development? How does it affect your adult life?
18. Describe your childhood best friend and your relationship.

Childhood Aspirations

19. What words of advice do you remember being given about your future? From whom? What influence did the advice have on you? Did you have a "Hope chest"?
20. When did you begin to think about "what you would be when you grew up? What did you think you might or might not "be"? Did your dreams change throughout childhood?

Physical Activity

21. Were you athletic as a child? Was this acceptable to your family? Have your physical activities and your beliefs about physical activity changed over time? Have you had to limit your physical activity? If so, how did you react?

Sense of Right and Wrong

22. Why and how were you punished as a child? How did you react? How has your personal experience with discipline or "justice" affected your attitudes about raising children or social justice? Describe your philosophy of right and wrong and how you think it developed.

Significant Events

23. Do you recall any special incidents that had a significant impact on you as a child? (for example, an accident, hospitalization, birth of a younger sibling, moving, best friend moving away, divorce, death, family violence, a school project, and so on.)
24. Do you recall any incidents in your childhood of a sexual nature? (for example, sexual exploration with another child, fondling by an adult, penetration by an adult, same-sex tenderness, and so on) Did anyone at the time suggest the activity was improper? How? How did you react to what happened? Did you discuss it with anyone? How do you think the incident(s) affected you at the time or later in life?
25. Did you participate in any special ceremonies in your early teenage years, such as a bat mitzvah? Quinciñera? Describe the event and its impact on you.

Puberty

26. Describe your relationship to your peers during your teenage years. How did you feel about yourself during this time? How were you treated by others your age? By adults?
27. When did you have your first menstrual period? Were you prepared? If so, how were you informed and by whom? If not, how did you handle it? Did it prevent you from participating in activities? What names were used for menstruation at that time?
28. How have you informed your own children about menstruation, sex, and romantic relationships?

Young Love

29. When did you first begin to develop romantic attachments to others?
30. What kind of life partner did you envision? How did you envision yourself as a partner?

Adulthood

31. As you entered adulthood, did you choose a role similar to the one you envisioned for yourself as a child? When did you first consider yourself an adult? Describe what adulthood meant to you then and now. If you were not a homemaker, and if you were not self-employed or employed by someone else as an adult, describe your life circumstances.

Employment

32. Describe jobs you had as a young person at home. Describe any paid jobs you had outside the home.
33. Did you obtain full-time employment immediately after high school? Why? Describe your jobs. What did you earn? How did your pay compare to the pay of men with similar jobs?
34. Did you enjoy working? Why or why not?

Higher Education

35. Did you continue your education after high school? Why? Where? Did you complete a degree?
36. Did you have any difficulties pursuing further education? (for example, family support, money, and so on)

Employment After Higher Education

37. When you entered the work force following higher education, did you experience any difficulties finding employment? If so, describe your experience.
38. Describe your various jobs. Did you enjoy your work? Why or why not? With a college education, what did you earn and how did your earnings compare with the pay of men in similar jobs?

Job Experiences

39. Did you experience any difficulties in your employment? If so, describe the difficulties. Were you every sexually harassed? (for example, did a supervisor or employer ever expect you to provide sexual favors in exchange for favorable decisions regarding your job, or did you experience a "hostile work environment"—comments, threats, requests, touching, and so on?)
40. Did your career progress as you had hoped or expected? Why or why not?

Working with Others

41. If you ever worked outside the home, did you work with other women? Were there women in supervisory positions? How were they perceived? Did they assist you in your job goals?
42. Describe any mentors you may have had (people who assisted or advised you in your jobs).

Marriage and Relationships

43. Did you marry or enter a long-term, committed relationship? When and with whom? Did you expect it to last forever?
44. Did your name change with marriage? Why or why not? If so, how did it change?
45. Did you ever have sexual relationships with anyone before or outside of marriage? If so, how did you feel about the experience? What are your attitudes about sex outside of marriage?
46. Were you ever pregnant (or think you were pregnant) outside of marriage? Did you ever have an unwanted pregnancy? What did you do? How did you feel about your decision at the time? How do you feel about it now? Have you ever told anyone about the pregnancy? An abortion? A miscarriage?

Children

47. Did you have children? How many? When were they born? How old were you when they were born?
48. What impact did childbirth (or adopting a child) have on you?
49. If you did not have children, what were the reasons?
50. Did you ever lose a child? How did you cope with the loss?
51. If you had children while you were working, how much time did you take off from work when the children were born? How did you feel about your decision? Were you paid during your absence from the job? Who cared for your children while you were at work? How did you feel about that arrangement? Describe any problems you may have had with childcare.
52. Describe your experience as a mother.

Both Partners Working

53. Did your partner work outside the home also? If so, did you both consider your jobs equally important? Why or why not?

54. When you were both working outside the home, how did you and your spouse divide all the responsibilities in your family? (for example, housework, childcare, repairs, car maintenance, social life, activities with family, paying bills, correspondence, and health care.) How did you feel about this division of labor?

Full-Time Homemakers

55. At any point in your life did you consider being a homemaker as your primary occupation? How did you prepare for this job? How many years did you work as a homemaker?
56. If your spouse worked outside the home while you worked as a homemaker, did you both consider your jobs equally important? Why or why not? How do you think society viewed your role? How did you feel about not receiving a paycheck per se?
57. If your spouse worked outside the home while you worked as a homemaker, how did you and your spouse divide responsibilities in your family? (for example, cleaning, food preparation, child care, repairs, car maintenance, social life, activities with family, paying bills, health care, and correspondence) How did you feel about this division of labor?

Couples' Finances

58. How did you and your spouse handle your income (from any source)? Did you share or have separate checking or savings accounts, for example? Did you prepare prenuptial agreements?
59. As a couple, how did you make decisions about how to spend money? Did you feel equally deserving of making spending decisions with your husband? As a couple, did you spend as much money for your needs and interests as for your spouse's?

Partnership Issues

60. Did you feel like an equal partner in your relationship? Why or why not? Did you attempt to make changes that would make you feel more comfortable in your relationship? Were your efforts effective?
61. If the relationship lasted, why do you think it lasted? Were you happy or unhappy in the marriage? Why?

62. If the relationship ended, describe the reasons why. How long did the relationship last? If it ended in divorce, who initiated the divorce and why? What were significant stresses?
63. How did the divorce affect you financially and emotionally?
64. If you divorced with children, how did you and your ex-husband handle child custody? Living arrangements for the children? Financial support for the children?
65. In the divorce, how did you and your ex-husband agree to share the assets and debts of your marriage? Do you feel the financial arrangement was fair? How did it impact you?
66. When you divorced, were you prepared to support yourself? If you found employment, describe your new job and how you adjusted.

Reflections on Single and Married Life

67. Looking back, what advantages have you experienced about being married? What disadvantages?
68. What advantages have you experienced about being single? What disadvantages? If you never married, what factors affected your decision to remain single?
69. Did you not marry because a woman meant more to you than a male-female relationship? If you are a lesbian, when did you know your sexual nature? How did you feel about that realization?
70. When your parents, family or friends learned of your sexual nature, how did they react? If you have children, what do you tell them? If you have kept your sexual nature a secret, describe the impact of your decision.
71. Describe any difficulties you have experienced as a result of your sexual nature.

Adult Influences

72. As an adult woman, what individuals have had a significant impact on your life? (for example, authors, bosses, friends, politicians, spiritual leaders) When and how have they influenced you?
73. If you have children, what advice did you or do you give them about their futures? Do you give the same advice to boys as to girls? (for example, advice about morals, marriage, religion, education, work and so on) Why or why not?

Adult Activities

74. What is your current occupation? Do you like it or not?
75. What activities do you enjoy for relaxation? How often do you do them? What are some of your favorite books or books influential in your life? What about movies, plays or other entertainment?
76. Throughout your life, what volunteer efforts have you undertaken for charities or nonprofit organizations? (for example, schools, Scouts or other youth groups, art groups, social service agencies, politics, church, and so on) What influence has this service activity had on you? What issues and organizations are most important to you? Have you contributed time or money to them?
77. Do you recall any incidents or issues in your adult life that have made a significant impact on you? (for example, accidents, hospitalization, moving, separation from a friend, divorce, remarriage, becoming a grandparent, sexuality, aging, career changes, death, or illness)

Attitudes About Women

78. Have you made specific efforts to impact organizations or issues that affect women or girls? Why or why not? Which organizations and issues have you been involved with?
79. Do you believe society restricts women? Do you feel you have the same freedoms and protections as men? Why or why not?
80. Do you consider yourself a feminist? Why or why not? How did you reach this conclusion?

Politics

81. What is your political affiliation, if any? Do you vote? Have you ever participated in politics? (for example, supported a candidate, run for office, demonstrated, and so on) Why or why not?

Women's Health

82. What are your current circumstances? (for example, your health, home, work, relationships, and so on)
83. Have you experienced menopause? What symptoms did you experience, if any? If so, was (or is) it a positive or negative experience? In what ways? Were you prepared?

84. What health issues have affected your life? (for example, have you experienced breast cancer, tumors, osteoporosis, sexually transmitted diseases, heart disease, clinical depression, disabilities, injuries and so on; discuss positive health experiences; include your sexual life)

Reflecting on Your Life

85. If you could change your current circumstances, what would you do and why?
86. If you could change your past, would you? Why? How?
87. What is your philosophy of life? If you could change the world, what would you do?
88. How do you feel about your life's accomplishments? What accomplishments are you most proud of?
89. How would you like to be remembered?
90. Would you consider yourself a luminary? (a "notable" person; someone who is a source of light; or a "shining" example of someone who has helped others or worked to develop her personal capabilities as fully as possible)
91. When did you start writing your life story (or working on the *Cameo Life Stories Questionnaire*) and how long did it take you to finish? How do you feel about the process? What do you intend to do with your story?
92. Is there any other aspect of your life you would like to describe? Please feel free to add anything else you might want to share.

Note: Thank you for participating in the Cameo Life Stories program! Your life story is very important. Feel free to enclose extra photographs, or photocopies of photos, of yourself, perhaps from different stages in your life. Mark your name and age on the back of each photo. Don't forget to complete the Cameo Release Form and send it when you submit your completed *Cameo Life Stories Questionnaire.*

Cameo Life Stories Questionnaire Release Form

Please complete and sign this Release Form, because it is the only authorization The STORIES Center will have from you on how to archive the information you are submitting.

☐ I give permission for my name to be used, in connection with the information I have provided, for research.
☐ I give permission for my name to be used, in connection with the information I have provided, for public education.
☐ I give permission for my name to be used, in connection with the information I have provided, for publication.
☐ I have enclosed a photograph of myself with my name and my age in the photo marked on the back, and I give permission for it to be used in any of the above applications.
☐ I give permission for my information to be used in any of the above applications, but do not use my name with my life story or *Questionnaire* answers.
☐ I want my *Questionnaire* answers or life story included in women's history archives, but I prefer not to provide my name.

Please provide the following information to help researchers, whether you provide your name or not. If you are submitting information on a woman who is deceased, give information applicable at the year of death.

Age __________ Marital Status __________ Race ____________________

Occupation ____

Current Religious Affiliation ______________________________

Current Residence (only city, state and country) ____________________

How did you receive the *Cameo Life Stories Questionnaire*?

____

Name (Print) ____
(Last name, first name, middle name, birth name)

Full Address ____

____

(Please notify The STORIES Center or the National Museum of Women's History of any address change. Your name and address will only be used to inform you about the Cameo Life Stories program.)

Home Telephone ____________________ E-mail ____________________

Signature ________________________________ Date ______________

Make a copy of your written information and this completed Release Form for your own use. Send a copy of both to: Cameo Life Stories, The STORIES Center, P.O. Box 9608, Scottsdale, Arizona, USA 85252-3608

Frequently asked questions

Do I have to answer every question in the *Cameo Life Stories Questionnaire*?

No. First of all, they won't all apply to you. That saves you some time. Start by answering the questions you are personally most interested in exploring. If you are concerned about sharing certain things, remember that you can create several versions of your final life story—one for yourself, one for family members and one for the archives, for example. Cameo Life Stories and the National Museum of Women's History would especially appreciate your answering the questions about women's experiences.

Are my answers confidential?

Absolutely, if you so choose. The key is the Cameo Release Form found at the end of the *Cameo Life Stories Questionnaire.* The written material you submit to The STORIES Center will not be shared with anyone unless you allow it by giving your signed permission on the Cameo Release Form.

Can I submit my life story as a narrative or must it be organized as answers to the *Cameo Life Stories Questionnaire*?

Your story is welcome in any written format. However, it will be helpful to scholars if information about your life is organized around the *Questionnaire*, because the *Questionnaire* will remind you to address women's issues you might otherwise leave out. Your answers to the *Cameo Life Stories Questionnaire* become your life story. Some women who have already prepared a narrative life story have gone back and inserted the *Questionnaire* numbers in their life story in the appropriate sections.

What is the difference between a life story, autobiography, memoir and Cameo?

Not much. An autobiography is a biography written by the person featured, and it usually includes a great deal of detail. Memoirs also imply significant length and, like autobiography, are most often associated with people of high profile. Life story is a term used more frequently with "ordinary" people. The term "Cameo" has been adopted by Cameo Life Stories as a shortcut way of referring to any version of a life story, and, like a life story, it can be any length.

What happens to my story when I submit it to The STORIES Center?

First, the Cameo you submit will be assigned a number and carefully filed according to the instructions you provide on the Release Form at the back of the *Cameo Life Stories Questionnaire.* You will be sent a letter acknowledging receipt of your life story and giving you the number assigned to it, unless you submit your story anonymously. We suggest you keep that letter and number with your important papers, for example, in a safe deposit box.

If you want your story to remain completely confidential, it will be filed under lock and key where no one will have access to it. If you choose to share your Cameo with researchers, it will be filed as a hard copy, as well as scanned onto computer for easier access by scholars across the country. The STORIES Center provides a safe and secure location for original life stories.

Is there a deadline for submitting life stories to the archives?

No. The National Museum of Women's History is going to be around for the next few centuries at least. Turn in your Cameo or *Questionnaire* answers when you are ready. The process of reflecting and writing may take awhile.

Can I add to my life story later, if I turn something in to the archives now?

Yes. Send your Cameo to The STORIES Center when you are motivated to do so; otherwise, life has a way of distracting us from our good intentions. Later, if you have more to add to your life story, send that in, too, with your assigned number, if possible.

Will future generations of my family have access to my life story?

Yes, if you indicate so on your Release Form. We suggest that you make copies of your Cameo and share them with family members now and tell them you would like your life story passed down to future generations as a way of teaching them about women and about the past. However, since not all family members can be trusted to care for our stories safely, your Cameo will still be available through The STORIES Center and the National Museum of Women's History. Family members may request access to your life story by using your name or the number assigned to your life story when you submitted it.

Should I send my address changes to The STORIES Center?

Yes, every time you change your address. This will help us contact you if scholars ever need to reach you about your life story. Please add the address and telephone number of The STORIES Center to your personal address directory and notify us of address changes.

Will I retain the copyright to my submitted life story even if I make it available to scholars?

Yes. The Release Form provides the opportunity for you to give scholars permission to publish portions of your life story. However, the copyright for your written work still belongs to you, if you want to publish it. If you give scholars permission to use your answers to the *Cameo Life Stories Questionnaire*, they will most likely contact you first, using the name and address you have provided on the Cameo Release Form.

Is the *Cameo Life Stories Questionnaire* available on the Internet?

Yes. To make the *Questionnaire* as widely available as possible, it can be downloaded from The STORIES Center website: www.thestoriescenter.org.

Can I make copies of the *Cameo Life Stories Questionnaire?*

Please do. Our only stipulation is that you copy it in its entirety, so that no questions are left out. Also, make sure that your copies include the name and address of The STORIES Center, so anyone finding a copy of the *Questionnaire* will know where to send her life story. Also copy the introductory letter. Your help in spreading the *Cameo Life Stories Questionnaire* is a great help in building women's history.

Where can I obtain additional copies of this book?

To order the *Cameo Life Stories Writing Guide for Everywoman: Penning Your Portrait in Words*, contact The STORIES Center at P.O. Box 9608, Scottsdale, Arizona USA 85252-3608. Telephone 480-421-1999. The e-mail address is cameolifestories@juno.com and the website address is www.thestoriescenter.org. An order form is also provided at the back of this book.

Do I need permission from The STORIES Center to start a Cameo Circle?

No. However, we would love to know that you are doing so. Women around the world are letting us know they have received the *Cameo Life Stories Questionnaire* and are encouraging others to write their life stories. This is always a thrill. It's also an opportunity for The STORIES Center to connect women interested in Cameo Life Stories who live in the same area but have not yet met. We can publish news of your activities in our newsletter and keep our coordinators informed, as well. ❦

CHAPTER NINE

Cameo Circles Bring Women Together to Write Their Memoirs

Despite your best intentions, working alone on your life story or Cameo may be difficult, even though it will give you more flexibility. Getting together with other women to discuss your life stories provides discipline, steady progress and the camaraderie of other committed contributors to history. Participants make progress on their *Cameo Life Stories Questionnaires* and have fun doing it.

Forming a Cameo Circle

Starting or leading a Cameo Circle does not require special training. This chapter contains basic information on how to organize and facilitate sessions of Cameo Circles, and the Suggested Reading List at the back should give you plenty of ideas for related reading.

However, some people are more comfortable if they have had a chance to discuss the Cameo Life Stories program with others and to participate in practice sessions. The best place to interact with other Cameo Life Stories volunteers is at the annual conference and at workshops. In addition, staff at The STORIES Center are always happy to answer your questions over the telephone or via electronic mail. They can put you in touch with experienced facilitators if you would like additional guidance.

State and local coordinators

Our goal is to appoint a Cameo Life Stories state coordinator in every state. State coordinators are volunteers committed to the Cameo Life Stories project. Their role is to train and provide information to Cameo Circle facilitators, serve as the primary state contact person for the Cameo Life Stories project, encourage the formation of Cameo Circles, and spread the Cameo Life Stories program among women throughout their state. Larger cities need coordinators as well. If you are interested in volunteering as a Cameo Life Stories coordinator or facilitator, call The STORIES Center at 480-421-1999.

Facilitators

Facilitators are women who are willing to help run their own Cameo Circle or be available to help other Cameo Circles get started. Facilitator training is a simple orientation to the Cameo Life Stories program provided by the state or local coordinator, and training can be held one-on-one or in groups.

Settings for Cameo Circles

Existing organizations may decide to focus on the Cameo Life Stories project for the benefit of their members. A book group, for example, may convert to a Cameo Circle. Larger women's groups—such as chapters of the League of Women Voters or the American Association of University Women—may have members who want to organize in smaller groups to work on the *Cameo Life Stories Questionnaire.* Groups have formed throughout the United States in senior citizen centers, churches, synagogues, educational institutions, singles groups, in neighborhoods, and among friends.

The Cameo Life Stories program is encouraged for use by domestic violence victims and survivors of sexual and other abuses. It has been introduced in training workshops as a tool to assist probation officers and professionals working with clients on issues of self-esteem and personal growth. The procedures followed in Cameo Circles are also being used in staff development and retreats for boards of directors.

Cameo Life Stories has a national domestic violence coordinator, a national hospice coordinator, and a national nursing home coordinator.

For more information on utilizing Cameo Circles in these environments, contact The STORIES Center.

Because no formal training is required to facilitate a group, I hope that individuals will not charge women to participate in a Cameo Circle. My intention is to make this program as inexpensive as possible and thus available to anyone with the desire to participate. As I discuss in Chapter 1, Cameo Workshop leaders might charge a nominal fee to cover expenses, including the cost of Cameo Life Stories materials. The basic, low-cost tool needed for Cameo Circles is the *Cameo Life Stories Questionnaire.*

The Golden Rule of Cameo Circles

Be kind to one another.

I have to amend the golden rule slightly, because we can't always assume, when we say, "Do unto others as you would have them do unto you," that the way you like to be treated is the kind way. Instead, treat others with kindness, and expect them to treat you with kindness in return. Treat others with respect, and expect to be treated with respect. Honor the dignity of others, and expect them to honor your dignity.

The underlying premise of Cameo Life Stories is that **every** woman is important; every woman is valuable; every woman makes history. It follows, then, that we must treat every woman with the respect she deserves, simply because she is a sister human being.

Just as curiosity about others is a natural human impulse, so is the tendency to judge others. Surrounding ourselves with other people who are just like us makes life easier to cope with, because we don't face as many challenges to our beliefs. Limiting our relationships to people we like is natural because it generates less conflict and is therefore more pleasant.

You may discover many similarities of belief in your Cameo Circle—and you may not. If not, you may stand a chance of learning more than you expected. Keep an open mind, and remember that the purpose of Cameo Circles is to help women write and share their life stories. It is not appropriate to judge each other or to make judgments about beliefs or practices or experiences other than yours. It is appropriate to discuss belief systems, practices and experiences, but do so from the perspective of amateur historians or sociologists. When you are sharing your own beliefs, do so without preaching. You will want others to respect you as you share yourself, but you cannot expect others necessarily to share your beliefs, just as others should not expect you always to agree with them.

Getting along with different personalities is part of life and something we've all had to learn since childhood. Luckily, society has developed guidelines to help us cope with the amazingly wide variety of people's personalities, and these guidelines are called "manners." You may not think of kindness as manners, but good manners embody kindness. Even when we may not feel naturally kindly toward a particular person, good manners help us avoid conflict. I have learned over the years not to trust first impressions because people's initial behavior toward one another may often reflect a temporary stress that gives a bad impression and because our interpretation of someone else's behavior may be tainted by our own stress.

Kindly manners carry us through the rough spots. Behaving kindly, even when we don't feel like it, usually ensures that we can expect kindly treatment in return, which makes our lives more pleasant. Most important, acting in a kindly manner, even when we don't initially feel kindly, can actually change our feelings. You may have noticed yourself how it often works, when you are unhappy, to "put on a happy face." Without going into the psychological underpinnings, let me just emphasize the truism. Sometimes our feelings follow our actions, rather than our actions always stemming from our inner emotions.

If an uncomfortable situation arises in your Cameo Circle, it is first important to strive for understanding by stepping outside of your expectations and observing, as dispassionately as possible, what is occurring.

Second, whether you achieve understanding or not, kindly manners should prevail. This applies to everyone, including people who may not be practiced in kindly manners.

Forgive me if this little homily seems unnecessary. I assure you it is extremely important, because if we do not honor one another, how can we expect society to honor women? Some of you may by thinking, "Why coddle someone? The world is a rough and tumble place, and it'd be better for everyone to toughen up and not expect kindness in a cruel world." Some people even think that kind behavior is too "feminine" and therefore to be avoided as a brand of inferiority. I believe that if women are kinder, so much the better for the world. Kindness among men would serve them all much better, and they can turn to women to learn from example.

It is one thing to be strong, and another to be kind. Some of the kindest women I know are the strongest. Whether you believe in kindly manners or not, they should be the standard in any Cameo Circle. For everyone.

The basics of kindliness

For many people, kindness is almost instinctual because they were raised believing in the inherent worth of others and the importance of treating them gently. For many others, kindness is not a way of life and treating others in a manner that communicates respect (whether it accurately represents their inner feelings or not) must be learned. For the benefit of all of us, here is a brief refresher list of the basics of kindly manners applicable in any social setting:

◆ **Smile.** Sometimes I worry people think I'm a simpleton because I smile so much. I don't want them to think I'm not serious, capable, or purposeful. The first message I need to send to others, however, is that I am approachable and receptive. They will learn more about me later. Smiles are the easiest, quickest tools we have to communicate kindness.

◆ **Extend a welcome.** When you meet someone for the first time, assume that they are shy and let them know, verbally or nonverbally, that you are very happy to welcome them into your circle (whatever the circle). Smile, shake hands, tell them you are happy to meet them, try to remember their names, and introduce them to others in your group.

◆ **Include newcomers.** If you are talking to someone, and another person approaches you as if to join in, say to your companion, "Excuse me." Then turn to the new person and welcome them into your discussion. Introduce each other if necessary. Then say to your new companion, "My friend and I were just discussing X." Then continue your original discussion if you can, stepping back and turning your head to include the new person in conversation.

◆ **Join conversation politely.** If you would like to join someone already in conversation, approach and stand attentively close to the circle of discussion. Someone in the group should include you. If they don't, wait for a break in conversation and say, "Excuse me. May I join you? My name is ________." If you are excluded, excuse yourself and look around the room for someone who is alone, someone who is smiling, or someone who appears to be listening to others politely—and try again.

◆ **Draw in others.** If you find yourself in a group where you know others or feel comfortable, share some of your good fortune with someone in the room who may not feel as comfortable. Extend yourself. Look around to see if anyone appears to need a friendly introduction. Jill Ker Conway, in her autobiography, *True North*, writes of being shy and entering a party of strangers. She decided to join an elderly man sitting alone, who turned out to be a leading businessman and philanthropist and became a good friend.

◆ **Raise your hands.** I believe in raising hands in discussion groups. This practice has fallen by the wayside, but it is good practice. It helps avoid interruption (the height of rudeness), and it is a helpful visual indicator of how many people want to speak on a given subject. Establish some mutually agreed upon signal for desire to speak.

◆ **Do not interrupt.** If you accidentally, unavoidably, interrupt someone else, immediately excuse yourself. "I'm sorry I interrupted. Go ahead." If the discussion seems to be moving away from your perfectly timed comment, wait anyway. If others are observing raised hands, they will see some urgency in your wave, and let you speak. If not, wait for an opening and say, "I'd like to address an earlier topic, in case we don't return to it."

◆ **Control negative emotions.** Speak with passion when you feel it. But never attack with anger. If you feel angry, say, "I feel angry about...." Don't hurl your anger at anyone. If you feel a strong sense of advocacy for a certain subject, be as persuasive as you can—but always ask yourself first, "Am I ready to take a stand yet? Is it time for decision? Is my influence premature for myself or for others?" Don't be afraid to express your enthusiasm. Enthusiasm is a joy, and it is not preaching.

◆ **Don't monopolize conversation or discussion.** This is an admonishment to me as much as to anyone. Some of us are talkers and some aren't. I feel I'm not participating in life if I'm not talking about it. Because I'm a talker, I have to be careful to observe group dynamics, keeping tabs on how many times I speak and noting clues on others' faces which show they might contribute if given half a chance.

◆ **Don't assume you are right.** Overconfidence can screen out valuable input. It can sometimes come across as arrogance, which none of us likes in anyone else! Even if you are right, how can you convince others if you are treating them like morons? Even if you are the boss, rather than a discussion facilitator, you will get more cooperation if you treat others as if you value their help, rather than demand or expect it.

◆ **Share the work load.** If you are a guest in someone's home—at a Cameo Circle, for example—and they have prepared food, at least carry your plate to the kitchen when you have finished eating. If the hostess waves you out of the kitchen, respect her wishes, but at least offer to help. If a function is catered, you don't need to help with the dishes, but always thank the host before you leave.

◆ **Thank-yous.** Thank-you notes are one of life's blessings. Follow-up thank-you notes are never inappropriate. I seem to be forever plunging into the moment ahead and I chafe at stopping to write thank-you notes. Ironically, I am always very grateful for the generosity of others—for their effort to spend time with me, to arrange a special occasion, to feed me, or to surprise me with a gift. I will go to my grave worried that I haven't adequately thanked everyone in my life, but I'm doing my best. Thanking people is one of the small incentives we have to keep on being kind to one another.

◆ **Ask forgiveness.** Asking for forgiveness is almost never out of line—even when you think the other person should be asking forgiveness from you. You'd be amazed at how many people expect apologies from others without examining their own behavior. Sometimes being the first one to apologize breaks the pride barrier and allows the other person to relax and apologize as well.

If you don't feel you've done anything wrong, but interpersonal conflict arises, say, "I'm sorry that we're bumping heads. I apologize if I've done anything to offend you, and I hope you'll tell me—gently—if I have." As a youngster I was so schooled in apology that I would say "I'm sorry" when I bumped into an empty chair. That is a bit extreme, but even good habits are hard to break.

◆ **Acknowledge your mistakes.** This may not seem to apply to Cameo Circles, but the ability to accept responsibility for mistakes reflects a habit of mind about life in general. When we hide our errors from others, it signals that we are afraid—afraid of punishment or disapproval, afraid to be seen as less than perfect. When we are silent about our mistakes, it shows a reluctance, if not an inability, to see and deal with reality. It also sometimes puts an undue burden on someone else. Making excuses is even worse, because it makes us look whiney, weak and dishonest. Confessing our mistakes shows maturity.

Once as a little girl I stole a piece of bubble gum from Joe Alick's small local grocery store, but my mother noticed as I got in the car, and she made me go back inside and confess. The man at the counter thanked me for my honesty and gave me a penny. Looking back, I appreciate his kind way of teaching me to do the right thing.

◆ **Don't criticize.** Don't criticize others in general conversation. Sharing your frustrations with a close friend is natural, and it sometimes lets us blow off steam and then adopt a more generous attitude toward the person we're criticizing. But complaining publicly reflects poorly on us as a kind and sensitive person, and we never know what damage we might do to another person.

◆ **Be on time.** When I worked for Preston V. McMurry Jr. (I always called him the "Renaissance communicator"), I was habitually late for appointments. Preston educated me in a positive way about the importance of being prompt. From his experience in sales, he said, he had learned that being on time shows respect for the client. In other words, being on time shows respect. Period. In addition, latecomers miss things and lessen the effectiveness of meetings, not to mention diminishing their own effectiveness as well.

Discuss kindly manners in your circle

It is wise to begin any Cameo Circle with a discussion about the manners of kindness which should be your standard operating procedure. That subject alone might provoke some lively repartee. You may not think it's necessary to bring up the subject in advance, especially if your church group is embarking on the Cameo Life Stories program, for example, but I can assure you it is far easier to have the discussion before a problem arises than afterwards.

What do you do if someone in the group consistently violates the rule of kindness? This is where the facilitator comes in. The facilitator can start a meeting with a review of goals and timetables—and the rule of kindly manners—as of way of gently reminding the group as a whole. If a particular person doesn't get the message, the facilitator or another group member should telephone the person privately, discuss the problem, then end on a different, positive note. I shudder at the prospect of having to make such a phone call myself, but if I had to I might say, "Some of the women in our group have had their feelings hurt because they feel you interrupt them."

I have been on both sides of this coin. In my enthusiasm for a project, I have sometimes crossed the border into rudeness without realizing it, so I empathize with others who might experience the same thing. On the other hand, I have actually had to leave an organization I helped create because others I worked with were too relentlessly insensitive. As hard as I tried not to take it personally, I felt their rudeness reflected a genuine lack of respect for me and others, which was unhelpful and unhealthy for a productive relationship.

In Cameo Circles, time constraints require limits on both writing and discussion, so group sessions are structured out of necessity. If the group would like more time for free-ranging discussion, you can vote to meet at other times, maybe for lunch or for a party. Not everyone needs to participate in these extra get-togethers, but never meet as your Cameo Circle without at least inviting everyone. If the group decides one member is too destructive to the group—or has problems which may require professional help—you may need to ask that person to leave the group, but I'm sure you will do that only with the greatest sensitivity, carefully weighing the needs and dignity of the one individual against the needs and dignity of the others.

Assertiveness and kindness go well together

One last word on kindly manners. It's no secret that many, many women have been raised to put the needs of others first, before their own. The purpose of kindness between people is to demonstrate respect and to encourage self-respect in each other. Kindness is different from self-effacement, self-abnegation, or continually putting yourself in the "backseat" or at "the back of the bus." To women trying to build their self-esteem, issues of interpersonal behavior can be confusing. At the extreme, imagine women who are the victims of physical and verbal abuse who learn to be afraid to express their own desires or take a stand on behalf of their own needs. When we encourage them to respect themselves and be assertive, it is never at the expense of respect for others.

Cameo Circle guidelines

Organization of Your Group

Cameo Circles should try to limit their group to 15 people or less in order to give each person time to participate fully. With larger groups, it is still valuable to begin the *Cameo Life Stories Questionnaire* together (group activity may be the impetus many of us need), but sharing may have to be limited because of time constraints. You may want to conduct an introductory session for a large group, then break into smaller groups for sharing.

It is helpful to have a facilitator or co-facilitators. You can also rotate responsibility for facilitating the group. If your Cameo Circle will be meeting on a regular basis, create a directory and provide a copy to each member. This will help you share the task of keeping everyone informed about meeting dates and topics.

Sit in a Circle

Each time you meet as a group, try to sit in a circle. Not only does a circle allow everyone to see each other most easily, a circle puts everyone in an equal position with no sense of hierarchy. A circle communicates inclusiveness.

Cameo Life Stories Workbooks

Everyone participating will need her own *Cameo Life Stories Workbook.* Copies of the 92 key questions are available on printed notebook dividers from The STORIES Center, or women may create their own workbooks by copying the essential *Cameo Life Stories Questionnaire* printed in this book. Ideally, each woman will have her own three-ring binder in which to store the *Cameo Life Stories Questionnaire* and her written responses to questions. The binders also store related papers such as sketches and notes, and they provide a portable writing surface in a group setting where there are no desks or tables. In addition, each woman will need blank paper, a pen, several sheets of blank paper, or a laptop computer at Cameo Circle sessions.

The facilitator or co-facilitators should read the *Cameo Life Stories Writing Guide for Everywoman* beforehand, including the *Cameo Life Stories Questionnaire.* If possible, have participants read this book and the *Questionnaire* in advance, also. Facilitators might want to prepare a "lesson plan" which includes warm-up exercises, introductory information, clustering, timed-writing exercises and discussion.

Length of Sessions

Generally, a good length for Cameo Circle gatherings is one and a half to two hours, including the first session. You may have to adjust the amount of time you set aside for each question as you go along. Allot four to five minutes for the clustering exercise before you begin writing. For timed-writing exercises, a rule of thumb is to give people 15 minutes to write, then five minutes each to share aloud. A group of 12 women will need an hour to read their written pieces to each other. Some people may not use their full five minutes; they may donate their extra minutes to women who request it. Obviously, if someone has something difficult to share and needs more time, the circle should respond lovingly.

Try using a timer or a watch to help women limit their remarks and leave time for everyone to speak so no one feels left out and everyone feels like an equally valuable contributor. Move from one person to the next without general discussion until everyone has had a turn, or discussion may bog down. When you open the floor for discussion, try to keep talkative folks from dominating. Take time to draw out women less apt to assert themselves.

Limiting your writing and speaking to specific time periods may seem constraining at first, but timed exercises are valuable. They provide goals and help maintain order. They keep the process moving. Anyone who wants to write more than the time allowed can continue alone. The group may also decide to schedule additional time for sharing.

Negotiate Your Group Goals

Use the democratic process when you have questions about procedure or scheduling. For example, groups who bond well and really enjoy getting together may want to prolong their Cameo Circle experience. This is easy to do, as you will quickly discover. The discussions the *Cameo Life Stories Questionnaire* generates can be fascinating—and lengthy! Be sensitive to circle members' goals. Who is in a hurry to finish her story? Who wants to make more time for discussion and camaraderie? Can you compromise?

Perhaps you can hold your regularly scheduled session and schedule socializing time immediately afterwards. The group may not be in a hurry to finish and may prefer giving more time and attention to each group of questions. Questions are grouped by general subject area. You may skip questions that don't apply; some questions are more detailed and evoke detailed answers. You may decide to be flexible as you go along in assigning questions for each session. If not, and you have limited sessions, you might consider assigning homework so circle members will answer some questions at home on their own.

Don't Neglect Writing in Favor of Talking

Talking is the fun part of Cameo Circles. I know. But, let me share with you something I've learned about writing. Both writing and speaking require the effort to formulate and express our thoughts. Because it's often easier to express things out loud, we communicate with our voices instead of on paper; however, the spoken words disappear and our desire to communicate is dissipated. Take the same energy and words you would use to speak, but direct them into your hands and onto paper. Then you can share aloud and also have something written to show for your effort. Writing may also help you formulate your thoughts better before you speak, which is helpful to your listeners.

So emphasize the importance of putting thoughts on paper. Too often when we just describe something verbally, we lose our incentive to write it down. Remember that you are penning your personal portrait piece by piece, so every piece counts. Capture your words on paper whenever you can.

Suggestions for the first Cameo Circle session

If participants haven't read the *Cameo Life Stories Questionnaire* in advance, take time to do so while you are waiting for everyone to arrive. The facilitator should briefly share with the group some general information about the Cameo Life Stories program and be prepared to answer such frequently asked questions (FAQs) as When did it begin? Where do the stories go? What is the National Museum of Women's History? Do we have to answer every question? Do we have to share everything? Is there a deadline for submitting stories to the archives? Answers to frequently asked questions are at the end of this chapter.

The facilitator should also review the following guidelines and allow some time for questions or discussion:

◆ **Kind manners.** Kindness is the cardinal rule in Cameo Circles, because it underscores the main premise of the Cameo Life Stories program—"every woman is important."

◆ **Confidentiality.** Your group experience will be most valuable if members trust each other enough to open up. Building that trust requires that nothing shared in your Cameo Circle should be repeated to anyone outside the group unless the person sharing specifically gives permission. Some information may seem harmless to you, but it's best to be safe and respect each other's privacy right from the beginning. Sharing the names of Cameo Circle members should not be a problem. We certainly want the world to know about Cameo Circles in general.

◆ **Openness.** Sharing our experiences and our feelings can bring us joy, relief, information, understanding, challenges, laughs, courage, friendship. Strive to share openly and honestly. Some women's greatest reward in sharing honestly is to learn that "they are not alone."

◆ **Respecting boundaries.** "Boundaries" is a term therapists use to describe a comfort zone which is unique to each person. We each have a fairly good sense of what we are willing to share with others. Most of us also can sense how far to expect others to go in sharing. No one is expected to "spill her guts" if she doesn't want to. If someone needs to share something which you might not think appropriate, hold your judgment. As an accepting listener, you may have provided an enormous gift. Set your own standard for what information you want to tell the group and only change your mind if you feel comfortable doing so.

◆ **Withholding judgment.** Answering the *Cameo Life Stories Questionnaire* is an experience in personal reflection and discovery. It is also an opportunity to gain greater understanding and acceptance of other women's lives. This is a rare gift in a world where many of us learn to control the image we project as a means of self-protection. The more exposure you get to other ways of thinking and feeling, the greater is your opportunity to develop wisdom. The knowledge you gain may make you more insightful about your own life.

◆ **Avoiding advice.** While sharing with others may be therapeutic, circle members should not assume the role of therapists, judges, or advice-givers. Expressing emotions is natural when a sharing and safe environment is created. In some cases, you might find it appropriate to privately recommend professional help to a group member. If you have a counseling professional in your circle, don't expect them to give professional advice. Instead, look to them for the wisdom to be a good listener.

◆ **Listening respectfully.** Everyone will be given an equal chance to speak. Not everyone is required to share aloud, although a person who will not share with the group at all should probably work alone. Her silence will eventually make the other circle members uncomfortable. When one woman is speaking, everyone else should listen quietly and attentively. So many of us have been trained to listen thoughtfully to others that we seldom get a thoughtful audience ourselves. Enjoy this blessed opportunity.

◆ **An attitude of gratitude.** We cannot prescribe that you feel grateful for the Cameo Circle experience, but most of us feel a happy sense of thankfulness to the other women who commit to getting together with us on a regular basis. At each circle gathering, try to begin and end with an expression of thanks.

Introductory Exercises

Remind the group that the three elements of Cameo Circles are l) reflecting, 2) writing, and 3) sharing. Do one or two exercises to practice these three elements. Some people are nervous about writing or sharing aloud. Many of us need help in retrieving our memories. Here are a few introductory exercises:

"Fruit Basket." Bring a bag of items of the same category—oranges, grapefruit, apples or other "identical" objects—and give one to each person. Ask each woman to carefully examine her particular fruit or object, then put their items back in a pile in the center of the circle. Mix up the items. Now have each woman retrieve her original object from the pile. This exercise points out the power of careful observation, which is helpful in writing specific, and thus more effective, descriptions. More importantly, it underscores the major premise of the Cameo Life Stories program—that every woman is unique and important.

"Scar-ology." Have each person draw an outline of her body on unlined paper, then sketch in the location of body scars. Give everyone five minutes to draw. Then give each woman one minute to describe one significant scar. One Cameo Circle participant pointed out that many women have "scars that don't show." Consider emotional scars as well as physical scars.

"Nicknames." List all the names you remember being called as a child—e.g., cutie, doll, peanuts—or labels used to describe you, like pretty, stubborn, precocious, dumb, fat, scaredy cat, and so on. Give everyone five minutes to write. Then give each person one minute to explain how one of those names influenced her. Ask each person to tell the group the name they prefer to be called in the Cameo Circle.

Do at least one clustering exercise, which is described in Chapter 7, "Suggestions for Good Writing." The facilitator can demonstrate an example of clustering, starting with a core theme—such as influential books, favorite toys and games, childhood fears, friends—then adding on details. Select a topic. Give people five minutes to sketch a cluster of words and ideas or pictures. Then give them about 15 minutes to convert their cluster sketch into sentences and paragraphs. This exercise is good for people uncomfortable with their writing skills. Suggest "double-spaced" writing to allow room for later editing. Give everyone a time limit for sharing what they have written. Because clustering usually brings out many more memories than the other exercises, the sharing process may also take longer.

Try to answer at least one question from the *Cameo Life Stories Questionnaire.* It makes sense to begin with the first set of questions. Give everyone five minutes to sketch a cluster of memories for Question 3, Describe your natural parents, stepparents, adoptive parents, or foster parents, or Question 5, Describe the first home you remember living in. Then allow 15 minutes to translate that sketch into written paragraphs.

In wrapping up your first Cameo Circle session, be sure to do three things:

1) Congratulate yourselves on the the success of your first meeting—you began writing your story.

2) Make sure the group is clear about the next step. If you will be meeting again, agree on the days and times. Set a specific date for the next circle meeting and select questions for that session so you can begin thinking about them. Arrange to notify absent circle members of the next scheduled circle meeting.

3) At the end of the session, and at the end of every meeting of your Cameo Circle, consider closing with the Friendship Circle. Those of you working together on your life stories usually become friends, and borrowing the Girl Scout Friendship Circle as a closing ceremony is fitting.

Stand close together in a circle; hold your arms straight down and cross them; with your arms crossed, clasp hands with the person on either side of you. This little ceremony can vary, but two elements are common. If you have time, each person in the circle expresses one thing they are thankful for and squeezes the hand of the person next to her. Girl Scouts usually sing "Make New Friends" while squeezing hands around the circle. When the person who started the hand pressing receives the last squeeze, everyone says "good-bye" together. You leave the circle by raising your hands over your heads, still holding your neighbors' hands, and turning to face the outside of the circle. As you turn outwards, your arms will automatically unfold and send you back into the world with the mark of friendship in your heart. ❦

CHAPTER TEN

Spread the Words

Be proud of yourself every time you put something about your life story on paper. However, completing your Cameo is an accomplishment that calls for celebration. It would be very fitting to celebrate within your Cameo Circle. If your family or friends are aware of your efforts to write your life story, let them share in your success as well. You might want to schedule a special time with family or friends to thank them for supporting you on your life journey or for their assistance with your life story writing. Don't be surprised if they ask you to share all or parts of your story with them.

Celebrate the completion of your Cameo

Do something special for yourself to celebrate. Circle the day you finished on your calendar. Tell everyone you meet. Reward yourself with your favorite meal or a day off. Buy yourself a new journal so you can keep writing.

Present yourself with a beautiful cameo—a brooch or pendant or ring. If a dear friend or family member has completed her memoir, consider commemorating her accomplishment with the gift of a cameo. A pretty cameo gift might even serve as a good inducement for a friend to begin writing her life story! When I called our North Carolina coordinator, Jan Proctor, about our new Cameo name and logo, she hurried to her jewelry box and found the cameo that had belonged to her grandmother, who died before she was born. Jan carried the simple but comely cameo to the finest jeweler in Raleigh and had it reset in a ring which reminds her daily of her heritage and her commitment to women's life stories.

Group celebrations make history in themselves. At a day-long Arizona fair in honor of the 150th anniversary of the Seneca Falls Convention, completed life stories were delivered to the archives in a special ceremony which symbolized the way women have transferred their legacies from generation to generation. As founder of the Cameo Life Stories project, I started a relay. From my hands a decorated box of life stories passed to a STORIES Center board member, to the dean of Arizona State University West's Fletcher Library, to the provost of the university, and finally to Governor Jane Dee Hull, who is an advisory board member of the National Museum of Women's History.

Create your own special event to celebrate the completion of many life stories. Call the news media and let them report your success, at the same time inspiring other women to begin their own very important Cameo.

Preserving your Cameo is also a way to celebrate. Consider submitting your life story to a local or regional historical society, in addition to The STORIES Center. Check with them to see if there is any other repository of life stories or women's history at a university or museum in your region.

Send your life story to The STORIES Center

Make a copy of your Cameo. Completely fill out and sign the Cameo Release Form found at the back of the *Cameo Life Stories Questionnaire* in Chapter 8 of this book. Attach a copy of the Release Form to a copy of your life story, and send them together (this is extremely important) to The STORIES Center, P.O. Box 9608, Scottsdale, Arizona, USA 85252-3608.

Your signed Cameo Release Form is the document that instructs The STORIES Center about how you want your life story handled; for example, whether you want it archived anonymously, whether you will allow it to be made available to historians and other scholars, whether you will allow portions of your story to be excerpted in academic publications, or other stipulations you might make.

How Your Life Story Will Be Archived

The STORIES Center and the National Museum of Women's History (NMWH) are committed to preserving women's life stories. They foresee no end to that commitment. A hundred years from now, your Cameo will be safely archived.

An Archives Committee composed of representatives from the NMWH, The STORIES Center, Fletcher Library at Arizona State University West and archive specialists is charged with the design and supervision of an archival system that, first, preserves women's life stories and, second, provides research access to the public stories. Requests to study women's life stories are already being made by doctoral students and other museums in the United States. The Archives Committee will ensure that the appropriate technology is employed in storing and sharing data. With the sophisticated capabilities now available through computers, life stories scanned onto disks can be easily shared with scholars throughout the world.

However, every woman who submits her life story through the Cameo Life Stories program is assured that no information will be shared unless she grants permission to do so. If a woman is deceased and a family member writes her story, that person will complete the Cameo Release Form and authorize sharing of the life story or not.

Each life story received will be assigned an archive number. Every woman who provides her Cameo to The STORIES Center will receive written acknowledgment that her work has been received, which will include her archive number.

It would be wise to keep that acknowledgment letter and archive number with a copy of the written life story in a safe place, such as a safe deposit box, unless you wish your story to remain anonymous. When you leave instructions with a trusted family member, friend or lawyer about the location of your vital personal documents, be sure to mention that your life story is stored with them.

Let family members know that you have started or completed your life story, and tell someone responsible where you keep it. It is helpful to write down your wishes about the future of your autobiography and place those written wishes with your *Cameo Life Stories Workbook.*

Share your life story with family and friends

Some women may choose to tuck their completed Cameo quietly into a safe deposit box and let others find it later.

You will be doing your friends and family members a great favor, however, if you begin sharing your life story with them while you are around to answer the questions it will inevitably stimulate. You may not have the opportunity to read your finished memoirs to an auditorium full of rapt relations, but occasions for sharing will arise once family members become aware that you have a story to tell. A greater awareness of the need to share stories generally arises when someone in the family begins to trace her genealogy or write her life story.

Part of your gift to your family is not only your own Cameo, but the realization that their stories are important, too. So when conversation turns to your life story, you may find other women in the family showing an increased willingness to talk about their experiences and life lessons. Encourage the women to write them down.

My youngest daughter, Jennie Anna, and her best friend Lizzy Gilbert loved their sleepovers at each other's homes when they were young, and Liz often joined our family for weekends at our cabin in the nearby mountains. When I tucked the girls in at night, Liz would sometimes say, "Tell us a story about when you were little, Mrs. Linzer." I was taken by surprise the first time she asked, and I couldn't think of anything especially interesting, but it felt so good to be asked. I was glad she gave me an excuse to reach back in my memory and remember myself as a girl their age, and I was grateful for the reminder to share my girlhood past with my own daughters.

Inside every woman is a girl, but our daughters and granddaughters and nieces and others can't see that girl unless we reveal her. Tell a tale or two about your girlhood for starters. They may not clamor for your entire résumé on the spot, but you will have planted the seed of curiosity about you, about womanhood, about adulthood. Wait and see where it sprouts.

What a cause for celebration it will be if your life story deepens your family bonds and encourages others to write their life stories, too.

Share life stories at a family reunion

My mother helps orchestrate family reunions for both her and my dad's families. In the summer of 1997, the Wertz side gathered in the cool, green Black Hills of western South Dakota near Mt. Rushmore. I connected with dozens of cousins I hadn't seen in 20 years, and all of us, male and female, enjoyed the catching-up process.

For the next reunion, I've been assigned the job of leading a life story workshop—like a one-time Cameo Circle—to encourage everyone to share something about themselves and to get started on their life stories. We'll probably group the "guys" together and the "girls" together at the beginning, then meet as a whole later on. (These gender divisions seem to occur after a large meal, when the women, who prepared and served it, gather in the kitchen to wash the dishes and start fixing the next meal, while the men take a nap or watch football on TV.)

A Cameo Circle is easy to do at a family reunion if you have somebody to watch the wee ones. The guidelines are in Chapter 9 of this book. A Cameo Circle will provide you a nonintimidating structure for sharing stories and a soapbox to emphasize the importance of recording and passing on memories.

Submit your story for publication

Elaine Kort tells me she just returned from a reunion of 11 childhood girlfriends. They were so dazzled by each other's stories they decided they need to write a book and go on the "Oprah" show and tell the world!

Joan Newth is just as enthusiastic about her women's group, girlfriends who have been assembling once a month for 35 years. Joan has the bunch busy writing their Cameos, with an eye to publication.

As Edith Mayo says on the back cover of this book, women have a hunger to hear about other women's lives. Publishing venues have traditionally been limited, but demand is opening the gates. Try submitting something you've written about your life. Check out *Writer's Market*, an annual guide to publications that, for the most part, pay for the work they accept. Look for a local avenue to express yourself—an organizational newsletter, a neighborhood newspaper, a city magazine. The STORIES Center would be happy to receive material you submit for its newsletter.

Self publish, if you prefer. Create your own newsletter and circulate it among friends. Print a book of life stories for your family. There are several helpful books on self-publishing available.

Keep writing

If you discovered you enjoy writing during the process of creating your Cameo, don't stop writing. If you feel you've already answered all the questions in the *Cameo Life Stories Questionnaire*, write in a journal or diary. Eventually, of course, you will have more to add to your life story. Remember that you can send your story to The STORIES Center any time, then submit an addendum any time in the future.

You might want to encourage your own writing by taking classes, joining a local writer's group, or becoming a member of a writer's association. The International Women's Writing Guild provides a newsletter, periodic conferences and connection to women writers in your area. For membership information, contact the IWWG at P.O. Box 810, Gracie Station, New York, New York 10028, telephone 212-737-7536, e-mail iwwg@iwwg.com.

Help others write and archive their life stories

Some of our Cameo Life Stories volunteers have begun gathering the written stories of other women for The STORIES Center. In talking about the Cameo Life Stories project to others, they discover women who have already written about themselves for their families. They provide these women with a Cameo Release Form to complete and sign, and they make sure the life story and the Release Form are safely archived with The STORIES Center. We encourage you to do the same.

Urge Women's Organizations to Participate

Commitment is the key to recording women's life stories. When an organization sponsors or endorses life story writing, it is a convincing reminder to women of the importance of their individual lives and the significance of their contribution to society and to history. When women who are active in civic and charitable groups write their life stories, they are also recording the vital role their organizations have played in shaping society.

The League of Women Voters (LWV) adopted this project from the beginning. Lila Schwartz and Ann Eschinger, successive presidents of the LWV of Arizona, consistently remind their members of the project in both state and local newsletters and at the state convention. Nina Sabrack, president of the LWV of Metro Phoenix and a former member of the LWV of California board of directors, introduced the life story writing project for Everywoman at the California state convention and the League national convention.

Arlene Johnson, president of the Unitarian Universalist Women's Federation, gave her blessing to distribute the *Questionnaire* at the Unitarian Universalist General Assembly in Rochester, New York. The Susan B. Anthony House in Rochester has provided the Questionnaire to visitors. The Sun City chapter of the National Organization for Women (NOW) made a commitment to life story writing, and Arizona state NOW coordinator Ann Timmer and other members in the organization dispensed the *Questionnaire* at the 1998 national NOW convention.

United Methodist Women of eastern South Dakota were instructed in the life story writing program by Hazel Hansen, and Rev. Linda DeAtley of the Willowbrook United Methodist Church in Sun City, Arizona, opened the fellowship hall to a Cameo Life Stories Workshop for 125 community women.

Workshops have been presented at the annual national training conference of Federally Employed Women, to adult probation officers, to organizations providing services to women, to senior citizen centers, to chapters of Business and Professional Women, and to singles groups, book clubs, political bodies and sororities.

Libraries offer one of the best opportunities for outreach to the community. At the Tempe Public Library, staff member Alexandra Barnard has been providing an ongoing life story writing venue for Everywoman. It is the hope of Helen Gater, Dean of Fletcher Library at Arizona State University, that libraries will become a major force in encouraging people to write their life stories.

Literacy groups are excited about Cameo Life Stories because the motivation to tell one's story is motivation to read and to write. Organizations that work with children, such as the Girl Scouts and agencies serving youth at risk, see life story writing as a way to focus young people on their role as the authors of their experience—choice-makers and agents in the consequences of their actions. FourWords is a self-esteem and writing program for young people sponsored by The STORIES Center.

Become a Cameo Life Stories volunteer

The Cameo Life Stories program needs coordinators, workshop leaders, facilitators and other volunteers. Chapter 1 describes these functions in more detail. It is the desire of The STORIES Center to decentralize Cameo Life Stories services as much as possible to make them available to the greatest number of women. We welcome participation.

Coordinators provide information about Cameo Life Stories to the larger community. They may fulfill the function of workshop leader or facilitator as well, depending on their skills, interests and time availability. Workshop leaders are women with a solid knowledge of the Cameo Life Stories program and some experience in facilitating groups. Often workshop leaders have a strong interest or background in writing, but this is not a requirement. Facilitators organize and guide Cameo Circles, groups of women who come together on a periodic basis to write and share portions of their life stories.

Additional volunteers are needed on the local and national level to help establish the Cameo Life Stories writing tradition. Volunteers are invited to help in the following activities:

- Publicize the importance of life story writing.
- Inform women about the Cameo Life Stories project and the National Museum of Women's History.
- Organize Cameo Life Stories workshops and register participants.
- Submit news and articles to The STORIES Center newsletter.
- Plan and carry out the annual conference.
- Make contact with women's organizations.
- Raise and donate money to provide Cameo Life Stories materials and support to domestic violence shelters and other women's service groups.
- Orchestrate a Cameo celebration.
- Record the life stories of seniors and women who cannot tell their own stories, such as women with disabilities and those who have passed away.

If you would like to assist a local coordinator or workshop leader, contact them directly. If you are interested in playing a role in representing Cameo Life Stories, give us a call. You can reach The STORIES Center at P.O. Box 9608, Scottsdale, Arizona, USA 85252-3608, telephone 480-421-1999, facsimile 480-421-0174, e-mail www.cameolife stories@juno.com or through our Web site, www.thestoriescenter.org.

Writing the stories of women who cannot tell their own stories

The autobiographies written for the Cameo Life Stories project emphasize many elements that never appear in a résumé or an obituary—reasons behind certain decisions, embarrassing but life-changing incidents, feelings and convictions, for example. These elements may be especially difficult to include when you are trying to tell someone else's life story, but it is still a worthy goal to preserve the life record of women who cannot tell the story themselves. A husband, a daughter, a son, a grandchild or a close friend might find this an especially fitting way to honor a woman who is no longer able to write or memorialize a woman who has passed away. Some of the suggestions in this book may help you interpret mementos bequeathed by a cherished friend or relative. Journals, jewelry, collections, clothing, letters and handiwork may give you additional clues to personality.

Be sure to fill out the Cameo Release Form and include the person's date of birth and date of death, as well as all names the woman has used in her lifetime. This will assist heirs in identifying their relations.

So many of us feel such loss and helplessness when we lose someone we love. Providing a written Cameo of a woman no longer with us is a beautiful tribute and a lingering testament to an important human life.

Recommend FourWords to young people

FourWords is a life story writing program for young women and young men designed to enhance their self-esteem so they are better able to navigate the road to adulthood.

FourWords is sponsored by The STORIES Center and was founded on the same premise as Cameo Life Stories—that life story writing confirms our individual value as human beings and underscores our sense of agency as the authors of our experience.

A Simple Four-part Program

FourWords has four parts which remind girls and boys how important they are and offers them tools they can use to make their journey to maturity happier, easier and safer.

A FourWords party. Every young person after the age of nine is encouraged to participate in her own FourWords, a simple rite of passage. During this brief but meaningful ceremony, the VIP (Very Important Person) celebrating her FourWords is encircled by friends and family, who provide her with the *Cameo Life Stories Questionnaire for Young Women*, words of wisdom, a box of symbolic tools for the journey of life, and a pledge to assist her on her journey.

Life Stories Workbooks. Young people receive a copy of a workbook to give them a place to begin recording the life story they are creating. Both the *Cameo Life Stories Questionnaire for Young Women* and the *Life Stories Questionnaire for Young Men* include questions which guide youth in writing about themselves and provide clues to the kinds of life choices they will be facing.

Words of Wisdom. The value of words on life's journey is emphasized. Young people are encouraged to write in a journal, voice their feelings and concerns, and turn to the wisdom of others, especially in books which are available to everyone.

Guides. Adults in the young person's family and community commit to help each VIP traverse the road to maturity.

The Meaning of FourWords

The name FourWords was chosen to describe a program for both girls and boys and to incorporate its four key messages:

1. FourWords' essential message is four words: "You are very important."
2. FourWords faces the future forwards, emphasizing growth and possibilities. "No matter where you stand, you are facing forwards."
3. FourWords is a young person's introduction or foreword to the Book of Life. It is the foreword to their life story.
4. FourWords stands for words—for the importance of writing about our lives, speaking up about our feelings and concerns, listening to words of wisdom, and reading words of wisdom, especially in books.

Support women's history organizations

The STORIES Center and the National Museum of Women's History

Like all not-for-profit organizations, The STORIES Center and the National Museum of Women's History need financial support to continue their essential work. Becoming a Friend of The STORIES Center provides monetary support for a good cause and provides you with a regular newsletter about Cameo Life Stories, life story writing in general and youth programs. Membership in the National Museum of Women's History makes you a vital partner in the creation of this exciting new American institution in Washington, D.C.

The National Women's History Project

Established in 1980, the not-for-profit National Women's History Project (NWHP) promotes public awareness of women's historic contributions to American society. Its motto is "Write Women Back Into History." NWHP has become an essential resource for teachers, especially at the elementary, middle, and high school levels. Books, posters, buttons, speeches and other materials explain women's history in a way that is accurate, entertaining, and geared to specific grade levels.

If you would like to know more, visit the Project's Web site at <www.nwhp.org> or ask for a free copy of the Women's History Catalog of books, posters, and videos. The mailing address is National Women's History Project, 7738 Bell Road, Windsor, CA 95492, and the telephone is (800) 691-8888.

The Susan B. Anthony House in Rochester, New York

Susan B. Anthony, pioneer leader for women's rights, lived at 17 Madison Street in Rochester, New York, from 1866 until her death in 1906. Here she met and planned with Elizabeth Cady Stanton and Frederick Douglass their campaigns for woman suffrage. The home is administered by a private, nonprofit organization and is open to the public. For more information call 716-235-6124.

Alice Paul Centennial Foundation

Alice Stokes Paul, a leading 20th century women's rights leader, was all but lost in history before a group of New Jersey women planned a celebration to commemorate the life and work of this New Jersey native in honor of her 100th birthday on January 11, 1985. For the last 15 years the Alice Paul Centennial Foundation has worked tirelessly to gain public recognition for the woman who played a pivotal role in gaining the right to vote for American women in 1920, initiated nonviolent civil disobedience as a political strategy in the United States, authored the Equal Rights Amendment in 1923, initiated the inclusion of sex equality in the United Nations Charter, and worked worldwide for women's equality throughout her long life.

In 1987 the Alice Paul Centennial Foundation saved a collection of Dr. Paul's books, papers and personal effects at a public auction. This collection was donated to the Smithsonian Institution's National Museum of American History and The Arthur and Elizabeth Schlesinger Library on the History of Women in America located at Harvard University.

When Dr. Paul's birthplace and home, Paulsdale, located in Mount Laurel, New Jersey, was to be sold by its private owners in 1989, the Foundation jumped at the chance to save this valuable women's history resource.

For further information you may write the Alice Paul Centennial Foundation, P.O. Box 1376, Mount Laurel, New Jersey 08054, call 856-231-1885 or fax 856-231-4223.

You can shape the future of women's history

Sharing your life story will help make history more complete and more accurate by expanding the history of women. At the end of this chapter is a list of additional steps you can take to actively support education about women's lives. Every step you take nurtures the study of women's history, which is essential to our maturation as a civilization.

Cameo Life Stories welcomes your assistance in encouraging the teaching of women's history and establishing the tradition of women writing life stories.

The seeds of this new tradition have already spread far and wide. The fruit that is born of women's life story writing will affect countless individual lives and countless generations. The rewards of women's life story writing will be

- greater self-esteem
- understanding of women's lives
- commitment to women's needs
- bonding between mothers and daughters
- connection between generations
- valuing of friendship
- knowledge of women's history
- dedication to writing
- commitment to reading and education
- pride in women's contributions
- membership in women's organizations.

Cameo Life Stories is changing lives. It is changing the world. We welcome you on this adventure! ❦

"I Can Make Women's History"

Your actions make history. Here is a checklist of steps you can take to nurture women's history.

How my work on my life story is progressing:

Date

__________ Today I read the *Cameo Life Stories Writing Guide for Everywoman.*
__________ Today I read the *Cameo Life Stories Questionnaire.*
__________ Today I started writing my life story.
__________ Today I started a Cameo Circle.
__________ Today I joined a Cameo Circle.
__________ Today I read another woman's memoirs or biography.
__________ Today I attended a Cameo Life Stories Workshop.
__________ Today I sent my Cameo (a narrative life story or answers to the *Cameo Life Stories Questionnaire*) to The STORIES Center.
__________ Today I shared my life story with family or friends.

How I encourage other women to write their life stories:

Date

__________ Today I encouraged a young woman to begin writing her life story and told her about the FourWords program (see Chapter 10).
__________ Today I started or facilitated a Cameo Circle for others.
__________ Today I attended a Cameo Circle Facilitator Training session.
__________ Today I volunteered to be a Cameo Life Stories coordinator or workshop leader.
__________ Today I arranged for news coverage of the Cameo Life Stories program or life story writing in general.
__________ Today I gave a copy of the *Cameo Life Stories Questionnaire* to a family member.

__________ Today I gave a copy of the *Cameo Life Stories Questionnaire* to a friend.
__________ Today I helped another woman submit her life story to The STORIES Center.
__________ Today I gave a presentation to other women about Cameo Life Stories.

How I help make the world a better place for women and children:

Date
__________ Today I supported a project that encourages the teaching of women's history.
__________ Today I joined the Friends of The STORIES Center.
__________ Today I joined the National Museum of Women's History.
__________ Today I joined a women's organization.
__________ Today I read a book or an article about women's history.
__________ Today I volunteered with or donated to: a women's organization, a social service agency serving women or girls, an agency serving children, a woman's campaign for public office.
__________ Today I gave a family member or friend a book about women's history, a biography of a woman, or a memoir written by a woman.
__________ Today I introduced my children or my grandchildren to women's history.

CHAPTER ELEVEN

Beginnings of the Cameo Life Stories Program

During 1995, the 75th anniversary of the 19th Amendment to the United States Constitution, I began reading about American women's 72-year struggle to win the right to vote and to have the same rights of citizenship as men. I'm not a very patient person, so I was especially struck by the tenacity and stamina of the suffragists, who strove so hard and so long for their goal. Some worked all their lives for woman suffrage but did not live to see the "Anthony Amendment" succeed.

Although the 19th Amendment was known by Susan B. Anthony's name, it was not the work of that tireless leader alone. The lengthy suffrage campaign involved the efforts of countless women and men, many whose names we will never know. And every contribution counted, no matter how simple. Some were organizers and strategists directing the actions of thousands. Some were speakers, traveling in grimy coaches and suffering disdain and hurled garbage. Some sewed banners, distributed leaflets, gave money. Some women declaimed in the legislatures, and many whispered in their husband's ears.

My reading about woman suffrage built my respect for women's perseverance in creating change. It also introduced me to new aspects of women's history. In particular, I was surprised to learn about the Seneca Falls Convention held July 18-19, 1848. It was the first convention in the world convened to organize for the rights of women as full human beings. When I realized the 150th anniversary of that pivotal gathering was approaching, I began to wonder how historians 150 years from now would explain the incredible changes in the status of women since that date in 1848 when women were virtually slaves.

The Spirit of Seneca Falls

In the fall of 1997, several of us in Phoenix, Arizona, organized a celebration of the 150th anniversary of the Seneca Falls Convention. Our goal was to honor the courage of those who, when it was denounced to do so, took a stand to improve the lives of women. Jennie Gorrell from Business and Professional Women (BPW) and I arranged the first meeting, inviting Joan Anderson Meacham of the National Museum of Women's History, Shaaron Cosner, Mary Melcher, Amy Ross and Ilene Gordon to tea at my kitchen table.

Out of that grew a dedicated committee we called the Spirit of Seneca Falls, and the League of Women Voters of Metropolitan Phoenix offered to serve as our fiscal agent. We were joined by Paula Goodson, director of the Arizona Governor's Division for Women, and Dana Campbell Saylor and Meaghan McElroy from her office; Carol Harris, a nursing professor at Arizona State University; Ann Eschinger, Nina Sabrack and Mary Wright from the League of Women Voters; Michael Carman, director of the Arizona Capital Museum; Roselyn O'Connell, who later became president of the National Women's Political Caucus; and Kit Prestwood, head of the Women's Resource Center at Arizona State University West.

All of us agreed that, with so much work yet to be done to improve the lives of women and girls, we wanted any anniversary observance of the Seneca Falls Convention to include programs that would have a lasting impact—that would educate young people, reinspire already committed women, and touch those who knew little about women's history.

Project goals

I wanted to create a program which would honor the efforts that every woman makes to improve her own life, the life of her children, the lives of other women and girls, and her community. I wanted to put my energy into a project that would accomplish the following:

- Provide a record for future historians of the role women have played in changing society, especially in improving the lives of women.
- Encourage women to regard their personal lives as being as valuable as the lives of men and other women, and valuable contributions to human history.
- Expand public awareness of, and respect for, the tremendous impact women have in shaping society.
- Increase support for each other among women of all ages and backgrounds through the sharing of our personal stories.
- Provide a safe place for the stories of women who have been afraid to share the truth of their life experiences.
- Motivate women to take more action to improve the lives of women and girls and society in general.

Questionnaire developed

In January 1998 I created the first draft of the *Everywoman's Story Memory Workbook*, a life story questionnaire specifically geared to women. This was not intended to be a general autobiography project or an attempt to help women compose literary memoirs. Instead, I wanted women to think about the factors that influenced their development and their decisions, to reflect on how being "born female" affected their lives, and to record their unique life patterns.

More than that, I hoped women would share the truth about their struggles, choices, joys, sorrows, family, work, friends, faith and moments of courage—and feel pride in their life journey.

I shared the initial questionnaire with dozens of women and received invaluable suggestions from women of widely varied ages, ethnic and socioeconomic backgrounds, religions, educations and life experiences. The National Museum of Women's History enthusiastically endorsed our work as a supporting aspect of their own long-term goals.

The first version of the *Everywoman's Story Memory Workbook* was distributed to 170 guests on February 14, 1998, at the first annual Susan B. Anthony Luminary Awards Tea honoring Arizona women who were shining examples of women helping women. On March 8 of the same year, during National Women's History Week, more than 1,000 women attending the Phoenix Women's Commission luncheon received a copy. During the week of July 18-19, Carol Harris, my daughter Jennie Anna

Swanson and I took copies to the national Celebrate '98 events centered around the U.S. National Women's Rights Historical Park in Seneca Falls, New York.

Sandra Lynch distributed the questionnaires at the national General Assembly of the Unitarian Universalists, with the blessing of UU Women's Federation president Arlene Johnson. Ann Timmer and friends from Sun City, Arizona, passed them out at the national conference of the National Organization for Women.

At a special reception we hosted at the Susan B. Anthony House in Rochester, New York, we introduced the project to presidents of national women's organizations, including the International Women Ministers Association. Nina Sabrack provided copies to delegates of the national convention in San Diego of the League of Women Voters of the United States. The Governor's Division for Women shared them with delegates from around the world at the Athena Conference, an international businesswomen's convention.

Countless copies have been passed along through churches, temples, senior centers, family reunions, book groups, libraries, and such organizations as the American Association of University Women, Junior League, the Girl Scouts, Federally Employed Women, Women at Work, Florence Crittendon, Women's Political Caucus, domestic violence shelters, rape crisis centers, veterans groups and others.

On wings around the world

Our best guess is that more than 200,000 copies of the original questionnaire made their way around the world in the first two years of the Everywoman's Story Project. They spread with the love and zeal of women who believe women's stories should be shared. The questionnaire was designed to be inexpensive and easily duplicated, and we intend that it remain that way, so **every woman** may participate.

It has been translated into Spanish. Nihal Nicky Muradoglu translated it into Turkish and has been giving it to friends in Turkey and Russia. Carole Ellison has mailed it to 121 friends and family, including those in Japan. Letters and e-mails arrive at The STORIES Center from Maine to Mexico, Canada to Florida, on a regular basis.

One of the most thrilling letters we received came to our first Arizona coordinator Shaaron Cosner from Krishna Ahooja Patel, who told us she was from India, living in Switzerland, and preparing to teach in Nova Scotia.

"Yours is the most exciting project I have come across," she wrote. "I feel fortunate in having a friend like Mercedes Paniker (chair of Femvision, Barcelona) who has passed on information about your group. It seems as if I have been waiting for such an opportunity all my life.... Every life experience is unique and each story is worth writing...."

Creation of The STORIES Center

My hope from the beginning was to establish the program so firmly that women would be writing and submitting their life stories for women's history archives for at least another 100 years.

Since the National Museum of Women's History is concentrating its efforts on establishing its CyberMuseum and a permanent building in Washington, D.C., it was clear we needed a separate nonprofit organization to nurture our program. My husband, Steve Linzer, took us to the next step and helped us form The STORIES Center. The acronym STORIES—Society To Obtain and Retain International Everyone's Story —reflects our primary goal.

Women in state after state volunteered to spread the word about the program in their areas, and they expressed the desire to meet one another and share suggestions. As a result, we held the first annual Everywoman's Story conference in Scottsdale, Arizona, January 23-24, 1999, with two special guest speakers, Sam Kathryn Campana, mayor of Scottsdale, Arizona, and Jackie Mott Brown, author and artist, from Ithaca, New York.

Donna Medoff, Carol Ellis and countless volunteers have worked to give The STORIES Center a firm foundation. Scott Linzer, my stepson, developed our website. My husband, Steve, and my daughters, Maren and Jennie Swanson, have lent their time and talents wherever needed.

Faced with a potential challenge for use of the name "Everywoman's Story," we carefully searched for a name that would represent our program forever. As I mentioned in the Foreword, cameos embody the qualities we wanted symbolized in a name—the focus on women, the beauty of women's lives, the heirloom nature of our life stories. As of July 1999, Cameo Life Stories is the trademarked name of this powerful project to gather women's life stories and protect them for posterity.

I believe each *Cameo Life Stories Questionnaire* communicates the love and encouragement of millions of women, living and departed, who say to each other, "You are important. You make history. You are not alone. Tell us your story." ❦

CHAPTER TWELVE

Excerpts from Women's Life Stories

Portions of women's life stories are included in this book to give you some examples of the way women write about themselves in answering the *Cameo Life Stories Questionnaire.* My hope is that you will read them and think, "I can do that."

When women speak from their hearts and their experience, you can see what interesting stories emerge. Only a few of the women represented write professionally or have had their work published. Very little editing has been done to anybody's material.

The writers of these life stories vary widely in education, age, lifestyle, locale, and interests. The excerpts represent an interesting variety of writing styles and subjects, which were suggested by the *Cameo Life Stories Questionnaire.* Notice the aspects of each selection that most appeal to you, whether it's humor, candor, detail, color, theme, brevity, pacing, subject matter, or dialogue. Think about how you might incorporate some of those features in your own writing.

Preparing a contribution for this book was a significant commitment. Each writer faced a unique set of hurdles and needed some degree of courage to do so. They are sharing their words with you, though, because they want you to experience the same satisfaction they have had in creating a personal Cameo. They believe in the power of writing about our lives. They want to inspire you to begin penning your portrait in words.

Evangeline Song

Evangeline Song is a Phoenix, Arizona, native with an elementary education degree from the University of Arizona. The oldest of eight children of Chinese immigrant parents, she has four grown children and seven grandchildren. For more than 22 years she has been a single parent. She is currently taking time off from the real estate business to delve into philosophy, history and writing.

Questions 1-10: Life's Beginnings

Chinatown Childhood

The Eva Harris Maternity Hospital at 1103 E. Culver Street in Phoenix, Arizona, was my birthplace on Sunday afternoon June 25, 1939, at 3:25 p.m. My father was accustomed to giving his name in the Chinese manner, which meant that he listed his surname first and then his given name. My birth certificate lists his name as Yee Kim Ling, which should have been noted as Yee (surname), Kim Ling (which means "Golden Chain") living at 140 S. Second Street, working as a grocer for 20 years. My mother's name appears as Ong Shee Yee and lists her as 24 years old even though her actual age was 23. Her Chinese maiden name was Dong, Shee Quai which meant "Fourth Turtle." She was the youngest of four girls in a small farming village.

My family surname is Yee, but my birth certificate lists my full name as Evangeline Ling. Stillman D. Little, the attending physician, got the honor of giving me my name since my mother's English was very limited, having only been here from China less than a year. "Evangeline" is not a name that anyone in my family would have chosen, which leads me to believe that Dr. Little loved the poet, Longfellow, who wrote the epic poem by that name. Both my parents had difficulty pronouncing my American name and my older stepbrother, Johnny, gave me the nickname "Vangie," which my siblings used, but my parents always used my Chinese name which sounds like "may siew" in our dialect. "May Siew" means "beautiful and lithe."

The world was at war in Europe and gradually the United States was also drawn into World War II, which affected the Arizona economy as well. My parents would awaken at 4:30 in the morning to open the grocery store to the migrant workers who congregated in front of our store to board the buses which took them out to the cotton or vegetable fields. They would purchase snack foods such as the Hostess individual Twinkies cakes, chocolate cupcakes, little tins of deviled ham, baby-food-size jars of wieners, cans of Beanee Weenees, and cracker snacks. After they left, the store would close and re-open around 8 or 9 a.m.

Everyone who was capable worked in the grocery store either cashiering, stocking, packaging, cleaning, or butchering. My mother ended up being the master butcher since she was young and strong and my father was experiencing heart problems. Occasionally, other relatives helped, including dad's brother-in-law, Ma Wing (his first wife's brother), and Charlie Fong, dad's cousin's son.

I was told that my father's first wife bore him three children, two girls and a boy, and was the first Chinese woman in Phoenix who learned to drive a car. Because most Chinese men who came to America in the late 1800s and early 1900s considered themselves sojourners always working to amass enough money to go back to China to make better lives for their families in their own villages, many sent their American-born children back to China to learn their native language and culture and to acclimate them to their father's village.

Such was the case with my stepsiblings. They had been in China living with relatives, when their mother left Arizona to go to the village and oversee the building of a three-story new home for when the family would go back to China to live. While she was there, she had to rely on her brother-in-law, dad's older brother, to help her with negotiations with the contractors. Rumor has it that he poisoned her to death. No one in my family has ever spoken about it in detail. My stepsister, Jenny, the youngest daughter, was about 12 years old and could only remember that her mother suddenly became delirious and would have crying episodes, was ill, and would cry out in fear of losing her children.

Shortly thereafter, she did die and my father went back to China for her funeral and also to ask for help in getting a new wife and mother for his children. Through a friend, Mrs. Hazel Lee at Joyland Market, my father was introduced in China to my mother who was 23 years younger than he, and they married right after the funeral. My mother was left by herself to get all her paperwork in appropriate order to pass the immigration officials and board the ship to come to America and land at

Angel Island. My father had returned to Arizona with his children a full month before my mother arrived.

Sam Kim Grocery was on the northwest corner of Second Street and Madison in what was considered "Chinatown." Chinatown consisted basically of one whole city block and half of another one from First Street to Second Street and from Madison to Jackson and halfway up to Jefferson, north of Madison. This part of town was the poorer section where Hispanics lived in houses with dirt floors and where prostitution flourished and was called skid row or the "red light district." This is the downtown Phoenix area where America West Arena is now located.

Life at the Store

As a child, living in the middle of skid row, I had no knowledge of its reputation or activities because I never saw or heard about them in my own routine. Daily life revolved around and in the grocery store. Our living quarters were in the back of the store, which was probably a converted storage area.

Without any discussion that I can recall, my parents moved their grocery store across the street to the southwest corner of Second Street and Madison. With the move came much larger living quarters which we would eventually need since my mother gave birth to a total of eight children, five boys and three girls. The refrigerated meat display cases were at the rear of the store. Since we were located in the "poorer" section of the city, our clientele consisted mostly of Hispanic families. We also had a large number of Native American shoppers who regularly came into town from the Sacaton Pima reservation. Chinese people were the only ones who had a Congressional Act prohibiting them from coming into America from 1895 through 1943, and those immigrants who were able to get here were relegated to the less desirable parts of town.

So my parents would stock items such as tepary beans, tortillas, chicharones (deep-fried pork rinds), chilies, tripe, brains, sweetbreads, tripas de leche, panocha (Mexican sugar), pan de huevos (Mexican sweet breads), 50-pound sacks of flour, rice, and chorizo to accommodate them. My older siblings helped us move, but they did not live with us. Jennie, 14 years older, and Johnny, 16 years older, lived with Bill and May (our adopted brother and his wife) at another grocery store that my father had also opened in South Phoenix at 7th Avenue and Cocopah.

A large number of the farm workers who frequented our store seasonally were of Philippine descent and a Philippine-owned pool hall and social hall was located directly behind our grocery store facing Buchanan, which bordered the railroad tracks. One sunny afternoon, I heard lively music, and I could smell the delightfully tantalizing aroma of food cooking outdoors coming from the pool hall. I ran over to the fence and quickly hauled myself up to peek over it.

I saw a large number of people eating plates of yummy-looking food with their hands and also saw some incredibly beautiful roosters with bright yellow, red, black, and brown prancy tail feathers strutting around. Their handlers picked them up, attached thin curved blades onto the back of one of their legs and then threw them up into the air. The cocks flew at each other cackling loudly and then I saw blood dripping and feathers flying in all directions. I'd never seen anything like that before and thought it was awfully strange.

Even though my mother had more than enough work to occupy all her waking hours, she still took the time to buy some baby chicks from the wholesaler, Firpo's Chickens, on Central Avenue, and would raise about two dozen at a time for our own personal use. We ate the best organically grown poultry and Chinese vegetables. She would put up chicken mesh wiring around a few poles to confine the chicks to a certain part of the yard. When the chickens were grown, she boiled some water in large galvanized tubs in preparation for the eventual plucking of the feathers.

She had such a commanding "knowingness" about so many things. She never whined nor complained about any of the work that she did; she seemed to relish every task at hand and was as purposeful and masterful as any artist creating a masterpiece. When it came time to slaughter the chickens, she quickly tied their legs together and cradling each chicken in her lap, she very quickly and humanely, with an extremely sharp knife, slit its throat and collected the blood in a container. The chickens were sacrificed very efficiently and beautifully prepared.

Once a year, around the month of June, mom would prepare a whole boiled chicken (literally a "whole chicken" with its head and feet still attached) and roast pork, rice and vegetables and would create a little altar. She would buy some special bundles of muslin-colored paper and at the altar, she placed three place settings of a bowl of rice, a pair of chopsticks, and the bowls of food and chicken in front of some lighted incense and candles. The children were asked to bow three times in front of the altar and then she would burn the bundles of paper at the end of this ritual. She never really explained this ritual so I could understand what it all meant, but we nonetheless participated in it until she and my father became members of the First Chinese Baptist Church.

When we stepped behind the butcher department, we entered the dining area of our living quarters. Towards the rear of that room was the kitchen area with a door leading to the fenced back yard behind the store. A kerosene tank was passed on the way to the only bathroom. The bathroom had a small single sink with exposed galvanized piping and a large area by the tub where my father had four galvanized 32-gallon trash cans with holes drilled through the bottoms for water drainage in which he sprouted his own supply of bean sprouts for sale in the store and at the local wholesale produce warehouses one block away. A sofa was at the opposite side of this 11 x 12 room and a piece of cloth covered the doorway to the next small room which had three beds in it. When we were small, we all slept in the same room. As we reached adolescence, we were able to convert some storage space into two other small bedrooms.

Learning about loss

Johnny was the handsomest, friendliest, smartest older brother any girl could have. I was completely captivated by him and looked forward to his visits because he was the only person who ever lifted me up into the air and played with me. He touched me with love and a joyful nature. He always smiled at me and made me feel wonderful. I saw him wearing a military uniform on the last few occasions that I saw him. By then he had enrolled in the Army reserve and was exempt from the World War II draft because he had been awarded a full scholarship from Yale and had gone to the University of California at Berkeley to get his Masters Degree in chemistry.

My father couldn't contain his pride in Johnny. He took me by train to San Francisco and on to UC Berkeley to see Johnny receive a huge trophy for having received the highest grade point average in his graduating class. That trophy ended up in large glass case on top of our refrigerated meat case in the middle of the store where no one could miss seeing it. It was like a religious icon. It was awe-inspiring in its size and importance. As a consequence, even though I never heard my parents tell us that we had to go to college, all my brothers and sisters and I graduated from college.

The next time I saw Johnny after his graduation was at his wedding in Sacramento. Father, my brother Danny, and I were driven to the celebration by two of Johnny's friends, David Sing (Yee) and Sing Yee, Jr. They drove straight through and we attended a lovely ceremony. His bride was very short, under five feet tall, but very pretty. She was the only daughter and she had a degree in social work.

A week after the wedding, a dinner reception was planned in Phoenix, Arizona, for several hundred guests. Johnny and Helen had been on their honeymoon and drove into town on Saturday. The reception was held on Sunday evening and because Johnny was supposed to report to work in California on Monday morning, they left town right after the dinner was over and the family pictures were taken. Monday morning at 5 a.m., we were contacted and told that Johnny and Helen were both killed on the highway to California. Helen was driving to give Johnny some "sleep-time" and while passing on a curve, she drove head-on into a semi-truck. What a tremendous loss that was. We were all so affected by that. He was such a personable, well-loved, and loving "brain" with enormous potential for good. He made an indelible, positive impression on everyone who had the good fortune to know him.

Johnny's death was the second one that I would experience in my young life. I was around eight years old when my baby brother, Eddie (the fifth child), followed me out of the store when I went out to play with the Mexican families' children living on the same city block where our store was located. I hadn't known that he'd followed me until I looked out of the door to the alley and saw him walking outside coming towards the house I'd entered. I just stayed inside watching him when I saw the large truck, behind which he'd been standing, start up and back right over him and take off.

I ran outside and saw him lying on the ground unconscious with some blood trickling out of his mouth. I scooped him up and ran home with him. Someone took him from me and I was just numb. I didn't know what to say or think. The police were called and they asked me some questions. One minute he was alive and then he was dead. My mother was devastated. She cried and cried for so long and she went to bed and stayed there, it seemed, for days. I know it was at least for a couple days.

At the funeral, which my mother was unable to attend, I was struck by how much longer he looked in his coffin. He was a year and a half old and he had such a happy, joyful personality. He laughed a lot for a little baby. Occasionally, in the evening after the store was closed, Dad would pile us into the car and give us rides around town and Eddie would laugh heartily every time we hit a little bump in the road. That little brother was joy and enthusiasm personified as soon as he awakened each day. It seemed that so many little things made him laugh. I don't remember anyone in my family saying anything bad to me about the incident, but I felt so guilty for not being able to save him by going out to get him and bringing him into the house with me sooner.

Surrogate mom

My mother had three more children after Eddie and I was instrumental in naming all of them. I was given a lot of freedom to take charge and make a lot of contributions to my family, such as shopping for clothes for my brothers and sisters. I started shopping for them when I was eight years old. J.C. Penney's was just two blocks away along with lots of other stores "downtown." There were Lerner's, Korrick's, and Woolworth's, and I got to buy underwear, jeans, shirts, and anything else we needed. I was also the surrogate "mom" or "day-care" mom to my seven brothers and sisters. I changed the diapers and fed them and looked after them because my mother was the major workhorse in the grocery store.

Instead of feeling angry and disgruntled about having to babysit, I actually enjoyed having my own "real-life" dolls to cuddle, change, and feed. I had free reign to wash them and dress them anyway I desired. I loved the sweet smell of Johnson & Johnson's Baby Powder and Baby Shampoo. As my sisters became older, I could even cut their hair, give them perms and arrange to have their pictures taken—just as if they were my very own children.

Because my father was 23 years older than my mother and had developed enlarged heart problems, she took it upon herself to manage and work at all the required jobs from butchering to cashiering and stocking. She loved working hard and she was adept at everything she tried. She was fearless, too. She once locked the front doors when the store was full of mostly male cotton-pickers because she was determined to retrieve some stolen items from a man who was going to leave without paying. She was looking out for shoplifters and she had seen him put several items in his clothing. When the large, burly, tired cotton-picker got to the locked front door, she rushed over and asked him for the articles. Shocked and chagrined, he did give some foodstuffs back, but not all of them and he, being larger, decided he'd just muscle his way out and he pushed her aside and unlocked the front doors. He hadn't counted on her being angry enough to give him a strong shove and making him fall flat on his face. Splat! We heard a glass jar break underneath him and he quickly got up and escaped. You couldn't help but be in awe of mom. I would later think that I didn't want to be as tough as she was.

The store was closed at 9 p.m. and then we would have dinner. Mom would start cooking before the store closed so we could eat as soon as it was closed. She also had a great gift of cooking. Everything and anything that she cooked was wondrously tasty and nutritious. She never had to read recipe books nor were any available to her. She knew no English when she first came to America, but she learned on the job and also learned to speak Spanish and some Indian words as well. She was a very warm, friendly woman. She never got to go on vacation while my father was alive because she had to take care of the store while HE went on vacation with some of his children. Being the oldest, I got in on most of the vacations he took. Mom worked without a vacation seven days a week for twenty years.

Then dad decided to sell the store and retire in 1957. Dad passed away in 1964 after a sudden heart attack. Several years later, Mom would get a job at Motorola in production and work there for almost ten years before retiring again. Mom would eventually visit China twice and Taiwan three times, and make other trips as well.

Hazel Wertz Hansen

Hazel Noreen Wertz Hansen grew up on farms in southeastern South Dakota and graduated from Mitchell High School in 1950. She graduated from Mitchell Business College and worked for many years in Sioux Falls as a bookkeeper and secretary. She married high school classmate Don Hansen in 1951, and they are active in the lives of their five daughters and 12 grandchildren.

Hazel continues to work part time and never has enough time for her many volunteer activities. She is active in the United Methodist Church, serving as an officer at the local and district levels of United Methodist Women. She also chairs the UMW reading program at her church and is proud of encouraging women to read about other women's lives.

Questions 1-10: Life's Beginnings

Growing Up on a Farm in South Dakota

In order to know about me, you need to know where I come from. I am proud of my heritage and know that most of the good qualities I possess come from the teachings of my parents and the good relationship we had as a family growing up during the 1930s and 1940s. We were taught to work and to have fun. Family times were important. We learned to be thrifty and make do with what we had. We planted victory gardens and recycled before it was the necessary thing to do. We were taught honor and integrity. Books were important in our lifestyle. Education was stressed. More than once my mother told us, "Your education can never be taken from you."

Mama

My mother was Beatrice Helena Renshaw. She was born November 15, 1901, on the family farm. Her parents were Henry Franklin and Nancy Jane Hudelson Renshaw. She was the fourth of five children. Charlie, Mary, and Leo were older and Howard was seven years younger. She went to Ebenezer grade school. She never attended high school but took a dressmaking class in 1921 from Mrs. Fife of Mitchell. Later she worked as a dressmaker when the income was needed. She was a beautiful seamstress and made all our clothes. She could take a used adult coat, wash it, turn it inside out where the nap was not worn, and cut a child's coat for one of us. I remember a pretty, light blue coat she made for our oldest daughter, Debbie, when she was three. Her best friend was Gladys Wertz, who lived west of her childhood home.

Mama was married on Monday, April 3, 1922, to Arthur Otis Wertz at the Congregational parsonage in Armour. They lived in the Renshaw home with her family until 1926 when they moved to a farm near Stickney. Life was not a bed of roses. Their fourth child, Harold Eugene, was born on December 27, 1930. The doctor used forceps to deliver him and this caused a brain hemorrhage. Little Harold died the next day. A second tragedy occurred in August 1935 when their second child, Dean, died from an accidental hanging while playing in the granary.

Mama never learned to drive, but she was a real helpmate to her husband. Besides the normal activities of being a farm wife like gardening, canning, and raising chickens, she would don her overalls and help pick corn in the fall.

I remember shocking grain, dragging two heavy bundles up together to make them stand and then adding more around them. I couldn't have been more than ten or eleven. I was very proud to be able to make a good shock. As a family we gathered dried cow chips for the winter to start a fire in the heating stove. The horse stood hitched to the wagon while we cleaned up one area and then Daddy would communicate with a "click,

click." The horse (either Pet or Ribbon) would amble forwards a bit until he heard "Whoa."

Planting potatoes in the spring was another family event, usually on Good Friday. We kids spread out, following behind the fresh plowed furrow my dad made with the plow, while he came back the other way covering up the row we had just planted. My favorite times were in the hot summer when I could take mid-morning and mid-afternoon lunch out to Daddy in the field. He would see me coming and stop the horses near the lone shade tree and wait for me. No matter how hot it was there was always a quart jar of coffee wrapped in rags to keep it hot. A treat for me was in the basket, too. This was a resting time and we enjoyed it. He would often take this chance to "catch a few winks" and give the horses a rest before leaving this nice shady spot.

During those days, people were concerned about heatstroke. We always had to come inside or lay down outside in the shade for an hour each afternoon. We didn't have to nap, just rest. This turned into some enjoyable cloud watching. Finding faces in the clouds and then seeing them disappear so fast was fun.

Mama taught me how to cook and bake. When I was nine, I could clean a pheasant, cut and fry it. With six children, we learned to do our share. She insisted that her three sons learn how to do laundry, iron and cook. This was in part because her own mother had not done that for her sons.

She played the piano, not a lot, but she played well. Most songs were from memory, and she sang to us often. Many of the old religious songs as well as some patriotic ones were her favorites. Years later I had her write down the words to several of the songs she sang to us. Those same songs are the ones that I recall when I have sung to my children and grandchildren. "One day I made a snowman," "Hear the popcorn pop," and "Four and twenty blackbirds" were my favorites.

She was a genealogist, as was her mother. I typed her notes on the Hudelson Family Tree in January 1955. She continued to search for more missing branches on her family tree. In her later years, she was also an ardent coin collector. She corresponded regularly with a number of people but especially with a distant cousin, Nettie Hudelson Coin, who lived in Oklahoma. They shared the love of coin collecting.

Mama was widowed the day after her 38th anniversary and lived alone for another ten years. She had taken up upholstery work and continued with it. Her work was always in demand. She had high blood pressure and was on medication and diet for that. She suffered a heart attack in June of 1967. We had a family reunion at the Plano school near Mary Lou's farm in 1968 and all her children were home for that. Glen, Donald and Gale all lived in California; Joyce in Watertown; myself in Sioux Falls and Mary Lou near Mitchell.

For years my parents lived on East Ninth Avenue in a "basement house," which the previous owners had fully finished with the intention of building the upper stories when money became available. High windows allowed a view of surrounding grass and trees. My children especially remember the huge, flourishing flower garden out back, where Mama would always let them pick bouquets of sweetpeas, gladiolas, daisies, and cosmos.

In 1969 she won a Chevrolet pickup truck in a drawing during Corn Palace week. Since she never learned to drive, she sold it and used the money to buy a small house which suited her better. It needed some fixing up, and she delved into it like a trooper, forgetting her heart condition. She ended up in the hospital again that next September and was released by her doctor to come to my house. On Wednesday, September 9, 1970, she died of a massive coronary. Don's Uncle Harold, who was a doctor at the Veteran's Administration Hospital in Sioux Falls, was with me at home when she passed away.

Mama is buried next to Daddy, Dean, and little Harold in the Pleasant Ridge Cemetery in Armour.

Daddy

When Arthur, my father, was still quite young, he was a frequent visitor at the Renshaw home. Beatrice and he lived on farms just three miles apart as the crow flies.

Arthur was the second child and the first son of Charles and Kathryn Conarro Wertz and was born in Lacon, Illinois, on April 29, 1901. The family had moved to South Dakota when he was quite young and had a dairy farm near Corsica. He enjoyed this and took his responsibilities there very seriously. Often I heard my mother comment on how he always "put the cows first." They were milked twice a day. His younger sister, Gladys, and Beatrice were best friends. Many times he came with the horse and buggy to pick up Gladys and take her home. We have pictures of him as a teenager having fun with Beatrice's brothers. His only brother, Keith, wasn't born until Arthur was 14. Many group pictures taken at the Renshaw's included the Wertz family and other neighbors. So Arthur had many occasions to get to know Beatrice.

Daddy loved to whistle. We could always tell where he was by his whistle. He had a good sense of humor. I vividly remember a Saturday morning in 1939. I was just six years old, and he had taken me to Mitchell to participate in the rural county declamatory contest as the representative for first and second grade from my school. I won, but he and I schemed to tell Mama that I had lost, with sobs and tears as needed. When she was thoroughly convinced and consoling me, we suddenly yelled out "April Fool."

In third grade, when I was to report back to my teacher what my ancestry was, my dad told me I was German, Scots-Irish, and Hillbilly. I don't remember my dad cooking much, but I do remember that I liked his oatmeal better than Mama's, and I remember him making baked apples on top of the Warm Morning stove.

Like a lot of things that need to be done on the farm, butchering was a joint venture with several neighbors getting together to share the work and make the job go faster. This was also the case with threshing. It was always fun to have the threshing bee at our house. The neighboring women came over and brought food. Pies were baked and tables were set to feed the men. This always included the neighboring men as well as the crew who traveled through the area with the threshing machine. A table was also set up with wash basins and towels for the men to wash up after this sweaty, dusty job in the fields.

Wendell Willkie was the Republican candidate for president in 1940 and ran against the New Deal president Franklin D. Roosevelt. My parents were Democrats, as many farmers were, but Mr. Willkie was coming by train through our area so we drove down to the railroad crossing to wave to him as the train chugged down the track. He stood at the back of the train waving to those who had gathered. This was a popular way of campaigning at that time. He lost the election.

Farming ceased to make a productive living for us, so my parents had a farm sale on December 2, 1943. The sale bill listed 13 cattle, nine horses, 26 hogs, 40 head of ewes to lamb in February, 110 White Rock hens, some cane, oats and barley. The farm machinery sold included one eight-foot John Deere binder, one four-section drag, one six-foot mower, one Case corn planter, one hay rake, one nine-foot disk, one gang plow, one Sulkey plow, one two-row cultivator, one one-row cultivator, one John Deere Seeder, one wagon and rack, and one small grinder. Many miscellaneous farm items and some household goods were sold also, like barrels, an electric fence control with battery, and a brooder stove.

After moving to town, my father got a job with the Anderson Ice Company delivering ice to folks around town who still had iceboxes. He also delivered to the restaurants and bars downtown. On hot summer days you could always see kids running out to get the chipped ice off the truck. He had to chip it just so to make it fit in each icebox. People who wanted ice could put a sign in their window much like they did for the milkman to indicate how much they needed. But Daddy knew what everyone wanted without the signs. He knew all his customers, and many of them had coffee for him or tempted him with goodies.

When he picked me up from the hospital in early June 1945 after my three-week stay with rheumatic fever, he carried me over his shoulder. When I protested that I was too heavy, he assured me that I was not nearly as heavy as some of the blocks of ice he carried every day.

At night he went to school to learn radio repair, which he used later as a second source of income.

The Home Place

The farmhouse I was born in has long since been torn down.My sister Mary Lou and two brothers, Donald and Gale, were born there also. While living there, we kids attended Grant country school in Perry Township, about a mile and a half away. My friend, Letha Rowley, and her brother Leonard, lived a mile west on our way to school. We had a Shetland pony named Caesar and a dog named Touser. In the fall of 1937 when I was just five years old, I started first grade. My folks made a cart that Caesar could pull. This is what Glen and I rode to school in. Sometimes we just rode double on Caesar. Letha and Leonard's grandpa Thomas lived across the road from them and sometimes we would meet him as he herded his cattle to pasture in the morning. He also had a bull leading the herd that scared us, so we would lean forward on the pony and look the other way so the bull wouldn't see us!

As I started first grade, Joyce started high school and was staying in town during the week. My first teacher I really liked because she had the same name as me—Miss Hazel Moran. This school had a basement with a coal furnace. Letha and I played hopscotch on the cement floor there. The school had a maypole. It was lots of fun to see how far we could swing out and keep going without touching the ground. I've never seen one since.

One of my recollections of that house was chasing out flies. I think we used those sticky rolls to catch the flies, but on particular occasions we would stand at one end of the room, each with a dishtowel, waving it ahead of us to shoo flies out the open door at the other end of the room.

We moved from there in March 1940, when Gale was still in the bassinet and only three months old, to a farm (the Christianson place) in Hanson County. This big house was six miles east of Mitchell on Highway 16 and three miles north. That house had an upstairs, a basement, and below that a corner hole that went even deeper, which Daddy used as a cream cooler. I remember being in that cement cooler once when Daddy spotted a tornado and kept a watchful eye on it at the back door while we were tucked safely in that corner below the earth's surface. We were so afraid for him.

One summer in the late '70s, my youngest daughter, Jane Ann, and I made a trip to Lake Mitchell to pull the boat over behind our red wagon, a 1970 Volkswagen squareback. We were in no hurry and I wanted her to see where I had lived during my third, fourth, and fifth grades. I drove the three miles north off the highway and turned down the long driveway and stopped the car at that house. We sat in the car a few minutes as I pointed out different buildings that were still there. The couple in the house had spotted us, and the husband came out to greet us and was curious as to why we had stopped. When I explained that this had been my home as a child, he invited me in to meet his wife.

What memories came rushing back. As I stood in their kitchen and recalled these childhood memories, I'm sure they were as excited as I was. I asked about the clothes chute, which they did not know about. It had been covered over. I showed them the spot upstairs where the drop started and allowed the clothes to fall clear to the basement. That's where we washed clothes and Glen and I played cops and robbers. Glen knew how to made a wooden gun with a clothes pin at the end as a trigger and a strip of an old inner tube stretched across the top that really stung when it hit! The cream cooler was also a surprise to them, since it had been boarded over.

Our home was lit by kerosene. Even now, Don will walk into the kitchen and wonder how I can work in the "dark." It's not really dark; the sun has not set. But it always brings to mind my mother saying, "It'll soon be time to light the lamp." We had several lamps that did not produce a lot of light but enough to read or play games by or just for visiting. At bedtime, Mama would carry that lamp upstairs to light the way and see that we were all tucked in before she returned downstairs. Just the year before we moved to town, we got an Aladdin lamp, and oh, what a bright light that gave off.

The kitchen had a pass-through to the large dining room and the dish cupboard opened to both sides. The big round, oak dining table was cozy in the evenings with the kerosene lamp lit. This is where we played rummy and where Mama sat so many evenings reading to us children. I especially remember *Lorna Doone, A Girl of the Limberlost,* and *A Byrd's Christmas Carol.* Daddy was an avid reader who especially enjoyed Westerns written by Zane Grey. He often brought books home from the Carnegie Library when he made trips to town.

The parlor or front room, as we called it, had a big, heavy rug that had to be taken outdoors in the summer to be dragged back and forth across the clean, mowed weeds in the yard, then hung over the clothes-line to beat. That room also had an organ, later replaced by a big upright piano. For three years I took piano lessons on Saturday mornings in Mitchell, until my mother was convinced that it just was not my forte. My first teacher was Mrs. Hermina McGovern who lived on the east side, and later, on the southwest corner of Fifth and Sanborn, I took lessons from Olive McGovern, whose younger brother George later ran for president of the United States.

Since there was no electricity on that farm, you have probably guessed there was also no plumbing. This meant all the water had to be carried from the well for drinking, doing dishes, baths, laundry and cleaning. This also meant there were no indoor bathroom facilities. Yes, we had an outhouse and kept the past year's Montgomery Ward catalog there. During peach season it was a luxury to use for our personal hygiene the soft pink paper that protected each peach in the crate. Once when I was out there, a garter snake peeked his head up through one of the knotholes in the floor. I quickly jumped up on the seat and screamed as loud as I could until my mother and Glen came running to see what was the matter. Glen laughed at me because it was "only a little garter snake." He just picked it up and threw it. I have never cared to see another!

Mother's Day was usually spent at Grandpa and Grandma Renshaw's. (It was also a time to celebrate my birthday on May 14 and Grandma's on the 11th.) Many of their neighbors and relatives gathered and group pictures were taken. Grandma was 70 years old when I was born.

My parents got the news from the radio. We enjoyed "Jack Armstrong, the All-American Boy" and "Li'l Orphan Annie" on the radio but had to have our chores done first. Glen and I each had a secret code ring that we sent for. The *Mitchell Daily Republic* came in the mail a day late with its pink funnies on Saturday. The detective, Dick Tracy, was a favorite in the funny paper. Later, I often wished I could have the powers of Scarlet O'Neill, who could press her wrist and make herself invisible!

Some of my chores in first and second grade consisted of picking up corn cobs for fuel starters, setting the table, and gathering the eggs. I still remember the chickens pecking at my arm as I reached in under their warm feathers to feel around for a nice, fresh egg. I don't think it took long for me to learn to wear long sleeves.

My life on the farm ended in December 1943 when my parents had a farm sale. I was in seventh grade when we moved to Mitchell and started life in a big town with 9,000 people.

Susan Carlson Gilbert

Born to the post-war baby boom in Salt Lake City, Utah, Susan moved to Bountiful, Utah, at age four. That community nourished her until she graduated from high school. After attaining a degree in English and speech from Brigham Young University, she married Paul Ensign Gilbert, and together they left the comforting arms of their native state for the unrest of Berkeley, California, in the late '60s. While her husband attended law school, Susan taught high school English in Oakland. Upon Paul's graduation, they moved to Phoenix, Arizona, where they continue to reside.

Susan has been a stay-at-home mother of four children, three of whom are now married, adding three grandsons to the flock. When her youngest child entered middle school, Susan entered Arizona State University School of Law and received her degree at age 50.

Susan has always been a teacher and leader in her church and a community volunteer. She envisions more time for writing and reading at the family beach retreat in Coronado, California.

Questions 1-10: Life's Beginnings

Return to Bountiful

When you grow up in a town called Bountiful, much is expected. The Bountiful, Utah, of today is an idyllic suburb of Salt Lake City. Nestled in the foothills of the Wasatch Range, with a sweeping view of the Great Salt Lake, the lawns of this prosperous middle-class community roll past property lines, and the vigorous petunias and geraniums shouting out from beds of black earth attest to the industry and work ethic of those living behind the doors of handsome brick homes. Only a dwindling number of apricot orchards and cornfields echo Bountiful of my mid-century childhood.

When I reflect on my own growing years, I do indeed think of bounty. My parents bought their first brick home on the GI loan in 1951. Situated at 276 East Twelfth South, two blocks away from the town center and just below Orchard Drive, our place in the sun was a half-acre that the post-war building boom had parceled out from an apricot orchard, evidence that even by the time I entered the scene, the bounty for which my nurturing community was named had begun to wane. The fruits of the earth, however, were still abundant and I matured along with them. The same seasons and elements that nurtured bountiful harvests of corn, tomatoes, apricots, and cantaloupe also nurtured me. Earth, water, air and sun grow fruits and vegetables. They also grow little girls.

Earth

Our plot of ground in a fertile apricot orchard turned out to grow rocks as well. My father worked two jobs to provide for his growing family (I am the oldest of five), and in his spare time set about landscaping his new home. After-dinner hours on long summer evenings were spent gathering rocks. My father and mother would rake. I would gather and throw my harvest into a gunnysack. Thus began my early questioning. Why? Rather than harvesting rocks, I could be out in the orchard, perched in an apricot tree with my dolls, flying away to China to see starving children on whose behalf I had been admonished to clean my plate at the dinner table.

When the rocks had all been gathered and delivered to the town dump, the slightly hilly land of our reclaimed orchard had to be leveled for lawns and gardens. My job this time was to ride on a broad board that my father pulled with a rope across the yard. The only problem with such an adventure, one that could have been as grand as an amusement park ride, was that the leveling process exposed more rocks, which I was sent scuttling to gather. Why were my parents so particular? Wouldn't the lawn cover up the rocks anyway?

The lawn was seeded and soon sprouted in the rich soil. Because my father would never have lavished his hard-earned money on the instant gratification of sod, I experienced the joy of watching the seedlings gradually turn the smooth face of the earth a faint tinge of green. As more sprouts joined their friends, the level floor of our yard became a lush green carpet, perfect for summer games of Mother-May-I and Kick-the-Can. Our yard became the favorite improvised neighborhood baseball diamond. Many croquet hoops and Fourth of July sparklers were stuck into that lawn, and never once did I hit a rock!

Growing a lawn means mowing a lawn, and as soon as the handles of our lawnmower were within my grasp, the job fell to me. The problem with the lawn flowing under the shading boughs of apricot trees is that ripe apricots fall to the ground and rot. I was disdainful of my mother's admonition to gather these pests before the mowing was started. The necessity of prying disgusting bits of produce along with their pits from the damp grass made my chore unbearable. I soon learned, however, that failure to do so was counter-productive to my task. Mowing over those rotting bounties of the earth hidden in the tall grass produced nasty and dangerous results.

Having once overcome this threshold of distaste, the actual mowing bordered on fun. I had control over a noisy, powerful machine, the smell of newly mown grass was in my nostrils, the warmth of the summer sun was on my back, and dandelions were in my way. Yes, once again my mother was out to get me. If I mowed over one single dandelion, she could feel it in her bones and was on the porch waving the dandelion fork in her hand. "Don't you know that if you don't get dandelions out by the root they'll spread? Mowing over them doesn't get rid of them." I rather liked dandelions. When the yellow flower turned to a puffy head of seeds, I loved to see how far those seeds would scatter. Apparently my mother was of a different opinion. My mother was also of a different opinion regarding lawn-mowing technique. To my mind, one shot back and forth across the lawn produced a perfectly adequate lawn-mowing job. To my mother's mind, the mow lines created by this method were unacceptable. A properly mown lawn must be stroked in two directions. In her book of lawn-mowing rules, a lawn must first be mowed north and south, then against the grain, east to west. I grumbled and followed mother's rules. Anyone passing our home must surely have thought good people lived inside because our lawn had no lines in it. Maybe they reached the right conclusion.

Our small piece of earth taught me many lessons. I learned, albeit reluctantly, about the virtue of hard work, the importance of proper preparation, the value of taking pride in doing a job right. One day as I was approaching my teenage years, my father invited me to join him on a hike up into the hills above our home. We passed from subdivisions and orchards into scrub oak and eventually pines. As we perched on a rocky ledge overlooking all of our valley, from foothills to distant lake, my father began to talk. He told me about the rock striations and the formation of the Wasatch fault. He told me about his childhood during the depression, his years in the army, his dreams for his family. This time I didn't question why he worked two jobs and spent evenings hauling rocks from his yard. As I looked out over the land called Bountiful, I wondered what was beyond. I knew I wanted to go there. I think my father knew I would go. He didn't question why, but had given me the tools to till new soil.

Water

Water management has been essential in making the arid Great Basin region, of which the town of Bountiful is a part, "blossom as a rose" as predicted by Mormon pioneer prophet Brigham Young upon entering the barren Great Salt Lake Valley in 1847. Consequently, my childhood home was crisscrossed with canals and irrigation ditches, to the endless concern of mothers, and the endless delight of children.

As a child, I felt a far higher use of a Mason jar was for catching various water critters than for canning the abundant harvest. My mother and grandmother told me stories of little girls who had fallen into rivers and ditches and drowned, but when I was in the throes of the hunt, hung over the muddy bank of a ditch, I paid their stories little heed. In my bed at night, however, I did lie awake to thoughts of early death by drowning and thus developed a healthy respect for water. Water was also the source for the scourge called polio, and I harbored fears that too much time spent in the city pool would somehow cause me to wear a brace and limp like a boy I knew from up the street.

The summer chills and thrills of running through sprinklers in our yard or skittling beyond the spray of rainbirds at the park, however, were no real match for the terror of my first swimming lesson. Our extended family had gathered for a reunion at a resort of sorts called Saratoga to the south and west of Salt Lake City. My father considered the occasion the proper time and place to teach me to swim. I had always been verbally precocious but physically timid, and my father's determination had the unfortunate effect of muting my verbal protestations and drastically increasing my timidity. With all of my aunts, uncles, and cousins within sight of my performance, my anxiety was increased considerably. My father chose the "Learn to Swim by Discussion" method of instruction. He described what to do, telling me to reach out my arms, to kick my legs, to turn my head, to take a breath. This was Swimming 202. I needed Remedial Water Awareness 90. After explaining all the finer points of staying afloat, he lifted me up by the straps and seat of my suit and hefted me off on my maiden voyage.

I was the *Titanic.* My fear was the iceberg. I was a sputtering, irate, humiliated shipwreck. I was sure I had come close to being the next little drowned girl of whom my mother and grandmother would read in the *Deseret News.* This water memory was not pleasant at the time, but as it has flowed through my mind over the intervening years, new ideas have sprouted regarding the experience. My father wanted to teach me a life skill, and in his awkward, abrupt way, this inexperienced young father taught his fearful oldest child to swim in the way he knew best. I was angry. I hated my father at that moment. But even as I thought I was drowning, I knew I was loved.

The church in which I formed my early tenets of faith, and to which I still adhere, believes in baptism by immersion. Shortly after my eighth birthday, I arrived at our church building for my baptism. I was somewhat apprehensive of this event, for since early childhood I had been taught by my elders and had discussed with my peers the fact that through baptism all of a person's past sins are washed away, and any no-no's committed afterward would go on a permanent record in Heaven. My days of lying, stealing, cheating and saying bad words were over.

Even at eight I was self-conscious, and I remember worrying that the little white outfit I donned for the ordinance didn't fit right. After my mother helped me dress, I sat on a long row of folding chairs with several other children my age, facing the baptismal font. One by one each child stepped forward with his or her father and climbed down the stairs into the lukewarm water. The father, also dressed in white, raised his right arm and pronounced the baptismal prayer. At the conclusion of the prayer, the child was lowered into the water, completely submerged, then brought forth again, completely cleansed of sin.

As my turn came, my heart was pounding. Perhaps I was thinking of the swimming lesson. My father said the words of the prayer and I entered the waters of baptism. As he lifted my out of the water, a kindly official whispered to my father that the ordinance would have to be repeated. My big toe had protruded from the water! Rather than an Achilles heel, I would go through life with an unrepentant toe! How embarrassing to be the only child to enter the waters for a second time that day. I'll never forget the day of my baptism. I'll always remember that sometimes good things emerge from uncomfortable situations.

My mother loved to scrub things. Water in our house was a tool for getting the dirt out. We rarely could afford "new," so my mother cleaned the old. I often thought she was wearing things out by keeping them so clean. We had a huge, shaggy, overstuffed sofa (or couch, as we called it) in our living room that reminded me of a green wooly mammoth. Mother kept doilies on the arms and back of this beast to retard dirt, but despite her best efforts, the hands and heads of five children and even the visits of her "eating" club ladies eventually slicked down the nap to her displeasure.

Filling a metal wash bowl with soap powder and water and armed with her eggbeater and a sponge, Mother set up shop in the middle of the living room floor. First, she beat the soapy water with a fury until a thick head of suds appeared on the top. Then taking her sponge, she carefully skimmed the suds off the water and worked the lather into the hide of the sofa. After this, all of the doors and windows in the living room were flung open so the fresh air would quickly dry the soggy fabric. The vacuum removed any residue of soap scum.

Numerous other water-based homemaking projects occupied my mother's time. She periodically administered a green dye solution to the arms of the above-mentioned sofa with a discarded toothbrush. She inexplicably refused to leave with the family for an occasional drive-in movie until the dinner dishes were washed (and dried). And she saw no need to invest in the luxury of an automatic timer for the sprinkling system that kept our lawn green all summer, preferring to set a bell-timer to remind her to turn on and off manually the twenty or more valves during the day.

I saw all kinds of ways for my mother to have a more leisurely life and vowed that I would marry someone like the rich doctor who lived on the hill. Watching my mother uncomplainingly engaged in these chores brought questions to my mind. Deep in my heart I admired her, and I wanted to be a wife and a mother more than anything. I saw no other role for myself. My husband would have a career and earn the money. I would care for the home and children. I did not, however, want to scrub sofas with an eggbeater. Water nourishes, but it can also drown.

Light and Air

I associate my childhood in Bountiful with open spaces, plentiful sunshine, and clean air. I rode my bide with abandon to the church, to the dentist, to the dime store, along paths worn in the fields, with the sun on my back, the wind in my hair, and my only care the dilemma over whether to spend my nickel on a root beer or a chocolate ice cream cone before heading home.

This was "happy valley" in many ways. Restaurants saw no need to post "No Smoking" signs because in Bountiful hardly anyone smoked. More than 90 percent of the population of our town was of the Mormon faith and adhered to the advice of the church's "Word of Wisdom," which prohibits the use of alcohol, tobacco, coffee or tea. I grew up thinking that anyone who smoked, had an occasional glass of wine, or drank coffee was bad. Very bad.

A new girl named Claire moved onto our block and one day, after I knocked shyly on her door, we became friends. Claire's parents were not originally from Utah, and they were not Mormon. I knew this, and as a child of an indigenous culture, I looked upon them as somehow different. After a summer morning spent playing in the open air with our dolls beneath the shade of Claire's willow tree, her mother invited me in to have lunch with them.

Under the scrutiny of my watchful eye, everything about Claire had seemed normal up to this point. "She's just a girl like me," I decided. (Except for the fact that Claire had long conversations with her doll and vowed that her doll spoke back to her.) At lunch, Claire's mother offered me iced tea. Iced tea! I couldn't imagine such nice people imbibing such a sinful beverage. A pleasant morning spent with a friend in the open air juxtaposed against iced tea thrust at me in the confines of Claire's kitchen produced one of my first paradoxes.

A favorite childhood retreat was to a tree house owned by a boy named Skippy who lived just through the apricot orchard from my home. Skippy's tree house was in one of the few really tall trees in our neighborhood, a giant black walnut. From the heights of this eyrie, I could scout the land. Almost as if I could soar as an eagle, with the sun on my wing, I would pretend I was off to distant lands, far over our mountains, beyond our lake. While my playmates read comic books and collected fire bugs, I was in Katmandu (wherever that is) and somehow knew that light and air would help me get there.

When I was in the fifth grade, arsonists set fire to our school in the fall, damaging several classrooms and forcing double sessions and cramped quarters. Mr. Van Dyke's class was reassigned to the stage, which had been enclosed across the proscenium arch, creating a cozy classroom without windows. All was well until Mr. Van Dyke turned the lights off one day and determined that the total darkness was the perfect setting for telling ghost stories. The rest of the class was in ecstasy. I learned how dark the total absence of light can be. Our second-session class was dismissed at six p.m. In mid-winter Utah, the shadows are long on the snow at that hour. By the end of the 15-minute walk home, my imagination was running wild, and from behind every juniper spindly arms reached out to grab me.

After dinner and dishes, the trek to my basement bedroom held even more perils. I was convinced that ghouls were lurking behind the water heater and under my bed. My father, noticing my reluctance to make my usual jaunt down the stairs, sat me down and asked questions. The next day at school, Mr. Van Dyke announced, "The principal received a call from a father this morning, and because someone is scared of the ghost stories, we will no longer be telling them." The audible groan seemed to be pointed in my direction, and I felt my face turn beet red as I tried to mimic the consensus of dismay. I was secretly exuberant. Mortified, but exuberant. My father had rescued me from the realms of darkness. Spring came, our school was repaired, and we returned to a classroom where light and air flowed through the windows.

I am part of the Bountiful harvest. Experiences with the land, the water, the light, and the air have taught me the values of hard work, order, faith, motherhood, and family. By working through the paradoxes presented by the juxtaposition of the complacency of daily life in a small homogeneous town and my inner desire to explore and grow, I have added to my garden the values of spontaneity, adventure, tolerance, self-expression, and individual worth.

As my father lay in a semi-conscious state dying of cancer, his five children around him, he began giving away trees. The trees in his yard, each of which he had planted and pruned, had been fed by the earth, water, air, and sunlight of Bountiful. The children around his deathbed had been likewise nurtured. To one he gave a quaking aspen, to another a blue spruce. To all of us he gave the best he had to give—his love. My mother and father now lie together on a hillside overlooking our lake. They can see all of Bountiful from their resting place. I thank them for feeding and watering, for pulling the weeds when necessary, and for allowing me to find light and air.

Valerie Jackson

Valerie Kay Jackson is a member of the Crow tribe from southeastern Montana and has resided in Arizona since 1983. She came to Arizona to pursue a degree in English, and she aspires to be a writer. Since its inception, Valerie has been an active member of Native Images, a writing program for Native Americans, and she enjoys sharing aspects of her heritage through her writing and public reading.

A single parent for more than 20 years, Valerie raised two sons while earning her college degree. She is happiest when involved in projects that involve children, communities and their development.

Question 15: What individuals most influenced you as a child?

Bones Like Lilac Bushes

My gramma, Susie Yellowtail, was a talented and loving soul who could nurse, deliver, stitch, grow, pick, can, butcher, or cook anything put before her. She was well-schooled in the ways of the white man. Having first gone to a boarding school in the town of Crow Agency after being orphaned at a young age, she learned agricultural techniques for being a good farmer. She learned sewing, so that she could make and wear white man's clothes.

Eventually, she went to school in Bacone, Oklahoma, and it was there she decided by becoming a nurse she could best serve her people. Susie Walking Bear went back East to attend Northfield Mount Herman, a small women's college. She went on to do her clinical work at Boston General Hospital in Massachusetts and was one of the first Indian registered nurses in the United States.

Much of my childhood was spent with my grandparents. Their farm lay across the river from our ranch in the Little Bighorn Valley in southeastern Montana. It was an exciting place. Gramma taught me many things over the years, how to sew and play "Onward Christian Soldiers" on the piano. She had a green thumb, so all us grandkids spent much of our spring and summers planting, weeding and picking everything in the garden. When I wasn't outside playing, I was at her side.

One day, Gramma left the washroom to answer the phone and warned me, "Do not touch the washing machine." Many times I had watched her do this chore and I felt confident I could do it alone. I began to feed the tips of towels and shirts into the wringer and was fascinated to watch the rinse water dribble down the white metal like rivulets on rainy windows. Suddenly, it grew ravenous and laundry no longer satisfied its hunger. The beast took my fingers into its compressing jowls and swallowed my wrist and my forearm. It was threatening to devour my shoulder when my terrified screams brought Gramma running to thwart the beast's grip on my arm. Popping the safety release, she saved me from certain death. My arm throbbed with a heartbeat all its own.

Gramma ushered me out on the side porch by a lilac bush in full bloom. "Look here," she said. "We are copied after things in nature."

I wiped my flooded eyes and tried to catch my breath so I could stop crying. She pulled down a fragrant green branch and held it inches from my face. Then she bent it in half. "See this? This is just like your bones." And I watched the young branch slowly take back its shape. Gramma reached deeper into the bush and pulled out a woody branch. Effortlessly, she snapped it in two pieces.

"This is like my dry bones, brittle and easy to break." All the while, my body was pressed into her soft breasts. With both hands, she rubbed my arm vigorously. I smelled tobacco and smoked hide mixed with the fragrance of blooming lilacs.

She wiped my tear-stained face with her apron and said, "It's going to be fine. You just bent it a little." With a gentle nudge, she pointed me toward the stairs and sent me down to the river to find my cousins.

My gramma Susie was a generous person and bestowed many gifts on me. The most memorable came to me on December 25, 1981. Several days before, I arrived home on the bus from New Mexico having just finished a tough semester at UNM in Albuquerque. I went across to tell Gramma that I had barely passed English 101, but an essay I wrote about Dr. Elizabeth Kübler-Ross pulled me through. I wrote about her theory on death and dying. I sat down on Gramma's bed and told her of the stages of grief people experience when a loved one has died. Gramma had never heard of Dr. Kübler-Ross, but she agreed that the theory made sense.

"In the old days, we buried our dead above ground. Now days we call Bullis in Hardin and he takes care of everything. They put you in an expensive box and stick you in a hole in the ground. Then the calaahs—the old grammas—wail the mourning song as the dirt is thrown on the casket by the relatives and off to the happy hunting ground we go." Her eyes twinkled as she laughed when she said this. I wandered around in her room as she caught me up on the latest mocassin-telegraph news.

I left and returned to my folks' home. The next day was full of presents for the little ones; they ripped open packages and then we "went across." Everyone in the family referred to visiting each other's households in this way, because to get to our farms we had to cross I-90, the railroad tracks and a bridge over the Little Bighorn River to get there and then reverse the order to come back across.

All of the women put food on the table and Grampa started to pray in Crow. Over by Gramma the great-grandkids started to fuss and fight; Grampa was famous for his long prayers and Gramma was the only person who could hurry him up with one of her deep throated disapproval sounds. She harrumphed and Grampa made a hasty finish.

The men and children and Gramma settled down to eat. My cousin gave her the turkey tail, her favorite part. Everyone began eating and a few minutes later Gramma's head slumped to the side. My father rushed to her and with his finger dislodged food from her throat. The men took hold of the buffalo hide she was sitting on and moved her from the chair to the floor. I checked her neck for a pulse. There was none. I listened to her chest as my father blew air into her lungs and all I could hear was the raspy sound of his air leaving her lungs and no heart beat.

Someone said, "Valerie, do CPR, do CPR." I told them it was no use—she was gone, but they insisted so I reluctantly straddled her lower torso. With my hands clasped I applied pressure to her sternum. Under my palms I felt her sternum give way—a cracking sound—then crunch. Looking up at the family surrounding us I saw terror and disbelief in their eyes. I looked at my father who was still blowing air futilely into her lungs.

"Daddy, it's no use, she is gone, stop now." He had to be wrested away from her. Gramma's mouth had turned blue. Someone finally called for an ambulance. When they arrived they put her on a stretcher and took her to the Indian hospital in Crow Agency 40 miles north. Everyone but myself and the kids followed the ambulance. I told the kids that Gramma went to the happy hunting grounds and she would have plenty of relatives to be with. Then they went downstairs to play.

I cleaned up the kitchen and put the uneaten food away. I went in my grandparents' bedroom to use the phone and called our many relatives to tell them Gramma had just died during dinner and everyone had followed the ambulance to Crow.

I sat down on the bed and took her night dress from the pillow and picked up her mocassin from the floor and buried my face in them and smelled tobacco and smoked hide. I will forever associate these smells with my gramma. They reminded me of that wringer-washer lilac bush day. I carried her dress and mocassin with me and walked to each window in her room. Outside I could see the bare branches of all the fruit trees she had nurtured, and just next to the house my favorite tree, the cherry, naked of leaves and coated with a delicate blanket of new-fallen snow.

Sadness flooded my heart, yet I appreciated and accepted the lesson she bestowed on me. I know that if any person on this earth could choose the time of their going across, I know she did. To her empty room I said, "Gramma, now you are free—your body is released from the aches and pains that plagued you." Her last gift to me was the peaceful crossing of her soul; because of this I no longer fear the journey to "the other side camp." Gramma left dignified and unafraid, surrounded by the family she loved. I know I will have the courage to do the same when my time comes. Thank you, Gramma. A-ho calaah a-ho.

Carole Ellison

Carole Ellison writes poetry to her now-grown children and has done so for the past 22 years. She is currently putting those poems in the proper book order for others to read. Carole and her husband, Bill, split their time evenly between Phoenix, Arizona, and Bellevue, Washington.

Carole participates in a Cameo Circle with women she met at the first national conference of the Everywoman's Story project, and she has encouraged all her friends and family to begin writing their life stories.

Question 15: What individuals most influenced you as a child?

A Loved Child

I was born in Yakima, Washington, in May 1939, the year that the movies "Gone with the Wind" and "Over the Rainbow" were released.

My mother was quite sick before I was born and, as a result, my birth cost my parents $1,000, an amount that is probably equivalent to tens of thousands of dollars now. They had no insurance then for things like hospital stays and doctor bills.

My mother, born in 1910, was the youngest and the most spoiled in a family of five living children. Her two older siblings, who had died before I was born, were seldom talked about except in hushed tones. One died as a result of an accident with a horse, and the other after a lengthy illness. Mother's older female siblings essentially raised her. She grew up on a farm and wasn't needed in the house because her mother and the older sisters did that work, so she would spend a lot of time outside with her dad and around the farm animals and equipment. Consequently, she didn't learn to do household things like cooking and cleaning until after she was married.

My father, who was born in 1900, was next to the youngest in a family of 12 children. His mother died when he was ten years old and he and his younger sister went to live with an older brother and his wife and children. The older brother and his wife took advantage of the cheap labor and treated my father and his sisters shabbily. The only complaint I heard about it was from Mom. Dad just said, "Well, those were hard times and there wasn't much money." He does have a scar on the back of his neck that my mother always said was put there by a brother's wife with a washing machine handle. Dad claims it was an infection that left a scar.

One thing I know for sure is that my father loved my mother. He cherished her. Every now and then she would get out of control and berate him up one side and down the other. He would just wait until she was through and then continue doing what he was doing, whether it was to finish a conversation or a task. My early visual memories strongly reflect love as being mutual between the two of them. When Dad would get up in the morning and walk out through the house and into the kitchen, Mom would pretend to "snag" him and they would embrace. Another visual memory of their closeness is that on some evenings he would be sitting in a big arm chair reading his newspaper or his beloved *Reader's Digest*, and Mom would lie across his lap and the arms of the chair and be hugging him. Good stuff!

My mother stayed in one town her whole life, even after she married my father. She never pulled up her roots for any other place. She talked about leaving as if she had longed for it (What-I-could-have-done-with-my-life-if-I-hadn't-married-your-father-and-had-you-kids-sort-of-thing), but even on short journeys away from home with my dad in later years, she could not wait to get back to her home and her garden and her roses.

Gardening and me? Well, once when I was in high school I planted a garden when my boyfriend broke up with me because he was going off to college and was leaving me behind. I took a shovel and spaded up a plot of ground under the clothesline—never mind the blisters and sore muscles—then raked it to soften the moist clods of dirt, and then marked out rows. I planted radishes and leaf lettuce and green onions and they grew and provided food for salads. Every time we ate from that garden I thought of my lost love—that is, until a better boyfriend came along. Gardens to me, ergo, seem to provide a means for working out one's frustrations.

I had only one living grandparent, my mother's mother. Her father had died before I was born, although my mother did a great job of keeping his memory alive by telling stories about him, how he was honest and well-respected in the community and a member of the school board. Grandma lived with her only son and his wife and my mother's maiden sister on a farm that bordered ours. She lived to the ripe old age of 87 and died when I was 12. Doing the math, that puts her birth in 1864, the year before the Civil War ended.

As a child I used to spend a lot of time at Grandma's house—not to see her, because she was always "nervous," always had a case of the "nerves." I would walk into the house, go up to Grandma's chair and stand by her and say, "Hello, Grandma, how are you today?"

And she would say something like, "Well, not as good as yesterday," or "I've felt better." She never ever answered, "I feel good! I feel great! How are you?" In line with a George Carlin line from the '70s, she never even told me to get out of the way! Looking back on it, it was as if I did not matter one way or the other.

What did matter was that I did not make my grandmother nervous. In her later years she lost her eyesight, which probably made her worry more. When Mom would stop by to see her with my brother and me in hot summer weather, she would have me wear jeans over my shorts. Grandma would always feel my legs and make sure they were covered so "I wouldn't catch my death of cold" from not wearing enough clothes. Later, I would take off the heavy jeans and go outside and play.

The person I really went to see in that house was Iva Chamberlain,my maiden aunt—a truly wonderful woman. She was like a saint who walked the earth. She loved me, accepted me for me and for who I could be, and did not try to make changes in me except by her own shining example. She was so much fun to be around. She knew how to do interesting arts and crafts and she baked cookies and always had the patience to show me how to do those things. She always had time for me.

When I was born—the first and only girl born into the family in 27 years—she started doing fancy work, embroidering pillow cases, crocheting table doilies and tatting lace. And when I married I was presented with an enormous box of her work, along with a special poem that she had written when I was born to welcome me into the world.

My aunt treated everyone with the same love and acceptance. She was the one who loved and accepted me and made me feel special. She believed I could do anything I set out to do. She believed I could leap tall buildings and change the world. And when I was with her, I believed it, too.

There have been reality checks in my life from time to time, but I shall never forget her undying faith in me. It warms me to think of it, and I continue to feel her love.

Eunice Nicks

Eunice Williams Nicks moved to Flagstaff at age five and grew up in Flagstaff. She was one of the first Native Americans to complete her entire public school education there. She attended Gregg Business College in Phoenix and found her first job at the state capitol in the Arizona Division of Rehabilitation. She married her first husband and settled in Avondale.

She later returned to Flagstaff alone. When she remarried, she and her husband moved to Tuba City, where Eunice taught school for five years. After her divorce, she attended Northern Arizona University, then worked for the federal Office of Navajo and Hopi Relocation until her retirement in September 1999. She has five daughters, seven grandchildren and two great-children. Eunice has been an active member of the Women's Business Association and a community volunteer. She loves to cook and does some occasional catering.

Question 17: What influence do you think race or ethnicity played in your development?

The Hopi Life

I have for many years had a desire to write about my heritage and role as a Native American woman and to give my children and grandchildren a legacy which they could be proud of. Memories laid between the pages of my mind are beautiful and wonderful as I recall the teachings of my grandparents.

I was born on a hot summer morning in a Hopi village called Moencopi in my grandmother's house with only my grandmother and a great aunt assisting. I was the first child born to my parents and was the first great grandchild. My mother was from Moencopi and my father from another village called Hotevilla. My brother and sister were born later.

When I was about four years old and my brother only one year old, my father died of pneumonia. My mother moved us to Flagstaff, which was 75 miles from "home." There were no jobs available on the reservation during those years, therefore the move.

Because my grandparents thought it was important for my brother to learn the Hopi language and to learn about the ceremonies, which are vital for the male members to participate in, it was decided that he would remain at home until he was older.

Although I lived in the Anglo/Caucasian world, I kept in close touch with the reservation. That was one of the conditions my grandparents set in letting me go with my mother—that she would allow me to go out there every chance there was so I would continue to learn about my culture. So during the summer months when school was out, my mother took me out there. When school was in session I would go out on weekends and during the holidays.

I experienced the life of a Hopi child and grew up among relatives who loved me and taught me well about my role as a Hopi woman and what was expected of me. My grandfather told me that I should never forget that I was very important to our culture and that life could not go on without woman. Hopis believe in this importance because women are the foundation of a home, and they are to be respected.

Grandmother taught me the importance of cleanliness, of keeping a home clean and of learning to cook as preparation for becoming a wife and mother. Women had the responsibility of raising children and housekeeping. There was much hard work—planting, irrigating, harvesting, fetching water from springs. Everything was laborious, but along with the work came great laughs and joys.

I participated in the social dances and learned to prepare most of the Hopi foods which are vital, especially for certain ceremonies and occasions like weddings, Hopi ceremonial dances, newborn-baby-naming ceremonies, and initiations. I am so grateful for my grandmother teaching me these things with great patience and love.

I recall the first time I made tortillas with her. I was about seven years old, with my black hair cut just below my ears and bangs cut straight across my forehead. Kneeling barefoot on the tabletop, I pushed the rolling pin back and forth over the cornmeal dough. I wore an old dress. I had two dresses to my name, which my mother washed every other day. In those days Hopi women were supposed to wear dresses, and my grandmother wore a typical, traditional dress, with a flour sack tied around her waist as an apron. Her long hair was braided and pinned into a bun at the nape of her neck. She was petite and had deep lines in her complexion, which I thought were pretty.

The table was used only for food preparation. It sat in the middle of the small one-room house, which was made of rock and adobe plastered with a white clay and roofed with big, board-covered beams. We never ate at the table. Instead, we spread a tablecloth on the floor and sat on small pieced blankets to eat. There was only one cot, in an alcove of the L-shaped house, so we also slept on the floor.

I am so thankful that I was able to stay so close to my family and the Hopi way of life and the teachings which now are so very important to me. I don't believe I ever appreciated it until I saw my own children growing up. I have sadly regretted not teaching them the language, which I myself speak fluently.

The happiness of life on the reservation cannot begin to compare with the "white man's" ways. I still live in the two cultures but will always go back to my Hopi way of life time and time again. Perhaps someday I may even return to the reservation to live permanently, because there I find such peace and contentment, which I need in my life. I always tell people that it is like therapy and rejuvenation for me when I go out there to my home.

Doris Frace

Doris Frace has been a resident of Scottsdale, Arizona, since retiring in 1996. A native of Minnesota, Doris earned her B.S. and M.A. degrees from the University of Minnesota and an MBA in business administration from Metro State University. Doris served as an education administrator in Bloomington, Minnesota, prior to retirement. She has one son.

Doris facilitates a Cameo Circle and is the Arizona Coordinator for Cameo Life Stories.

Question 19 : "What words of advice do you remember being given about your future?"

Childhood Aspirations

The most significant thing I remember about my childhood is the total lack of advice given to me about a potential future career.

I cannot recall any family member, teacher or friend ever planting a seed in my mind that I could be anything I wanted to be—a leader, a manager, "the boss"—even though I was considered to be a bright child.

In the 1950s, my high school of 800 students employed only one counselor, with whom I never met, and friends were too occupied with day-to-day happenings to bother about the future.

As a child, I always felt loved and cherished by parents and relatives. However, empowering your children wasn't a parenting skill in the 1930s and '40s.

Children absorb insights of what is expected of them by observing implicit behaviors as well as by hearing what they are told. For example, what I was about 13 years old, my father built me a beautiful hope chest, which my aunts and grandmothers would fill with beautiful gifts of dishes and linens on special occasions. I learned how to embroider pillowcases and dish towels, which were placed in the chest, and I got into the habit of buying special treasures for my hope chest with extra money. Clearly, the unspoken message was that I would marry and that this dowry I was accumulating would be a great asset for a young wife.

The lack of accomplished female role models was a detriment for young women growing up in this era. Although such women existed, there weren't many of them, and they primarily were invisible to young girls.

Women in the books we read—Heidi; Nancy Drew; Meg, Jo, Beth and Amy in *Little Women*—had wonderful qualities, but usually they didn't grow up to become professional women with interesting careers. Even the women we met through the radio and later on television—Stella Dallas, Molly of the *Fibber McGee and Molly* program and Loretta Young—were devoted wives and mothers.

In the mid-1950s, when I had an assignment to write about an accomplished female, the only two women who came to mind were Eleanor Roosevelt and Queen Elizabeth. Successful women such as Elizabeth Dole, Margaret Thatcher and Barbara Walters play an important role for today's teenagers, for they are living proof that girls can become successful in their own right if they are ambitious and hard-working.

I believe we all have a small voice deep within us that is our navigational compass, and it will guide us successfully through life if we listen to it. This intuition kept telling me that knowledge and continued learning were keys for my success.

Consequently, I always knew that I somehow would graduate from college and that this would be an important step for my future. Like so many of today's youth, I had no inkling of what would happen to me after college or what opportunities college would provide.

Having grown up at a time when women had three career options—teacher, nurse or secretary, I wisely reasoned that I would have more flexibility by combining two of the options, business (secretarial) and education.

In college, I enjoyed and excelled in business classes, so I met with two business professors about my career direction. Both men discouraged me from pursuing marketing, accounting or sales and warned me that these were predominantly male fields in which I would have a very hard time. I consequently became a business education teacher and eventually entered school administration.

To this day, I am amazed and disappointed with myself because up until the 1970s it did not enter my consciousness that I could advance my career and broaden my options. Up until that time, it never entered my mind to study to become a principal, superintendent or administrator, even though I was ambitious and hard-working. It seems that in about the 1970s, something connected, and women began to get the message that they were capable of making the same career efforts that were available to men.

To this day, I regret growing up in an era when women weren't encouraged to pursue science and math. At least one recent study has shown a strong correlation between higher salaries and the amount of math a person has, and science is, of course, responsible for the technical and medical innovations that have enriched our country.

Rev. Francine Sample

The Rev. Francine Sample is a minister, motivational speaker, trainer and management consultant. She earned her bachelor of science degree in social work from Temple University and her master of arts in administration from Antioch University, and completed doctoral course work at Arizona State University. She is currently pursuing her master of divinity degree from Golden Gate University.

For most of her career she has worked in government. Her most recent position is curriculum and training coordinator for the City of Phoenix Public Works Department. She is also adjunct faculty for Ottawa University and Prescott College.

Francine has a strong love for gospel music and is an active toastmaster, mother of two and grandmother of four. She is the senior associate minister of Bethesda Community Baptist Church in south Phoenix.

Question 43: Did you marry or enter a long-term, committed relationship? When and with whom? Did you expect it to last forever?

Relationships

I entered several long-term relationships with men, each of which I expected to last forever. My first real long-term relationship was with a great musician who eventually got hooked on heroin and likes that lifestyle. As far as I know he is still addicted. We met in 1970 and divorced in 1976.

My next relationship was with a charming man who was a very ambitious guy and a great provider. Our first ten months were great, but he began to get upset about my choice to continue my education. He started by telling me regularly that he was able to take care of my children and me and going to school was a waste of time. He would bring the topic up every three or four months with a little more aggression each time. He eventually began complaining that a real man can take care of his woman and a real woman would take care of the house. We used to argue a lot because he didn't want his woman (me, at the time) to work. I didn't need education, according to him.

When he realized the arguing was not effective and the loss of sleep didn't stop me from attending classes and studying, he started to become physically abusive. I was shocked when he hit me for the first time. I didn't even try to defend myself. I just froze. I had no real concept of this behavior in a loving relationship. Not physical abuse. My perception of love is that you never hurt anyone you truly love. Not deliberately. After the first time he hit me, the next day he cried and said he was sorry. He said he couldn't believe he would try to hurt me. He said he didn't know what came over him and asked me to forgive. He was so apologetic and seemed so sincere. I really loved him. I didn't want to lose him. He was a great provider and a wonderful lover so I gladly accepted his apology. He brought me flowers and jewelry to make up for his behavior.

Less than four months later he hit me again. This time I defended myself. He punched me with his fist in my face. I knew he was deliberately trying to hurt me and cause me to bruise in hopes that I wouldn't go out of the house. I saw red and I charged at him with full force. He was in the hospital for six days. When he came home from the hospital he left me. Six months later he filed for divorce. He told me he was not going to stay with "no woman who tried to kill him." I couldn't believe it. He agitated the entire scene. I was just defending myself. I had always been taught that if you choose to defend yourself, don't give your opponent a chance. If you don't choose to defend yourself just walk away. Well, I knew walking away was out of the question. He would have just thought I was scared and he may have gotten worse. Besides, I was so angry that it was too late to walk away. That relationship lasted four years.

I married again in 1979. I didn't even like this man. But he pursued me non-stop and he was great with my children. Everyone thought he was a great guy and would be a fantastic stepfather. He stayed on my heels until I gave in and married him. We didn't have sex before we married. That was a big mistake. I enjoyed making love and I had some of the most creative lovers, so I know what good lovemaking is about. I knew on my wedding night that this marriage was not going to last. Sex was poor. Poor! Bad.

I had more headaches in that relationship than I ever had prior to or since that time. My husband was afraid of sex. He thought of it for reproduction purposes only. He wouldn't take off his underwear until he got in the bed and under the covers. I don't think I ever really saw him naked unless I went to the bathroom when he was in the shower and pulled back the shower curtains. Then he screamed and squeezed his knees together.

Doom. That marriage was doomed. In August of 1981, I packed my brown station wagon and my children and left for Arizona. My husband didn't want to leave Philadelphia so I left without him. He never came to Arizona and I never returned to Philadelphia. I divorced him in 1984. My children loved him. They thought the world of him. They were quite angry with me for leaving Philadelphia, leaving their family (cousins), leaving their friends and schoolmates, and leaving their stepdad.

I have not entered a long-term relationship since I arrived in Arizona. I had several short-term relationships but nothing lasting. Nothing I even wanted to last. I truly have no patience for poor conversation, lack of ambition, lack of direction, or poor sex, nor will I tolerate it. I will not share my lover's intimacies with others either.

Since my call to the ministry my lustful desires have decreased tremendously, much due to my efforts to gain self-control. My prayer is that God will send the right person my direction and all my needs and desires as well as his will be met and we will complement each other and truly enjoy each other as man and wife ordained with God's grace. He has to love God and God's word as much as I have learned to.

I don't go shopping for a man and I by no means feel I am nothing without a man. I love my independence and I know I am capable of taking good care of myself with God's help. It will be nice to have intimate and long-term companionship if that is God's will. I know now that it has to be God's will and not Francine's will because my choices haven't been the wisest. They've been based on flesh. Lust has its costs. But I really have no regrets. I've had many wonderful opportunities to do my research on intimacy. I've also spent precious time with many wonderful men.

Today, as a woman of God, I am so thankful that I serve God who is a forgiving God and chooses to use people because of what they can bring to the kingdom. I am out of the dark now. I see the light. It's truly shining on me.

Laurie Eynon

Laurie Eynon is a former English teacher and church youth worker who grew up in Milwaukee, but has lived most of her adult life in Columbus, Indiana.

She is a freelance writer, an architectural tour guide, and a part-time health club employee when she is not playing tennis, traveling, or at the movies. She has two grown sons and a bevy of wonderful women friends who keep her from slumping into V-8 and tuna fish times.

Question 43: What has been your experience with relationships?

V-8 and Tuna Fish Time

I dread the arrival of the feeling even before it strikes. I begin to pick up subtle clues that all is not well. "Red alert! Red alert!" my mind signals my body. "Remember how bad this feels? Well, fasten your seat belt; it's going to be a bumpy ride!"

I won't be able to sleep or eat. I won't be able to concentrate on a book or a TV show. All activities will seem pointless and joyless, even those I normally love. Though exhausted, I will lie awake at 4 a.m., answerless questions churning in my head. Though despondent, I will be too numb to cry. And I can see no end to my hopelessness.

I will lose weight dramatically, perhaps 10 pounds in 10 days. This last phenomenon is the only positive effect of my condition. I may be miserable, anxious, depressed, but, by God, I'll be thin.

The mere idea of food nauseates me. A large knot halfway down my esophagus prohibits the swallowing of food. Because I know that I must eat or perish, I force myself to eat, standing up over the kitchen sink. I should eat good stuff, I reason, not the usual comfort food like ice cream or mashed potatoes. My condition is way beyond comfort food. I need survival food. So I open a tin of tuna fish and ingest enough to give my body some protein. Then, for vitamins, I wash it down with V-8.

And all because some man has broken my heart.

Interestingly enough, if there were a real emergency—tornado, fire, accident, illness—I would be passing out first aid kits and serving chicken soup. I am a good person to have around in an actual crisis. But let a careless, shallow man tell me he's leaving, and I fall apart.

I remember the first boy who ever dumped me. I was 14. He was 17 with a little green Fiat. I had felt his attention waning, but the day I saw him taking Lois Lubinski home from school in the Fiat, I was devastated. I walked home to find my mother at the stove, her attention focused on stirring supper. She didn't seem to notice my tragic visage. I went to my room and threw myself down on my bed. No tears came, but where did that huge knot in my throat come from? At dinner, I was unable to choke down whatever my mother had been preparing.

In the ensuing days, I considered converting to Catholicism and entering a convent. Nuns must be immune to such devastating feelings. Besides, it held a certain dramatic appeal.

Though I'd like to think I have grown intellectually, emotionally and spiritually since I was 14, the way I grieve over relationships hasn't changed much. It still hurts the same way, no matter how smart I am, or how many times it's happened, or how unworthy the man turned out to be in the end.

And I rarely suffer in silence. I spill my sad story to anyone in listening range. Unwary acquaintances in line behind me at the supermarket innocently inquire, "How are you?" and I spew histrionics:

"I'm miserable! Tom and I broke up and I feel so bad even though all my friends warned me about him, but I thought I was different, but I guess I wasn't and now I'll probably spend the rest of my life alone and depressed."

Even the check-out clerk seems embarrassed.

I have spent a good part of my adult life trying to avoid those V-8 and tuna fish times. I have accommodated, denied, compromised, bit my tongue and laid down like a doormat, just so the man du jour would stick around and I would not have to feel bad.

And it rarely worked.

When the man goes out the door, my spunk, my self-worth, and my sense of humor go out the window. It is a tribute to my self-centered and irrational desperation for a man that, when I heard about Linda

McCartney's death, one of my first thoughts was, "Oh, now Paul's available!"

Just to let you know, I'm not some naive young girl. I'm a highly educated, competent woman. I've raised two children, taught school, written plays, organized major events, and traveled the world. I should know better.

It's partly a cultural thing, I know. Generations of women were indoctrinated with the idea that marriage was the be-all-end-all of life. Catching a man was the highest goal we could aspire to. I apparently bought this popular myth. So I've never been all by myself, without some man as an appendage, for more than a few weeks at a time.

Mary Ann McQuinn

Mary Ann McQuinn was raised in the rural Appalachian foothills of eastern Kentucky. She is one of eight children born to parents with less than an eighth-grade education. Strong family encouragement led Mary Ann to excel in school, and with the help of scholarships, grants and part-time jobs, she earned a bachelor of arts degree in journalism

She is an award-winning writer and has 15 years of experience in public relations at the state and national levels.

Now, at the age of 38 and single with no significant other, Mary Ann has embarked on a journey to motherhood. McQuinn plans to chronicle her life growing up in a work tentatively titled "Girl from Kentucky."

Question 49: What impact has not having children had on you?

The Decision

The decision was hard. I thought about it for years, agonized over it, shed a few tears—and then, and only then, took a deep breath and picked up the phone and called a fertility treatment clinic.

I was 38, single, and faced with the harsh reality of taking responsibility for parenthood. If I were to be a mother, then I had to start now and, with no significant other in my life, I had to do it alone, knowing that family and friends may not understand or approve, knowing that there would be no grandparents on either side. Knowing that the responsibility for raising the child would be completely mine. I welcomed it. But I had no illusions of ease. I knew it would be a journey of difficulties, trails and tribulations, laughter and tears.

Every five years, I set life goals. When I was 30, I decided to have a child by the time I was 35 due primarily to the increased risk of birth defects after 35. The years rolled by too quickly, however, and one day I saw a prominent gray hair in the mirror and realized that I was 38 years old and time was running out. I couldn't afford to wait any longer for "Mr. Right." Waiting could mean no children.

I felt naked. Raw. Exposed. I did not want to have to make this choice. Why did I devote so much time to a career? Why didn't I spend more time socializing? It was hard to admit that if I were going to be a mother, I would have to do it alone. Picking up the phone took a tremendous amount of courage. What would the clinic think? Would they accept a single woman as a patient? (Some don't.) Would they judge me? Would it be too expensive?

Where did I start? I typed in fertility as a search term on the Internet and discovered a clinic less than three miles from my home—fate. Now, it was time to call. What to say? Finally, I just dialed the number. And giggled. And sputtered. Finally, "Hello, I'm single, and, uh, I was, uh, thinking about, you know, having a baby through artificial insemination and uh, I don't know how to get started."

Finally, after an eon (30 seconds) the friendly receptionist rescued me and told me the initial visit was less that $500. There would be expenses for some blood tests, a psychological evaluation, donor sperm, vitamins, and medications—all in all, not out of my reach. And yes, they did take MasterCard and Visa.

Then, she dropped a bomb—now taking appointments for three months ahead. Devastation. And then that little three-letter word—BUT—we have a cancellation. Can you come in day after tomorrow? Fate again. Yes! Of course! You bet! And so the journey to motherhood began.

Alberta Meyer

Alberta Meyer spent most of her life in her home state of Missouri. She was a career employee for the state, working with the Division of Employment Security and as the first woman executive secretary of the Missouri Highway Reciprocity Commission. She was a charter member of the Jefferson City Business and Professional Women and BPW state president from 1954 to 1956.

Alberta served as chair of the Missouri Commission on the Status of Women from 1965 to 1967. In 1965 she was the first recipient of the Service to Women Award from the Omicron Chapter of Phi Chi Theta, a national professional business fraternity. Her interests include theater, television, radio, spectator sports, books, women's rights and wrongs, and anything chocolate.

Question 68: If you never married, what factors affected your decision to remain single?

The Meyer Family I Have Known, but Mostly About Me

It is hot in the month of August in southwest Arkansas and especially in Little River County. I endured the heat each year of the twenty I lived there. I was glad of it as I was growing up because I could have watermelon, and ice cream, and out-of-doors birthday parties.

When I was a child I thought the millennium would bring the end of the world. It was so far away, and now as I write this, in a few months we'll go into 2000. I never expected to live to be this age, 84 plus (and counting—or waiting?). My birth date was August 14, 1914, when the Archduke of Austria was assassinated and World War I followed.

I was born at 11:30 am on Friday in Ashdown, Arkansas, county seat, population less than 2,000. I was born at home, a small white frame house, in a high headboard solid cherry bedstead, a bedroom suite I came to love mostly because of the pretty little writing desk. The house is long gone and so is the bedroom furniture. I have regretted many times that mother did not want to bring it to St. Louis when we moved from Arkansas, but she was "tired" of all that old furniture and sold most of the furnishings she had grown up with.

I weighed eight pounds and had a bit of black curly hair and strong lungs which colic allowed me to exercise. Three locks of hair from the first haircut are still in my baby book. I was named for my maternal grandfather and paternal grandmother, both of whom had died before my parents were married. It was no secret I was supposed to have been a son and Albert would have suited nicely.

Some may think it is not natural, but I am completely honest when I say I have never thought of myself as a wife, or dreamed of marrying or regretted not doing so.

My adult opinion of men as a "class" is not the highest! I like men—some men—as individuals. Some of my best friends have been men, and some of my most important help has come from men, but I never thought I'd have to marry one. One reason may be that I've always had to compete with or against men. A man was never a high priority for me.

I think the Pulitzer Prize winning novelist, Edna Ferber, expressed my sentiments. Her friends could not understand why she had remained single over the years. "Surely you have met someone you would have married," one said. "I have," admitted Miss Ferber, "and I met one man who would have married me—but unfortunately it wasn't the same man!"

My family never pushed for, suggested, or evidently expected me to marry. One aunt was unable to accept that I was unmarried and "tsk, tsked" a lot, although she agreed I had a good single life. I never thought of myself as a "domestic goddess" and I was over 40 years old before I had an apartment of my own. I hate housework and related tasks and ironing! Me with a man's shirt? Forget it! It was a miracle for me when "wash and wear" came along.

Yes, there were boyfriends. I went steady in high school and was only 14 when I had my first date with him. He was on the football team, could borrow his brother's car, had a pretty tenor voice and made delicious ice cream sodas in his drugstore job. He gave me a tennis racket for graduation. He moved away after graduation; so did I a few years later and I saw him again 50 years later when we had our Senior Class reunion. He was a good man but not for me.

There were others—flirtations, blind dates, the whole bit—for some reason I never met a man I couldn't "live without!"

The only time I seriously considered matrimony came when I was in my 70s. My path crossed with a man I had known years before, right after World War II. He had married a girl in my circle of friends and after the war they stayed in Jefferson City. He was attractive and smart, attentive, thoughtful and had many qualities of a good husband. All of his wife's girlfriends loved him and he loved that. He and I were in Little Theater together, he shared my interest in baseball and drama. His wife became ill with breast cancer. I comforted him during her illness and after her death we dated for a while. He decided to take a job at a college in Iowa.

I never saw him again for over 20 years, although he had invited me to the wedding when he married his second wife. We were both retired when our paths crossed again. He and his wife were moving to Arkansas, and en route they stopped to visit a mutual friend who lived in my apartment complex. We recognized each other in the parking lot. Soon after they were settled in their new home and I had begun to spend most of my time in Arizona, his wife developed Parkinson's disease and was in a care center for about four years.

He was a good caregiver, but caregivers need some attention also. So he began to come to Arizona for short respites. It was fun and I enjoyed the attention. He was attentive with long distance calls, cards, gifts. He even flew out to drive with me to Missouri several times. He was more of a romantic than I am and I probably misled him into thinking there might be a future for us. After the death of his second wife, he couldn't adjust to his release from responsibility plus the fact that, in spite of his belief he was a "liberated man," he wanted a woman around the house—his woman. I sensed that. We shared enough interests that I would have been amenable to "living with him" and dividing time between Arkansas and Arizona. He thought he was in love with me. I didn't care for him that way. I think his religion was a factor in his wanting a wife, not a companion.

When I came to grips with the situation, I realized that, despite my high regard and respect for him and the physical attraction we had felt through the years, it was not enough for me to surrender my single life. I probably hurt him, his pride maybe; within the year following he suffered a stroke, fell in love with his caregiver, married her, and to date I have not had a written or spoken word from him in four years.

My observations have told me that marriage compels sacrifice of its participants. There is not true 50-50. Maybe close to 49-51 for some couples, whether favoring the man or the woman. I'm not that generous. I guess I've never loved a man enough for marriage. Or feel that a man really loved me enough.

I do not know why I feel this way. My parents were a happy devoted couple through good and bad times. Many of my friends appear to be happily married. And I've known wives who look upon single women as "husband hunters"—a sign to me of a not very happy marriage—but there have been very few wives with whom I would have traded places.

Now that I am nearing 85 I will admit maybe I have missed out on too much—the comfort of a loving family, grandchildren. During my active years there was so much on my plate I didn't think of myself as a mother or grandmother. The single life is not for everyone but that is probably a good thing, although today many young women choose not to marry. I take responsibility for my choice, but I must point out that old age can bring loneliness, which some wise person has said "is a terrible price to pay for independence."

Jean Budington Bateman

Jean Bateman began serious writing a few years ago. She has been a professional working woman most of her life, designing fabrics and then selling fabrics and furniture for health care and the educational environment in New York City and later in Arizona with her own company.

Now 75, she has two children and three grown grandchildren. She retired from business to devote more time to her writing, especially poetry, and she has been published in numerous magazines, literary journals and anthologies.

Question 71: Describe the impact your sexual nature has had on your life story.

Coming Out Party

Walking in the door, I waited for my eyes to adjust to the diminished light. I had been told I would find what I sought at this place, a gay and lesbian book shop. Dressed in a black pants suit with soft pink shirt, I was apprehensive, unsure of what I should ask, afraid of what this stranger would say. What she or he might think of me for asking such questions. The olive-green shag carpet stuck to my feet, and I could see unmatched bookcases holding battered paperbacks seemingly tossed on the shelves.

Bent over a low shelf, a bearded man in jeans and a black tank top was looking for a title, humming softly to himself. Why did a man have to be here at this time? I looked at general headings, such as Fiction, Mystery, Non-fiction, Poetry. Apparently these books were similar to those in any used book store. And then I saw other titles that suggested more. Men Loving Men, Women Loving Women. I hoped no one would see me staring at these titles. No one should know of my interest. And after all, I was seeking information, not books.

In an adjoining room, I saw the proprietor, a left-over hippie, her hair long and stringy, dressed in jeans, a tight printed T-shirt, and bare feet. Well, I thought, I like to go barefoot, too. I realized I was over-dressed for this visit.

Another man entered and I was becoming tense because I wanted to talk to the proprietor alone. I pretended to look at books and saw a large illustrated volume that I had been wanting to buy, *The Wall*, the story of the Vietnam memorial. Great, I thought, this book will give me an opening.

"How much is this damaged book?" I asked, pointing to the deep dent in the cover, the torn dust jacket.

"Twelve dollars. That's a good price, even though it has been banged. The insides are perfect." She pushed a strand of dark greasy hair back behind her ear and looked up at me from behind her desk, covered with scraps of paper and three partly filled styrofoam coffee cups. I was conscious that the men had left, so I began.

"I, uh, I'm told that you can help me find women," my voice low. No answer. She simply stared at me.

"I'd like to meet some women." The words slipped sideways from my throat. "I was told that you could help me." She continued to stare at me as though I were speaking Spanish and she did not understand. At last I realized she wanted me to beg.

Again I tried, "How do I meet women?"

She swivelled in her chair, turning her back to me, reached into a file, pulled out a card and copied a first name and a phone number on a torn bit of paper.

"Call this woman, and she will guide you." She handed me the paper. "And, oh, yes, tell her that I sent you."

I took the paper, staring at her in disbelief. I bought the book about the Wall and left quickly, wondering how I came to this point.

Soon after my husband died, I had gone back to work and began to think about the big picture of my life. Where I was going, what I wanted from the rest of my years. Though I had been married twice, seventeen years each time, and had two children, I realized that the most important adult relationships in my life had been with women. These friendships were different from my love for my husbands. I called a friend in New York who is lesbian, and spoke to her at length.

"Nan," I said, "I need to talk to you." My voice was low, hesitant. I could hear my breath bouncing off the receiver as I tried for control. "Nan, I have been thinking about my friendships with women, and I find that they are most important to me."

"Go on," she said. "Go on."

"I don't know where to begin, but I feel I have had deeper feelings for women than I have had for men. I am truly happy about having my children, but something is missing." I felt most uncomfortable. I could not, would not, use the "L" word.

Slowly I became comfortable and told her of my wishes. And of my fears.

"All right," she said, "now you have found out who you are. The hard part will be finding someone." Nan wrote me, suggesting different sources for connecting. The Gay and Lesbian Hot Line: Me, call that number? No way. A national group called SAGE, for mature lesbians: No chapter in this city. A bookstore: Why on earth would I look in a bookstore? There were a few other suggestions, equally distasteful. The word lesbian repelled me. To me it meant rejection, hate, weird, queer, abnormal.

I forced myself to go into a chain bookstore and stealthily look at Women's Studies. Fortunately, that category was on a side aisle where almost no one could see me. I felt it would be disastrous to be caught looking at such books. I happened on a book called *Invisible Lives: The Truth About Millions of Women-Loving Women* by Martha Barron Barrett. Reading this book changed my life. I learned that connections to women can often be found in a bookstore. Thus I made my trip to the bookstore that my friend had mentioned in her letter.

I called Ginny, whose name was written on the slip of paper, and heard a warm voice invite me to the Breakfast Club. First names only are used, I discovered.

"Come to Carlos' at 10:30 on Sunday," she said, "and ask for me when you enter the restaurant."

Again I dressed in my black pants suit, my uniform. Again I should have worn jeans. As I entered the restaurant I smelled the wondrous odor of Mexican food, but I could also hear the clatter. Glancing quickly in the main dining room, I saw and heard a large group of loud women. I was so embarrassed that I nearly turned away. But I had decided to do this thing, and I asked for Ginny. She was one of perhaps thirty women sitting at two long tables.

I glanced around me and saw all manner of women, some in neat jeans and tee shirts, some in ragged jeans and tank tops, exposing tattoos. One woman had a blue lizard crawling down the back of her left shoulder. I saw a "bracelet" of barbed wire drawn on another's upper arm. Three young women each carried a pack of cigarettes rolled into the sleeves of their T-shirts. Two very large women wore full-length jean cloth dresses and long hair seldom brushed.

"Hey, so glad you could make it," said Ginny, sincerely warm, pointing out an empty chair at the far end of the other table. "There's room for you down there." I was losing my courage, but joined a white-haired lady and a younger woman at the table. They introduced themselves as Laura and Michelle.

"I'm Jean Bateman," I said, forgetting about first names only.

The air was soaked with chiles, salsa, onions and machaca. I ordered a chimichanga, with sour cream and guacamole, surprised at how hungry I was.

Evidently Laura was newly out, a term I quickly learned. "Out" to the world about her sexual nature.

"You know," she said, "we have our own music, our own books, our own performing artists." It took me a moment to realize "our" was the Women-loving Community.

Michelle offered, "Over at that table is a couple you should meet. They live quite near you." We had already exchanged our home locations. I went to their table and introduced myself, again forgetting the first name rule. These two women were Linda and Mary, and upon learning this was my first function, they stood up, gave me a warm hug and invited me for Saturday evening dinner.

At their home, I was introduced to each one who came.

"Hi, Jean, welcome to the Community," from Michelle and Laura.

"Oh," I replied, "I'm not new, I've lived here 15 years."

After several more "Welcome to the Community" greetings and my dismissal, I realized that each was talking about the Lesbian Community while I was referring to my neighborhood. Finally, I understood.

Linda and Mary referred me to another group, a monthly Saturday evening pot luck. My lesbian world was opening, but still I could not use the "L" word, the word that made me feel ostracized, the object of scorn. As I left my first pot luck supper, a woman somewhat older than most, closer to my age, pushed her business card into my hand.

"I wrote my home number on it," was all Janice said. I smiled and took her card. Later she invited me to a country western bar.

It is hard to explain how difficult it was for me to drive to the bar. I parked across the street in a grocery store lot, so no one would know I was entering a lesbian bar. As I walked toward the entrance, I was conscious of a man walking close behind me. It was not the nicest part of town, I was alone, and I began to panic. Then I realized he was a guard, accompanying me to the entrance. What relief.

I forced myself to open the windowless door, and found the inside very dark and choking with cigarette smoke. An attendant greeted me.

"Welcome. Come on in." I mumbled a reply, already feeling my chest tighten with the smoke. The song that the DJ was playing was "Earthquake," and I felt it appropriate. The floor, and my body, shuddered with the deep vibrating chords. A visual wall of smoke obliterated people's faces and the crowd was thick, making walking forward difficult. I brushed bodies, dodged cigarettes and made my way to the right rear, hoping against hope I would find Janice.

Glancing at the dancers on the crowded floor, I saw many cowboy hats, of black felt or straw. Most wore cowboy boots, western shirts, and tight jeans. Some had beaded key chains hanging from a pocket. I stopped a moment to watch a couple move through intricate dance steps and hand movements as they glided gracefully over the polished wooden floor.

Suddenly, and gratefully, I heard a loud whoop, and there, glass in hand, stood Janice.

"You came!" she shouted over the music. "I didn't think you would." She introduced me to perhaps twelve women, some with long-neck beers, some with glasses of amber liquid. One tall woman in western gear immediately invited me to dance. I had no idea how to do the two-step, but my partner explained, demonstrated and was patient. Soon I managed, when I looked at my feet. I was enjoying this scene, but before midnight my asthmatic lungs could no longer cope with the smoke. My first experience at a lesbian bar, and I was excited. My life in the community was opening. It didn't happen overnight, but slowly I became one of the group, even though, at 75, I was older than most.

My friend Liz, 69, later told me of the old days when, as a young woman, she went to gay bars for both men and women.

"Often the police would raid the bars, and each girl would grab a man by the arm, in fear of arrest." Liz spoke bitterly, the creases between her brows tight with anger. "We women were particularly concerned, because the police searched each of us to be sure we wore women's garments: slacks with the zipper on the side, bra, panties, or a woman's shirt. If we did not wear at least three women's items, we were arrested and thrown in jail for the night for impersonating a man." I was shocked, unbelieving. I had had no fear of arrest in the women's bar. It was difficult to relate to her situation.

"You simply don't understand," said Liz. "You weren't part of the disgrace, the fear we felt in the old days." She brushed back a bit of iron gray hair.

Michelle gave me a sour look. "You don't understand," she echoed Liz. "You can't understand how it used to be. And I can't just drop the old stigma. I can't, I won't, stand up on a chair and shout to the world who I am. There is still danger."

Recently I was able to witness the Community at work. Martha was in an automobile accident, her car had rolled over three times, and she was in the hospital, bruised and broken. Hank, a mutual friend, realized he had not heard form her, long after he should have. He tracked her to the hospital. Hank called Sue. Sue called Liz, who called me for clues as to who might care for her dogs. I called Nora, who called Maxine. Maxine called Liz back and said she would care for Brutus and Big, since she, too, lived out of the city close to Martha's home. This cycle of calls was repeated later to tell of her injuries, of her progress. Women volunteered to go in shifts to visit her, to tend her when she was released from the hospital. I saw the power, the warmth of my Community.

Martha's well-being was of great concern to me, because nearly a year ago she had invited me to join her and some friends on a rockhounding trip. I went, not that I particularly enjoy hunting for crystals, but because I thought a day in the country would be great fun. I brought a book, pad and pen, and a chair, and was prepared to sit out the day in the woods. Martha arranged for me to ride up with Liz, whom I did not know at the time, and when we arrived at the designated spot, I found some loose crystals on the ground and I was hooked. The thought of merely sitting vanished and I followed the group up a wooded hill, finding crystals and bugs.

Later, our pockets filled, Liz and I started down from the mountain in her van and the air conditioning died. As we went ever lower towards the valley, the car grew hotter and hotter.

"I am so embarrassed," Liz wailed. "Why did my car have to do this today?"

"It's all right," I replied, "at least the motor is running, and we are heading home. Things could be worse." She was not reassured.

Since that day I have felt that the others found crystals and I found a diamond—Liz—who is now my mate, my love. It all began with that rockhounding trip.

A group of older lesbians met for lunch the other day.

"I am not yet totally out," I opened the conversation, twirling my iced tea in its own puddle. "But I am at last comfortable with who I am." I sipped my tea, loving its cold wetness, its wedge of lemon. "I feel that my late blooming has been an advantage. I don't come to my new life with a lot of torn baggage."

Liz looked at me, her eyes warm.

"And, oh yes, I can now say 'lesbian.'"

Nina Sabrack

Born in Cleveland, Ohio, Nina graduated from Ohio Wesleyan University and earned a master of arts degree in Russian history at the University of Chicago. "Nothing will convince you to get politically involved more than studying Russia's struggles," she says. "For centuries there, any attempt to give voice to the people was crushed by the powerful few. In contrast, we are part of the greatest experiment in history, with citizens governing themselves through peaceful means. We need every American to keep the process free and fair."

Nina has taught at the secondary and college level. After years of political organizing, she joined the League of Women Voters. "League is grassroots politics at its best," according to Nina. Today she serves as president of the League of Women voters of Metropolitan Phoenix.

Question 76: Throughout your life, what volunteer efforts have you undertaken for charities or non-profit organizations?

Working for the League of Women Voters

Why would a woman devote much of her life to volunteering to increase civic participation? I've worked for years with political organizations and now with the League of Women Voters. A powerful League slogan is, "If you pay taxes or breathe air, you are political." It's true, but many Americans do not join the process.

My inspiration for my work comes from my family. They were working class people who staked their claim to democracy. My parents worked at the polling place and devoted many hours to political work and discussions. Their parents had come to America seeking freedom, and my parents did their best to keep the door open for civic participation.

As a teenager I witnessed a powerful political event: the mayor's race in Cleveland back in the '60s. The papers dubbed it, "Grandson of a slave faces grandson of a president"—Carl Stokes and Seth Taft. Tensions in racially divided Cleveland ran very high. Yet I saw Clevelanders ignore the ugly and divisive fake issue and vote for Carl Stokes, whom they deemed most likely to act on their behalf. This showed me average citizens can see through the static of emotionally hot rhetoric. The voters weighed the candidates' stands on things that actually mattered to them.

Since those days, it's gotten even harder for Americans to keep their roles as citizen decision-makers. Many no longer vote. In fact, a recent League survey of nonvoters revealed that the chief reason many women do not vote is that they believe they do not have sufficient reliable information.

So that's why I work for the League. Candidates' nights, study of issues at the local, state and national level, and helping people register to vote are rewarding activities. To see ordinary citizens come together to get answers and take action inspires me.

Since joining League I've learned about the long struggle to get women the vote. Many thousands of women gave of themselves to make sure my voice would be heard as a full citizen.

That's why the Cameo Life Stories project is so very important. Women telling their stories inspire and educate all the rest. So many political reforms and solutions we benefit by have come from women. Women's work in PTA, in church groups, and often on their own deserves to be recorded.

Terrie Carter

Terrie Carter was born in Idaho and grew up in Phoenix, Arizona. After graduating from Maryvale High School in 1982, she worked in California, where she met and married her first husband. When she fled the marriage as a victim of domestic violence, she returned to Phoenix.

There she was trained as a registered nurse and became an active volunteer on behalf of domestic violence victims.

Terrie is married to Oscar Carter and has two sons. She is currently living in Las Vegas, Nevada. Terrie serves as the national domestic violence coordinator for The STORIES Center and as Nevada coordinator for the Cameo Life Stories program and the FourWords program for young people.

Question 77: What incidents have had a significant influence on your adult life?

Tomorrow's Dreams

I know you don't know me, but I am you; my story is yours and yours is mine. As survivors of domestic violence, we are sisters in the biggest sisterhood of all. My name is Terrie and my story began long before I ever married the man who would welcome me to this sisterhood.

I was born to a woman I have never met by the name of Rena Carolyn Neyman at Booth Memorial Hospital in Boise, Idaho, on September 1, 1963. She loved me enough to give me up for adoption, and 14 days later I was chosen by the people I now call Mom and Dad. I have two brothers who are twins and a sister. They are also adopted. I am the oldest of the four kids. My parents have always told us we were special because we were chosen.

I graduated from Maryvale High School in 1981 at the age of 17 with my whole life ahead of me. I tried to get a job with the Phoenix Union High School District as a sign language interpreter, but my parents decided I needed to go to California to live with my aunt and find a job.

I flew into John Wayne Airport in January of 1982 and found a job at an insurance company. I never went for an interpreter's job because I was told that I probably wouldn't be able to do it and the people in Phoenix didn't want me so why would I think that anyone else would. I found out six years later that I was offered the job as an interpreter and my parents told them I no longer wanted the position.

After I received my first paycheck, my aunt decided I needed to move, and I couldn't afford to get an apartment of my own. I decided I needed to find a roommate, and that's how I met Dan. I moved into Dan's place in February and by March, 1982 I was engaged.

Our first date was dinner and a movie. My choice, he said. I told him where I wanted to go, and he stated that on his way to work he came across a wonderful little place and thought of me. I agreed to go there instead. He then wanted to know what time and I told him seven.

He said, "Why don't we go at six and have a few cocktails before dinner?" I agreed. That's the moment I was chosen. He knew I was the one. For the second time in my life I was special because I was chosen.

Our courtship was romantic and there were flowers and love letters. It was extremely quick. Only one month after I moved in, he asked me to marry him while we were watching M*A*S*H*. The dreams and ambitions that I had for my life were quickly going south. I dreamed of a career and eventually going to Washington, D.C., to help change the world. Everyone told me my dreams were too high and that I should just be a good wife. I was told by my grandmother that I would be a failure as a wife, career woman and a mother because I wanted it all. Today, in her and my mother's eyes, I have proven them right.

Dan told me he would not marry me until I was nineteen years old, so on September 4, 1992, we were married, only three days after my 19th birthday. I should have gone to Disneyland instead. We were married in a garden with the works—white gowns and tuxes with tails, three bridesmaids and groomsmen, even a flower girl. This was supposed to be the happiest day of my life, so why did everything in my gut tell me I was wrong? I didn't listen, anyway, because I didn't know then about a woman's intuition.

The wedding gown was beautiful, white with just enough lace and covered buttons and a train. I wanted to wear ballet slippers, but Dan wouldn't let me, so five-inch heels were the order of the day. The bridesmaids were in lavender dresses with off-the-shoulder sleeves. The flowers were Sterling Silver roses with white daisies. Dan wore a white tux with tails and the groomsmen wore light gray tuxes with lavender cumberbunds. The wedding went off without a hitch.

Dan's friends were all there and my family—my mother, father, brothers, sister, grandma, and Aunt Pat—and two of my best friends from high school. There was an extra seat in the front row next to my grandmother that was reserved for my grandfather who was there with me in spirit. We had a reception after the one in the garden, and Dan and I were the last ones to leave instead of the first. My brother Shawn was drunk and sick behind a dumpster. By the time we arrived at the hotel it was almost morning.

My wedding night was not what I had expected. It was the night I found out Dan did drugs, and not just that, but that he did them intravenously. I can remember thinking, "If I leave now I will really prove my grandmother right," and hearing my mother say that getting married is for life—until "death do you part."

Dan lied about the kind of drugs he was doing, and I was naive enough to believe him. I remember the look on his face when I walked in on him. I've never seen that kind of evil before. That was my first encounter with Dr. Jekyll and Mr. Hyde, who would become a huge part of my life.

It's funny that I don't remember a lot of the time frames. I just know that my world started to crash on my wedding night. It wasn't long after the wedding that the honeymoon was over.

I remember the first time he hit me. What I don't remember is what it was about. He just hauled off and slapped me hard enough that the back of my head hit the door jam and there I was in the corner. I asked him to stop and the tears were stinging my face. The next thing I knew he was on top of me with his hands around my neck, banging my head on the floor. I was begging him to stop and then as quickly as it started it was over, and he was crying, asking for my forgiveness, telling me he loved me and didn't know what he would do without me. The honeymoon was back on, or at least what I thought was a honeymoon. I don't think he was ever so sweet or would ever be that sweet again.

We weren't married for more than six months before he got me fired from a job I really enjoyed. He would call me all the time or show up at the office and want me to go to lunch, only he wouldn't let me go back to work. My boss was concerned and asked if there was anything he could do for me. At the time, the abuse was still a big secret and I was in protective mode. I thought maybe if I only did what Dan wanted, everything would be okay. Dan thought I was having an affair with my boss. I really can't blame my boss for firing me; he did have a business to run. I thought Dan loved me so much that it was hard for him to stay away from me. Funny.

Once I wasn't working, Dan wanted everything just the way he ordered. He wanted his drink made when he came home in a glass with three ice cubes and mixed to his taste, although there were times he wanted five ice cubes and that's when I was beaten. Funny thing, after I left Dan I didn't have ice or glasses in my house for almost ten years. My friend Julia would come over with a ten-pound bag of ice and I would set it in my sink and let it melt.

Other things set him off. Everything really. I never could please him no matter what I did, and the drinking and drug use was worse than ever. One night he scored some cocaine and laid out a line on the table and told me that it was mine. I told him that I didn't want it because it was something I was strongly against; it was bad enough that he did it; I didn't want to join him. I was sitting at the table and he got up, grabbed my hair, pushed my head down, and told me to do it. He then hit me so hard that he knocked me over, chair and all. I still refused and the beating commenced. My lip was bleeding, my eyes were swollen shut, and four hours later I did the line of cocaine because I hurt too bad to fight for what was right.

I don't really know how long after this incident I was doing it intravenously, but in a sick way, this was the only time Dan and I were close and the only time we communicated. Dan was into every drug know to man—cocaine, heroin, Valium, ludes, acid, mushrooms. You name it, this man did it. We never did anything or went anywhere when he wasn't high or drunk.

Everything escalated, the abuse and the drug use, until one day I woke up in an intensive care unit with black eyes, swollen lips, and a very sore rib cage. They told me I overdosed on cocaine and heroin. I don't remember doing drugs that night. I just remember the fighting. The doctors and hospital staff never asked who beat me up, and when I was ready to be discharged they never asked me who I wanted to pick me up. They just called Dan and released me to his care. This was the first time I realized that our vow "until death do us part" was going to come sooner than anticipated, and death would be by the hands of the man who vowed to love me until death.

I've been racking my brain, but for the life of me I can't remember the names of any of the other players in this saga, only faces.

On June 6, 1985, Dan and I, along with one of those faces, went to the circus. It was Dan's first circus, and I hadn't been to one since we were married. Dan and his friend were drunk and high and I had an awful time, but what else was new? When they dropped me off at home, they went to the bar, and I went to bed. I don't know what time they came home. What I do remember is the knife. I opened my eyes and there was a knife to my neck and the stench of alcohol was filling the room. I then realized Dan wasn't alone. They both took turns raping me, but I left and hid behind the chair in my room, which seemed to be my favorite place to hide when things hurt too bad to stay. They were just raping a body.

After it was over and Dan's friend left, the party was just beginning. The beating commenced. Dan said I must have enjoyed his friend more than him. To this day I still can't figure out what is enjoyable about rape. Although I was married to him, in those days it wasn't called rape because I was his property and you can't rape what you own. I left and went home to my parents, but before I went Dan told me what to say about my face. He always did.

My mother asked me what happened and I told her I ran into a cupboard door and she believed me again. Before I was married I never had a black eye, fat lip, or broken bones, but since my wedding day, I became the clumsiest person in the world and my mother believed it. Never once out of all the times I came home after a bad beating did she ask if Dan did this to me, and that's all I wanted—someone to care enough to ask that question. Well, no one did. I don't think I've ever been so alone. Even in a crowd of people I was alone. I stayed with my mother and father for three weeks before I went back and eight weeks later I found out I was pregnant.

The news of a baby should be one of the happiest days of a woman's life, but I sat in the doctor's office calling him a liar and crying. I did not want to bring a child into the hell I was living in. I also didn't know if it was Dan's baby because of the rape. Life couldn't get any worse.

The nine months of pregnancy were the longest and the worst of my life. The abuse had escalated to the point that all I had to look forward to was death. Dan moved me to Lancaster, California, where he grew up. I had no where to go and no one to turn to. I felt that if my parents cared they would have asked. The police didn't care because they always told me that I deserved it if I stayed, that I should do what he wants and not make him mad. My brother Shawn said I deserved everything that Dan gave me. The doctor told me that the bruises on my abdomen must be from the baby. Well, I knew better.

Josh was born on March 2, 1986, and I was in the hospital for four days. I didn't see Dan while I was in the hospital and my mother picked me up to take me home when I was discharged. Dan was busy partying with his friends, if that what you would call them.

Dan moved Josh and I into this two-bedroom, one-bath townhouse not too far from his mother. I knew that this was where I was going to die. Dan's appetite for weapons had become enormous. The beatings continued and the marriage had been over for many years. Dan was dating others and I was getting the leftovers. By the time the marriage ended I had Josh, herpes, chlamydia, TRIC agents, endometriosis, and post-traumatic stress disorder.

The month of May 1986 was the beginning of the end. On May 8, which happened to be my first Mother's Day, I went to a Catholic church for mass and to ask the priest there to help me. I was coming out of the closet and I thought that I was the only one in there. Boy, was I wrong. Domestic violence didn't have a name back then because it was an accepted practice, and the only person I could come up with to help me was a priest. It's funny, because he ended up telling me what everyone else ever told me. He told me to go home and fix my marriage because I must be doing something wrong.

I felt that my last hope of surviving this hell was just taken away from me. When I arrived at the house, Dan was back early and found me gone. Well, this was the proverbial straw that broke that camel's back and I received my due. This was beating number God-only-knows-what because I lost track. Anyway, it didn't hurt like it used to because I had died a long time ago. Somebody just forgot to tell my body. Happy Mother's Day.

The month of May was bad. I was hit at least once a day whether I needed it or not. I knew that I needed to do something, so I disassembled some of his guns. That was the end of my safety plan. That one thing probably saved my life.

May 16 started off like any other day. Josh and I woke early and I fed him, then fixed breakfast for Dan. When breakfast was over, I started on the breakfast dishes and Dan was in the living room brooding. Josh was fussy and I was trying to keep him quiet. Me, I was hurting. The bruises on my face and body didn't have a chance to heal before I received new ones.

Suddenly I knew my face was in the dish water and I was in for a fight for my life. I don't really remember a lot of the day, but I do remember it was the worst beating that I have ever received. The beating lasted all day, and by the end I was just wanting to die. Josh hadn't been fed or changed all day long because when Dan wasn't beating me, one of two things was happening. I was either unconscious or he was raping me on the floor of the kitchen.

The day had almost come and gone when Dan got up and I remember him saying, "That's it. I'm going to get my gun and shut you BOTH up!" That was the moment that I got up off the floor and looked for a way out. I could hear him upstairs looking for the gun and all its parts when I crawled over to Joshua and picked up him and the key to the car and left. I thought to myself, "He can kill me because I'm already dead, but he's not going to kill my son."

The next thing I remember, I'm sitting in the driveway of Dan's lifelong friends. Ray and Kurt were in the driveway barbecuing when I arrived. Ray opened my car door and I told him that Dan had Josh and was going to kill us. He told me it was OK, that Kurt had Josh and I was safe. My face looked like I just went 12 rounds with Rocky and I lost.

Kurt had just started a new job and received his first paycheck that day. They were having a barbecue to celebrate, and I had rudely interrupted. I knew one of two things would happen. They would either call Dan and tell him where I was, which meant that I would die that day, or they would help me escape.

Ray and Kurt decided that I needed to get out of Lancaster and back to Phoenix. Ray called and booked a flight on America West Airlines. Kurt then called my father to let him know that I was coming home and when. Then he gave me his whole check. They put Josh and me in the car and drove us to LAX, which was a two-hour drive.

I boarded the plane with a two-month-old child, looking like I was hit by a Mac truck. The steward took Josh from me and helped me down the ramp. He sat me in the front row and wouldn't allow anyone to sit next to me. After the plane took off, the steward came and sat down next to me to help me take care of Joshua. The plane ride lasted about an hour, and all I really remember was the steward handing me his sunglasses so I could lift up my head. That gesture was one of the kindest things that anyone has ever done for me.

When I arrived at my parents' house, Josh and I went to bed. My parents told me that when I was ready to talk they would listen. The next day I went to the doctor to be checked out. I had a closed head injury, two black eyes, a cut in both corners of my mouth, broken ribs, and a broken finger. A couple of days passed and then I decided I needed to tell my parents what happened. After I told them, my mother told me that it's over with, I'm safe, and I should just forget about it.

The divorce was finalized on January 7, 1987, but Dan was always in my rear view mirror, sitting outside of the house, or calling me on the phone. For five years he knew my every move. One day I received a letter in the mail. It said, "BOO, I know where you are!" That was the day I got mad and stopped running. I started going to counseling and found a wonderful haven called Sojourner's. This is where I found out I wasn't alone.

I started working in the domestic violence community and telling my story. I also founded Family Guardian Angels, which is a foundation for domestic violence education, through which I have helped develop a program to teach doctors and nurses about domestic violence and the questions to ask possible victims. This program is now up and running in the major teaching hospitals under Dr. Dean Coonrod's close supervision. I also went back to school for my RN license. I met Deborah Linzer when I started Family Guardian Angels and that is when I joined her army.

I chose to write about my life with Dan for a few reasons. One of the main ones is to let other women know that they are not alone. Although this has been a difficult story to write because I had to relive the experiences, I am also putting it out for the universe to see. This was like writing a letter to my abuser and offering forgiveness. I know that I married Dan for a reason and this is it, this is my gift to the world. There are two words in the English language that mean the world to me and they are FREEDOM and SAFETY. My hope is that one day all women will be able to feel about these words the way I do.

It took a few people to put my life back together again. They are my guardian angels and I would like to thank them. Julia Laney helped me grow up into a wonderful adult and stayed up with me many nights when I though I would go crazy. She is also a survivor of domestic violence and she is my mother. My son Nikos, because he was my gift from God. My son Joshua for saving my life. Diane Young, for giving me power and courage and saying things like, "Anger is just one letter away from danger," and "I didn't create it, I didn't cause it, can't cure it, so don't carry it." She is also a survivor of domestic violence and she is my sister. Doreen Nicholas, for being a mentor and showing me that Terrie is an important person. She taught me that domestic violence was nothing more than power and control. She is also a survivor of domestic violence and she is my sister. Dr. Dean Coonrod, for putting his faith in me and listening to what I had to say. You are a true friend and mentor. Virginia Dumas, my nursing instructor, for giving me two words—"walk on." Deborah Linzer, for giving me the opportunity to share with the world.

Most of all, I would like to thank Oscar for teaching me how to love again. It took 20 years, but on January 1, 1999, I married my high school sweetheart, Oscar O. Carter AKA: Tingi Lau, who is my heart and my soul. We took our vows at midnight in Las Vegas at the Candlelight Chapel and I started a new life, a life with a man who has worshiped me for 20 years. He has been my best friend for many years and for our wedding day we wrote our own vows.

This is not the end but the beginning of a whole new book in my life.

Jacqueline Mott Brown

Jacqueline Mott Brown was born in Lincoln, Nebraska, inheriting the pioneer spirit of her ancestors. She's a graduate in sociology from the University of Kansas. Jackie has a son and a daughter and spends the winter in Ithaca, New York, and summers at her Lake Skaneatles cabin, which can only be reached by boat.

She is a Renaissance woman, who believes we are all one in the universe—we just wear different uniforms. She is the author of Parrots in the Kitchen, 29 Stepping Stones: A Wisewoman Journal, *and* Everywoman Memory Bank. *She is presently prodding women to unleash their potential and creativity, and she is an authorized Cameo Life Stories workshop leader.*

Question 77: What incidents have had a significant influence on your adult life?

New Friends

They were in close formation, this time five of them inches above the cobalt blue water, their brown bodies looking too prehistoric, too heavy to fly. In unison they swoop and soar, maneuvering by flicking only two or three feathers at a time.

Mesmerized, I leaned on my rake and called up to them. "You are amazing. I am jealous." How I ached for such effortless control—direction. Oh, to savor the day as a pelican. My life had fallen apart all around me—in piles like the seaweed, bits of plastic, and fish bones that I was assigned to clean up this morning.

"No mowing. Just needs the beach and the yard. Be sure to make marks on the sand so they'll know we did our job. Put the debris at the road. I'll pick you up at 11. We'll do Sutton's estate next—the palm fronds—big job." Harry talked fast and drove off before I could respond. It seemed to me at the time that he was the oddest, most protective friend I'd ever had.

Sometimes I'd see the con man's face in a pile of leaves. He was there with his mother. They were a team. I would shudder and blink back the tears.

I could be on the Oprah Show, I thought while loading a large green plastic bag and dragging it to the road. Oprah would probably say, "Oh, my God! Now I've heard everything—he used his mother to run a SCAM!?" This is what I said too after they disappeared into the ethers with my last penny. Me—an educated world traveler. How could I be so stupid, a "victim" like I read about in the newspapers. The banker says it happens all the time, but it's too embarrassing.

I was soon too distracted by gulls galore, terns with red beaks and the scurrying sanderlings that made me laugh at their legs blurring in haste to outrun the waves. The Gulf of Mexico, like a giant heart, sent beat after beat onto the sand, the only constant I could depend on.

The west side of Mrs. Blake's estate was my favorite. Each week I looked forward to the "Aromatherapy Salon." The thick, syrupy sweet gardenia hedge row knocked me over in the hot Florida humidity. "This is just a temporary job!" I explained out loud to the greenery. "I'll call myself an exterior decorator for now, but actually I'm an interior decorator for these wealthy Floridians. But they sap more energy than I can muster up right now, so that will have to wait."

Each week the gardenias looked sturdier, stronger—and I did too. "I think we need each other," I confessed.

Years ago I read Mary Catherine Bateman's book *Composing a Life.* You may have many careers in your life as your needs change, and this is okay, she said. That sentence resurfaced when I first heard Harry, the lawn man, with his job offer. "Hey," he'd said, "you need a job? My helper quit. She's a crack head and keeps having babies to get government assistance. Just a raker—it'll be easy—five dollars an hour.

"OK, Harry," I'd agreed. "But just for a few weeks."

I had worked my way up to mowing with the John Deere tractor in a few months. It was then I noticed that the dark cloud of gloom had lifted. "I am cheerful and positive again—I'm me," I yelled.

The pelicans flew over in their formation. I looked up and said, "I'm in control and directing my life just as you do. I'm ready for my fabric samples again!"

Leaning on my rake I called, "Thank you, thank you. I'll be back to visit on my day off."

Arlene Flecha

Arlene was born in San Juan, Puerto Rico. She spent most of her life in a town named Canovanas in the northeast part of the island. Upon graduating from the University of Puerto Rico with a degree in environmental science, Arlene worked at the Caribbean National Forest as an environmental interpreter. On her 25th birthday, Arlene decided to start a new adventure and moved to the Washington, D.C., area. Since then she has been working for the U.S. Bureau of the Census as a personnel management specialist. Her hobbies include dancing, reading, bike riding, and singing. Arlene currently sings with the Alexandria Singers.

Question 77: What incidents have had a significant influence on your adult life?

Facing My Fears

On October 1997, I started the most challenging adventure of my life. I moved from Puerto Rico to Alexandria, Virginia. Not only did I leave all my family but also started a new career in human resources. If I would have known back then that I would have to advise management regarding complex personnel issues, I would not have accepted the job. I never imagined that my English was good enough to keep a job like this. I also did not know that I could live without my family for so long.

Above all, I never thought I could be able to live on my own. I am still surprised that I have managed to make it for almost two years.

My decision to move was motivated by my desire to become independent and to know myself a little bit better. I wanted to see myself in a new scenario where I could start making my own decisions without having to depend so much on my family's opinion. No one who knows me well would have ever conceived the idea of Arlene living far from her family, especially her mother. Since I was a little girl I was very close to her. Being away from her scared me. Her presence made me feel secure. I loved sharing every thought and feeling with her.

However, as I grew older I felt that our closeness was interfering with my process of becoming an adult. Although she always respects my decisions and advises me as a friend, I felt we were too dependent on each other. Our bond was so strong that it sometimes felt as if I were her mother and she were my child. I also love my sister dearly. She has always been my best friend. However, when we were little, I always resented the fact that she was considered the outgoing one and I was the "mama's girl." It seemed that she had all the courage and I had all the fears.

I had dreams, but I did not have the confidence to pursue them. I still remember one time I had the opportunity to shine and I rejected it because of my fears. I always loved the English class. In seventh grade our teacher organized a spelling bee. The student who made it to the finals would represent our class in the intermediate school competition. I spent so much time learning the words. I was so excited about it. The day of the seventh grade competition I was the second runner up. I was given the word EDUCATION. I knew exactly how to spell it but my fears overwhelmed me. The thought of having to represent my class in the auditorium scared me so much that I chose to misspell the word. I regretted that decision so much. I knew the word. I knew that if I had overcome my fear I could have been the winner. I could have shown that I could make it, but I did not dare to shine.

A similar experience occurred in my senior year of high school, but this time I handled it in a different way. I applied for a special program that selected outstanding students from all over the island based on their academic achievements and their scores on the college board. I applied not because I thought I was smart but because I really wanted a new experience. I had spent two years in an all-girl Catholic school and

I was ready to get out of there. I wanted something exciting and this program seemed to provide it. I was selected to participate in the program and I accepted the challenge.

The first three months were a nightmare. I could only visit my family every two weeks and the workload was becoming overwhelming. I was constantly anxious and I could not sleep. I felt so out of place. All my classmates seemed to be having so much fun. Being far from their families was rather a relief for them. I was always worried about failing in my classes. I was convinced that everyone else was smarter than me. This was especially true in the English class. Based on my College Board scores they assigned me to the advanced English class. What a shock when I realized that all my classmates had lived in the United States. They spoke English fluently without an accent. As we say in Puerto Rico, I felt like a cockroach attending a chicken dance!

On the first day of the class the teacher announced that we had to prepare a written and oral presentation of the book *Lord of the Flies* for the following week. I felt I was going to die. An oral presentation in English! I spent so much time getting ready for this, but I was convinced that I would only make a fool of myself. I knew my presentation could not be as good as the others. Once again, as I did years before during my spelling bee, I decided to quit. I explained to my teacher that I would drop off from his class because I did not think I had what it takes. Mr. Munoz looked into my eyes and told me that he would not allow me to do that and that he knew I could make it.

The weekend following our conversation my family came to visit me. I will never forget the date. My heart was beating so fast. I felt so desperate. I told my parents that I was ready to quit and that I wanted to go back home because the program was too demanding. However, I felt my father would be disappointed and quitting would only strengthen my lack of confidence. It would prove I was not good enough. In spite of my fears, I decided to give myself some time and stayed.

The following week I gave my oral presentation. It was not perfect but I made it. As the months went by it seemed that I felt more comfortable with the classes and that I was not missing my family as much. On my graduation day, I received one of the sweetest surprises of my life. Mr. Munoz gave me the golden medal for my accomplishments in the advanced English class.

While in college, since I felt more comfortable with my ability to communicate in English, I applied to participate in the Hispanic Association of Colleges and Universities. The letter of acceptance took me by surprise. This time I would be on my own for 10 consecutive weeks in Washington, D.C. It happened that my parents divorce coincided with the first week of the internship. Though I had learned to detach from my mom, this was a very difficult time of our lives. I debated whether to accept the internship or stay with her. In spite of my feelings of guilt I decided to take the opportunity. I think the moment I made that decision something magical occurred within me. I had learned and I had grown. We agreed that we would stay in touch by phone but that I must take advantage of this wonderful opportunity. By the end of the internship, I realized that my English was good, not because it was perfect but because I could communicate. That summer I fell in love with the D.C. area and I wished that I could return to live there someday.

After graduating from college with a bachelor's degree in environmental sciences, I obtained a job with the U.S. Forest Service in Puerto Rico. The job required me to offer training and tours to different audiences. It was time to face my greatest fear, public speaking. The girl who did not dare to participate in the spelling bee and was scared to death about delivering a ten-minute oral report now had to talk to an audience. This job was quite an experience. Of course, the first time I had to offer training I could not sleep the night before. I spent a lot of time preparing my index cards. I wrote down everything I wanted to say. I planned it carefully. When I stood in front of the audience I thought I would pass out. But somehow I noticed that as I started to talk the fear started to dissipate. I felt more calm. I even forgot about looking at my notes. It was a matter of relaxing and letting the words flow. Suddenly, I started walking around the room. I did not have to control anything, just relax and I did it. Next thing I knew, the Forest Service sent me to work as a volunteer for the 1996 Olympic games. I spent three days offering talks to the visitors regarding the history of the games and the history of kayaking and canoeing. I still cannot believe this.

All of these experiences prepared me to be where I am today. Detaching from my family and facing my fears was a process. From all of these experiences I have learned that I am much more than I can ever imagine. Comparing myself to others and expecting perfection from myself takes me nowhere. I also know that my fears only prevented me from seeing my real potential and that if I let them, they can stop me from going where my dreams want to take me. These memories give me the strength to face the new challenges life presents me everyday. I have learned that every time I choose to face a fear the outcome is far better than I ever thought. I am so glad that I decided to accept this new challenge and I am very happy to see how much the shy little girl has grown.

Joan Anderson Meacham

Joan Anderson Meacham is currently the vice president and a founding trustee of the National Museum of Women's History in Washington, D.C. Her professional career included positions as registrar, Yale University Graduate School; program director for state scholarships at the Educational Testing Service in Princeton, New Jersey; executive director of the Madison-Chatham, New Jersey, American Red Cross Chapter; and associate director of the New England Board of Higher Education, Wellesley, Massachusetts.

Joan serves on several national non-profit boards and is a member of many community service organizations. She has been a state and local officer in the League of Women Voters, president of the National Celebration of the 75th Anniversary of Woman Suffrage, and national co-chair of the Woman Suffrage Statue Campaign. Joan resides in Rio Verde, Arizona, and spends much of her time in Washington, D.C., working on the development of the National Museum of Women's History.

Question 78: Have you made specific efforts to impact organizations or issues that affect women or girls?

"Time for the Ladies to Come Upstairs"

On a beautiful, crisp day in the fall of 1993, five women sat contemplating a seemingly overwhelming task. We had just committed to moving a marble statue that weighed more than seven tons from the lower level of the U.S. Capitol to the rotunda. The statue was called the "Portrait Monument." It was commissioned in 1920 to honor the passage of the Nineteenth Amendment to the constitution, which gave women the right to vote.

The statue was accepted for inclusion in the capitol rotunda by an overwhelmingly male Congress (the one woman present was Representative Jeanette Rankin from Montana) with great fanfare in 1921. Then, in a gesture that spoke volumes about the prevailing prejudices of the time, it was relegated to a hiding place in a basement storage area just three days later. The statue was still in that crypt 72 years later as we were discussing its fate.

We hadn't come together at my house to discuss the movement of the statue. We had more pressing business on our minds. As the members of the steering committee for the national celebration of the 75th Anniversary of the Passage of the Nineteenth Amendment, we were up to our ears in details. The planned events were only two years away, and we needed money, resources, people and, of course, more time. I had been elected president of this ambitious project, primarily because my beloved husband had passed away several months earlier and it was presumed I would have more volunteer hours to dedicate to such a massive undertaking.

There were only five of us that cool morning, enjoying a planning retreat in my quiet home on the inland canal in Cape May, New Jersey. We had already committed to staging a re-enactment of the most highly publicized suffrage march deployed in the 72-year battle for equal rights. The original peaceful demonstration occurred on March 3, 1913—the day before the inauguration of President Woodrow Wilson. Our march in Washington, D.C., on August 26, 1995, was planned to follow the same historic route, approximately a five-mile trek around the Washington Mall. Other events on our schedule included a one-day symposium at one of the Smithsonian museums on August 25. As we began to build a detailed list of our goals for this celebration, someone in our group mentioned the plight of the only suffrage monument in the United States. As I listened to the story of the statue for the first time, I knew that we had to rescue this important part of our history and restore it to its intended place in the Capitol building.

This huge monument was created by a prominent sculptor of the day, Adelaide Johnson. The National Woman's Party, a suffragist organization founded by Dr. Alice Stokes Paul, had commissioned the statue following the ratification of the woman suffrage amendment on August 26, 1920.

Because there were so many competent and dedicated suffrage leaders throughout the struggle for the vote, it was determined to memorialize the three founders of the movement. These were Lucretia Mott, Quaker minister, anti-slavery leader, wife, mother, grandmother and mentor to so many; Elizabeth Cady Stanton, also an abolitionist, wife, mother, grandmother and reformer; and Susan B. Anthony, Quaker, teacher, reformer, abolitionist and orator.

Our suffragist foremothers were vilified in society. Many had endured imprisonment and force-feeding. Alice Paul and her colleagues in the National Woman's Party were sent to work houses and prison on several occasions. Members of the Congress of 1920 were reluctant to place "these radical women" in the capitol rotunda. Finally, after effective lobbying from Alice Paul and others, which is a story in itself, the "Portrait Monument" was placed in the U.S. Capitol Rotunda. The dedication ceremony was held on February 15, 1921, Susan B. Anthony's birthday. Just a few days later, in the middle of the night, the monument was whisked down to the basement area and stored away from sight.

For years, members of the National Woman's Party and other women's groups would go to the capitol to clean the statue. Legislative attempts were made to return it to its rightful place in the rotunda to no avail. In 1959 the basement storage area was renovated, renamed the Crypt and opened to the public. The statue, minus its original inscription, was still there, with no attempt to identify the sculpted women or the tremendous things they had accomplished. However, now that this area was no longer a broom closet, the National Woman's Party would occasionally organize rallies and ceremonies at the base of the monument.

As I reminisce about that autumn day in 1993, I am amazed at our enthusiasm and innocence as we confidently prepared a list of the major tasks ahead. Our ultimate success was due, I'm sure, in large part to the talent and dedication of the women in that room that fateful day. I remember looking around the table at the members of my team.

Barbara Irvine was the founder and president of the Alice Paul Centennial Foundation, Moorestown, New Jersey. This organization has preserved Alice Paul's historic childhood home as a museum and leadership training center for women and girls around the country. Edith Mayo was curator and designer of the only two displays dedicated to women in the Museum of American History at the Smithsonian Institution in Washington, D.C. Maureen Savage was first vice president of the League of Women Voters of Cape May County, New Jersey, while working as an adjunct history professor at St. Elizabeth's College in Convent Station, New Jersey. Caroline Sparks, Ph.D., was founder and president of the Feminist Institute in Washington, D.C. Two other members were unable to attend the retreat, but were with us in spirit—Allie Hixson, Ph.D., a founder of the ERA Summit based in Washington, D.C., and Molly MacGregor, executive director and one of the founders of the National Women's History Project in Windsor, California.

Our Foremothers With Our Forefathers

I was serving as president of the League of Women Voters of Cape May County and was president and founder of the Cape Women's Resource Fund. Speaking for all of us as I added this project to our list of goals, I remarked, "It is time to have our foremothers with our forefathers." That phrase became our rallying cry. Little did we know that resistance to allowing these remarkable women to reside in the rotunda along with some of our nation's male leaders would prove to be as strong in the 1990s has it had been in the 1920s.

Plans for the three-day commemorative celebration continued during the next several months, with notices going into the organizational newsletters of women's organizations throughout the country along with encouraging suggestions for local and statewide observances as well. Interest began to grow. Lobbying efforts began on Capital Hill regarding the suffrage monument, with little interest or support in the early stages. Phone calls and letters began to come in from women's groups, and the National Women's History Project included our announcements in all their national mailings.

The board of directors of the National Woman's Party agreed to allow us to use office space in the lower level of their headquarters in the Sewall Belmont House, the formal home and office of Alice Paul. Interns were obtained through Caroline Sparks, who was now on staff at George Washington University. We were gearing up, with no outside funding for the hectic summer of 1995. Telephones with no hold buttons were donated; we used a slow but dependable fax. Our task force center resembled a local political campaign office of the 1950s.

That early spring, Karen Staser, a new resident of Alexandria, Virginia, was touring the capitol and chanced upon the suffrage statue in the crypt. Thinking it was unfinished, since there was no sign or inscription, she made a mental note to look into who the three women were and hurried on to the Sewall Belmont House, which would be only open for tours for another hour or so.

A brief description of the suffrage monument is warranted here. It is massive. The three suffragist leaders rising out of marble are the sculptor's portrayal of these courageous visionaries bringing women out of bondage. The marble base was intended to represent the fact that women once had few rights; they had no guardianship rights of their children, could not own property and could not vote, for example. Behind Lucretia Mott, Elizabeth Cady Stanton and Susan B. Anthony is a section of unfinished marble. This represents the women of the future who will work for equality and also that "women's work is never done." This part explains Karen's guess that the statue was a work in progress.

The next stop on Karen's exploration was the Sewall Belmont House, a national historical landmark and a jewel of Capitol Hill. She wandered into the wrong door, on the lower level, where she was greeted by one of our task force interns. Suzy informed Karen that the museum was upstairs. As Karen turned to leave, she saw a poster by the Feminist Institute regarding the statue. She exclaimed, "That's the unfinished statue I saw down in a corner in the Capitol Crypt!"

Suzy explained the 75th anniversary celebration and the lobbying efforts for the "Portrait Monument" to be returned to the capitol rotunda. Karen enthusiastically replied, "I want to volunteer to help with this project, and my husband works for Senator Ted Stevens, chair of the Senate Rules Committee. Perhaps he can talk to the Senator about the suffrage statue."

Karen was as good as her word. She contacted Caroline Sparks, saying she would help in any way we needed with the national events and that she had informed her husband of our attempt to return the statue to its rightful place by August 26, Women's Equality Day. Caroline was busy organizing the Suffragist March for August 26, obtaining permits, and getting approval for the historic route we would use. She met with Karen and Sherry Little, a staff member for the Senate Rules Committee. Sherry immediately became dedicated to the Statue Campaign and was from then on a staunch supporter and efficient liaison in the Senate.

At about this time I came to the D.C. area to spend the summer, coordinating the interns, handling inquiries from potential participants and the press, and keeping in touch with activities on the Hill.

In the meantime, Jeff Staser, Karen's husband, spoke with Senator Stevens. To our great fortune, a suffragist grandmother had raised the distinguished Senator. She had even taught him the suffragist rallying songs! He told Jeff to have the legislation prepared, a unanimous resolution, and he would see that it passed the Senate immediately. I have been told that Senator Stevens commented, "It is time the ladies come upstairs."

The resolution passed within that week in July and we were ecstatic! We thought we were half way there. By this time Karen and I had met and immediately bonded. We were much alike and enthusiastic about the unbelievable task before us. Undaunted and tenacious, we tackled the daily problems, working in intense heat and barely keeping our heads "above water." Thank goodness for Karen and the interns. I look back at those summer months and marvel at our fortitude. I was living in the Sewall Belmont House, where I could work day and night for our cause. Karen brought her two daughters in to help. Sara, 16, faxed and helped answer phones while Katie, the youngest, stuffed packets and put stamps on mailings.

Some conservative members of Congress met our efforts with mistrust. Still others demonstrated a complete lack of interest. (Sadly, many of these individuals were women.) Senator Stevens continued to speak up for us to his colleagues at every opportunity. When the resolution was brought to the floor, U.S. Representative Connie Morella spoke eloquently for the return of the monument to the rotunda. Other members of Congress certainly supported the statue move. However, House leadership, due to several misunderstandings, fought the move totally.

The three-day commemorative events began on August 25 with the suffrage monument still in the crypt, and we scheduled a historic rally in the crypt in front of the statue. Press coverage was extensive; hundreds of supporters joined us inside the capitol and out on the grounds. We vowed to continue our efforts to obtain legislation in the House and then joined nearly 10,000 people in the Suffragist March, taking the same path as our earlier suffrage foremothers in 1913.

Our three-day celebration was a success, with a memorable and educational seminar at the symposium planned and executed by Edith Mayo, a commemorative program sponsored by the National Archives, a Suffrage Stamp Ceremony hosted by the National Museum of Women in the Arts, and our Suffrage March. There was also a performance at the Ford's Theatre sponsored by the National Park Service, featuring Fred Morsell as Frederick Douglass, one of the first supporters of woman suffrage. At the conclusion of events we found ourselves exhausted but determined to continue our crusade to rescue the statue.

Karen and I cleared out of the Sewall Belmont House, and records were archived. I returned to my new home in Phoenix, Arizona. By this time, Karen had talked to me about her exciting concept of a National Museum of Women's History (NMWH). We had included a flyer regarding such a museum in our latest mailings to the public. I found myself thoroughly committed to Karen's ambitious undertaking—a museum dedicated to preserving, presenting and sharing a more comprehensive view of human history. Karen was proposing an institution designed to inspire girls, boys, men and women and counter 5,000 years of cultural stereotypes. What luck that such a visionary leader had wandered into our offices in 1995!

Setback on Capitol Hill

By October of that year, thanks to continued lobbying by individuals and women's groups throughout the country, as well as support from Senator John Warner, who had become chair of the Senate Rules Committee, the unanimous resolution was brought to the floor! If there is even one objection, this type of motion will not pass, which is exactly what happened. U.S. Representative Sue Myrick led the way and objected to spending any funds to move the statue with the current budget constraints. She, along with two other Congresswomen, expressed support for the statue, but not for spending any public funds. In response, Senator Warner sent word that he would personally guarantee private funding and urged the House to re-introduce the resolution. The answer was no. The resolution was killed. Immediately afterwards, a memorial bust for a man was approved, along with a $75,000 allocation of public funds, the same amount of money needed to move the suffrage statue. There were no objections.

Karen Staser by now was moving to incorporate the NMWH and I had agreed to serve with her as national co-chair of the "Woman Suffrage Statue Campaign" and to work with her in the development of NMWH. We refused to give up because we had already made more progress than ever before in the history of the statue. This statue campaign would be continued by NMWH as its first project.

Senator Warner, along with Sherry Little, now suggested that we schedule a press conference and announce that we would raise the funds for moving the monument. Since the holidays of 1995 were fast approaching, we agreed to schedule it on February 15, 1996, once again on Susan B. Anthony's birthday. Senator Warner agreed to participate. He and I spoke to hundreds of women from all major national women's organizations, along with women from the Federation of Republican Women and the Democratic National Committee and Congressional staff. We had ample news coverage and were on our way with a national grassroots campaign.

Notices were sent to all women's state organizations requesting $1 per member. The monies began to trickle in. We opened a bank account, spoke wherever persons would let us, wrote news releases and, in July 1996, had a major bipartisan fundraising reception at the National Museum of Women in the Arts. Several corporations helped underwrite the fundraiser and we were delighted with the huge and bipartisan participation.

In Arizona, a nine-year-old girl had read about the statue and began her own campaign to help. Arlys Endres spoke first to the state League of Women Voters. She was so captivating, she was asked to speak to many women's groups. She wrote to every member of Congress and the Senate and came to our July 1996 fundraiser, bringing along her parent and her brother David. The NMWH board of directors had approved travel allocation for this delightful family to come to Washington, D.C., to see the monument. All in all, Arlys raised more than $2,000 for the statue campaign. Her national recognition created human interest, which helped the campaign tremendously.

There were other dedicated individuals throughout the campaign. We heard from Girl Scouts, Boy Scouts, elderly women, men; people of all ages and all walks of life supported us. And the letters! We received beautiful letters of support, some so poignant, all expressing gratitude to the campaign and hope for our success. The groundswell was fantastic.

Later that summer, we received a call from Abbott Laboratories. I answered the phone and the spokesperson told me that the CEO had read about the statue and wanted to help. I was asked how much we still needed and informed her that we were $25,000 short of our goal. In a few days, Karen and I were told to come and pick up the check! We practically floated to the Metro and to the Washington office of Abbott Laboratories that wonderful summer day!

We had the money, but we were not over the hurdles yet. Back on Capitol Hill, a key congresswoman did not approve of the statue from an artistic point of view. Other members of Congress complained the women were too ugly, or just as frequently, that they were too old! Then a previously stated concern from the former capitol architect came up. He complained that the statue was too heavy, which proved unfounded when the issue was thoroughly reviewed by professional engineers.

Some people even suggested that we substitute statues of other women who appeared more attractive or contemporary, or that we attempt to satisfy other conflicting political agendas. Finally, the House leadership agreed to place the resolution on the floor once again.

This time it passed, due to the help of so many people and women's organizations, particularly the National Woman's Party and Business and Professional Women. The campaign succeeded with the help of individuals like Coline Jenkins Sahlin, great great granddaughter of Elizabeth Cady Stanton; Barbara Irvine; U.S. Representatives Connie Morella and Carolyn Maloney; Jeff Staser; Molly MacGregor; Jan DePlain; Shelly Heretyk; Sherry Little; as well as news media representatives and major donors like Abbott Laboratories.

Our NMWH trustees, Edie Mayo, Ann Stone and Joan Wages, also conducted noteworthy efforts, with weeks spent lobbying on the Hill and dedicated hours preparing letters and special mailings. And the National Museum of Women's History had concluded a successful and historic project. Teamwork and dedication were the keys.

The three-day effort to physically move the statue began on Mother's Day 1997. And we were allowed to watch. Karen, the NMWH trustees and other campaign friends spend the weekend in the capitol cheering the workers and making friends of the president of the restoration firm which handled this awesome task. Patricia Ghiglino, the president, and her husband, Reinaldo Lopez, a sculptor and foreman of the statue relocation, are now staunch supporters of the Museum. Patricia is the treasurer of the board of trustees and Reinaldo has sculpted our first artifact, a bust of Sojourner Truth, which has already been shown at the Women's Rights National Historical Park in Seneca Falls, New York.

The Rededication Ceremony for the statue was held in the U.S. Capitol Rotunda on June 26, 1997. For Karen, other members of our founding board of trustees, and me, the day marked the end of several years of dedication and hard work. We dedicated this time in our lives so that a generation of women and girls, along with their husbands and brothers, can now view the memorial in its rightful place—right beside many of the great men who have led our country.

I am capturing the inspiring story of the struggle to move the statue in a book. The plight and adventures of the statue in many ways parallel the Women's Movement, and there are many more important and interesting incidents to tell than I could include in this synopsis.

Women continue to face challenges to their freedom at home, in the workplace, and in the political arena. However, looking back on that amazing day in 1993, it is very satisfying to know that I was privileged to play a part in placing our foremothers with our forefathers. Finally, after 76 years, "the ladies have come upstairs."

I hope readers will join me in the continuing formation of the National Museum of Women's History and will visit our foremothers in their place of honor, the U.S. Capitol Rotunda.

Roselyn O'Connell

Roselyn O'Connell was elected president of the National Women's Political Caucus (NWPC) in July 1999 after 20 years as a Caucus member. The mission of the NWPC is to identify, recruit and train qualified women for elected and appointed offices.

Since moving to Arizona in 1984, Roselyn has provided leadership as state chair of the Arizona WPC and as chair of the Greater Phoenix chapter.

For several years she has been the director of public affairs at Planned Parenthood of Central and Northern Arizona, where she is responsible for public policy development, legislative affairs, advocacy and grassroots organizing. She is a graduate of Western Oregon State College.

She is married to her high school sweetheart, George O'Connell, and their grown family includes George's two daughters and Roselyn's three sons.

Question 81: Describe your participation in politics, if any.

My Commitment to Women in Politics

I remember seeing a picture of President Dwight D. Eisenhower on the front page of the *Sioux City* (Iowa) *Tribune* around the time I was eight or nine years old. It was one of those grainy black and white photos, and what I remember most was that he was with a number of other men (all who seemed quite old to me then) and they were wearing hats.

What I knew about politics then was what I gleaned from listening to supper-time conversation between my father, the staunch Roosevelt Democrat, and my mother, daughter of a devout Republican farmer who had nothing good to say about Roosevelt. I learned from those discussions that Democrats were for "the little guy" and Republicans were for "big business."

My mother, who yearned for nothing more than a peaceable family, did her best to deflect incoming anti-Republican flak. Most of the time she was pretty successful and, quite honestly, she did not come by political discussion easily. Occasionally, though, she rose to the bait and offered a half-hearted but truly aimed anti-Democrat verbal missile which escalated the discussion to a new dimension. Usually, however, the Democrats won out as the good guys and my father settled into his favorite chair in the front room knowing he'd won another round.

Things really got interesting when the two clans came together for birthday and anniversary parties. You could count on a least one good argument over which politician was good for the farmer and how bad (or good) things were going for the country. Miraculously, there were never any fist fights, and hard feelings were generally forgotten until the next family gathering. Besides, heated discussions over the best brand of farm implements (now there was a real pride of ownership issue) went on much longer and often included statements like "I wouldn't have a blankety-blank John Deere tractor if you gave it to me." The ultimate put-down for politicians went like this: "I wouldn't cross the street to see that blankety-blank." And so it went.

But getting back to the photo of President Eisenhower, I remember wondering if only men could be important enough to run the country. I don't remember anyone ever talking about women being elected to office. And in the '50s, in small-town America, very few people were thinking about women and elected office. It seemed like a remote possibility then to me, a very little girl who lived on a farm near a town with only 70 people, a general store, a barber shop, tavern, jail, church, school, and a grain elevator situated along the railroad tracks. In those days, there were small towns about every seven or so miles along the railroad line, with granaries to fill the box cars with the heartland's finest corn and oats.

Fertilized by political discussions, much as the young plants in my family's cornfields received doses of sun and rain, I began to understand the relationship between power and politics. It was very clear, even at that young age, that only men played in that arena.

But then Helen Hoenig became president of the high school student body, and the potential for other political achievements by females at last seemed real. I really wanted to run for a school office and work on student government and finally made it when I was a senior in high school. I've been running for leadership in political organizations ever since. Recently, I learned that people who serve in student government are very likely to run for public office eventually, a path I haven't taken yet. My job right now is to identify, recruit and train qualified women to run for office, a commitment I serve passionately, knowing that political equity is still a long ways off for women.

Just as I knew those many years ago that a political system without the equal participation of women is incomplete, so I know now that unless more women are elected, things will happen in the same old way. Until women began to be a part of the national dialogue about what is important to families, issues like child care, reproductive health care, and economic parity were discounted. It is only by getting women to the table that attention will be paid to the things that women care deeply about.

As president of the National Women's Political Caucus, I know there has been a great deal of progress in getting women elected and appointed to public office since my childhood. I've been committed for more than 20 years to the work of putting women in public office so that other little girls can see there is a place for them as leaders of this nation. And I hope that in my lifetime we will see a woman as president of the United States. A woman President on the front page of every newspaper. Some little girl will see that photo and understand that someday it could be her.

Barbara Mark Dreyfuss

Barbara Dreyfuss grew up in Minneapolis where she worked in retail sales and modeling and became a radiological technologist. There she acted in community theatre, chaired the first Minnesota Community Theatre Festival, and created Masketeers, a troupe taking plays to elementary schools through the National Council of Jewish Women.

She later entered the management world as a San Francisco branch manager and became a personal financial advisor. Currently retired from the world of finance, she is a sculptor and writer. Barbara recently published her first book of poetry, Kaleidoscope, *and is working on* Dying to Recover, *a book giving hope to people suffering from chronic fatigue immune dysfunction syndrome.*

Barbara is close to her three children and seven grandchildren, even though they live in various parts of the world. Since 1994 she has resided in Scottsdale, Arizona, with her husband, Norman Dreyfuss.

Question 84: What health issues have affected your life?

Fore!

After the 1961 pleasurable experience of the birth of my youngest son, I managed to avoid any confinement in hospitals until the late '60s. One memorable summer the family vacationed at a Northern Minnesota resort for a week of fun and relaxation, which included golf.

Though quite a novice at the sport, I enjoyed golf and played nine holes one morning with my customary loss of a ball in the rough. Evidently when I went into the brush to retrieve the ball, something bit me, something very small, as I never saw it, but my entire midriff itched. I scratched as delicately as I could, but it reddened and swelled to such an extreme that I could not wear anything but a muumuu. Muumuus, which were full and formless Hawaiian dresses, thankfully fell under the category of appropriate resort attire at the time. Every night I felt my midriff, hoping the swelling had gone down.

One night as I touched the swelling, I felt a hard lump about the size of an almond on the side of my left breast. I became alarmed, and I knew this had progressed far beyond a simple insect bite, so we packed and returned home immediately.

I called my doctor, who saw me that afternoon. After examining me, he called a surgeon, who saw me within the hour. The surgeon determined that I had to go right to the hospital for the surgical removal of the lump.

I said to Dr. David Gaviser, the surgeon, whom I had not known before this experience but who had an unusually warm and compassionate manner, "Please look carefully at my face. Now I want you to remember my face, and promise me you will speak with me before they put me out for the surgery. Promise that you will tell me my name and what procedure you are about to do."

"Of course I will do that for you, but why do you want me to do that?" he asked and laughed a little.

"I do not want to be confused with another patient whose right leg is to be amputated. Please promise me you'll do it."

"Of course I will," he agreed.

I went home, packed some hospital stay essentials, including of course my cosmetics, and checked in early the same evening.

Upon arrival at the hospital, I had to begin the ordeal of signing papers.

"Just sign here...and here," ordered the admittance clerk. One of those "heres" gave permission to remove my breast if the lump proved to be malignant.

I swallowed hard, took a few very deep breaths and signed the paper, believing that my life could be changing drastically. Fears entered my being, but I pushed them aside in order to take care of business.

"May I see my chart please?" I asked after the identification bracelet was placed on my wrist.

"What for? There's nothing in here."

"I just want to see my name and number."

"OK, but I don't get it. Here is your empty chart."

"Thank you." I compared the number on the chart with the one on my wrist I.D., and they were one number off. Self-fulfilling prophesy or just one of many mistakes that are made hourly in even the most efficiently run hospitals?

"See the number on the chart?" I pointed to my number.

"Uh huh."

"OK now will you please look at the number on the I.D. bracelet you just put on my wrist?"

"Oh, my God, how did that happen? Sorry."

She corrected the number on the I.D., and I went by wheelchair to the pre-operating room to be prepared for surgery. I asked them to delay the anesthetic until my doctor came in to see me. They promised that the initial injection would only relax me, would not put me out and that I would be able to communicate with my doctor.

Dr. Gaviser stopped to see me as the orderlies lifted me onto the gurney that would take me to the operating room. He took my hand. "You are Barbara Mark, and I am going to remove a lump beside your left breast. How do you feel?"

"Drowsy and thankful that you are the doctor doing the surgery. I trust you implicitly."

As I awoke from the surgery, I saw Dr. Gaviser's face. He was looking at me and smiling. "Is it gone or is it still there?" I asked, referring to my breast.

"It's there."

"Thank God."

I stayed overnight, and after breakfast a doctor I hadn't seen before came rushing into my room pushing a wheelchair. He turned out to be the pathologist who tested the now-absent lump.

The pathologist entered my room. "Good morning, Barbara. How are you feeling? Do you feel ill? Do you have any more lumps?"

"No to both questions," I answered, surprised at his disappointment.

"Are you sure?" he asked, expecting a reconsideration of my original response.

"Yes, I really am sure. I feel just fine, and there are no more lumps. Just the one."

"I brought a wheelchair. I'd like you to go to the lab with me. I want to show you something."

"Fine. I have nothing else to do but wait for lunch."

He helped me into the wheelchair and wheeled me down to the lab where he placed slides on the fluorescent viewer.

"This is a slide of Bubonic Plague."

Next to those slides, he placed the slides of the lump removed from me just hours before.

"This is the slide of the lymph node we removed from you."

"They look exactly the same," I observed.

"They are."

"What does that mean? I have Bubonic Plague? Oh, my God. Who's going to take care of my children? Oh no, please no. How did this happen?"

Before I became completely hysterical, he stopped me. "It means you are a very luck lady. He explained, "The venom of the rat flea that bit you was confined to the lymph node, to be trapped there, saving you from what could have been brutal effects of Bubonic Plague."

"Unbelievable. Oh, thank God. Thank God." Tears of joy poured down my cheeks. The visions of someone else raising my precious children disappeared, and I knew that I would appreciate every moment of every day much more than ever before.

I was elated, shocked, and so very, very grateful. He was thrilled to write my case up in the medical journal, and my young children were happy to have their mom back.

Linda Herold

Linda Herold, publisher of The Herold Report, *understands that women relate to one another in a unique way that benefits both the individual and the community.*

Coming to Phoenix, Arizona, in 1997, she was struck by the diversity and experience of women and the vitality of their business environment. She saw an opportunity to forge an alliance of women and to create a forum for the exchange of information and ideas. She established The Herold Report, *a quarterly subscription publication promoting local women, communicating useful information and encouraging interaction among colleagues in an atmosphere which benefits everyone. She also serves on numerous community boards.*

Question 90: What is your philosophy of life?

Living Fully Engaged

Reviewing my life from the vantage point of 50, there are three things that I know, without a doubt, have meaning for me—being fully engaged in contemporary life, pursuing beauty, and cultivating friendship.

It has always been important for me to know and experience the world of the moment. I am thrilled and fascinated by the things I have not known. I need to know, see, hear, feel, smell, and experience that which is presently going on around me, the essence of life in the moment. This is what makes me feel part of my era in history. My explorations take place in the here and now. Discovery is in the book or magazine I have never read, the art I have never seen, the room I have never been in, the place I have not visited, the person I haven't met, or the taste I have not savored. Being fully engaged, surprised, saddened, or perplexed with my world, yet completely a part of it, is how I live my life. I do not believe this is possible unless we relinquish the past. To be fully engaged in the present it is necessary to let go of the past. One cannot live in two worlds at once.

I am in awe of the beauty of the world. Beauty is a gift, and creating a beautiful life is both a challenge and a pleasure for me. The great thing about beauty is its abundance. Beauty has an inspirational effect on me. Almost daily a beautiful experience creates a watercolor concept in my mind. When time permits, I act on it, wishing only that I could devote the requisite energy to become an accomplished artist. I feel most complete when I have accomplished something beautifully, whether an environment, an event, a friendship, a painting or even a work project.

We are all connected, all part of the same universe. What we do and say impacts on others, both in obvious ways and in ways we will never know. I take great pleasure in friendship, sharing experiences, and reciprocating kindnesses. What I aspire to in relationships with others is grace. Grace is kindness, practiced spontaneously with suppleness and ease, tactfully, naturally, elegantly.

For me the love of life, love of people, and love of beauty developed over time. Having been an unloved child and young girl, I had to discover and decide for myself what my life would be like. Accepting that I was alone in the world early on forced me to look inside, always asking What do I want? How can I achieve it? It also made me feel compassion for others who feel the same loss of love. Being alone also afforded me the opportunity to pursue my interests unencumbered. My late teens and twenties were difficult and wonderful. This was when I explored the world great and small and came to "know" what I wanted in life. In my adult life, I have learned to ask the universe for interesting experiences and opportunities. With patience and perseverance, I have been rewarded with an ample share of love and joy, beauty and companionship.

Betty Morrison Carlton

Betty Morrison Carlton is a retired teacher, counselor, curriculum coordinator, staff developer and secondary school administrator in the Huntsville City School System in Huntsville, Alabama. She is actively involved in teaching with the continuing education program at the University of Alabama in Huntsville and has been using the Cameo Life Stories program with her adult students.

Betty has a B.A. in social science for the University of Alabama in Huntsville, and M.S. and A.A. degrees from Alabama A & M University. She has also done extensive graduate work at Vanderbilt University School of Education at Peabody in administration and supervision and is continuing her studies at Vanderbilt's Divinity School. She has four adult children and six grandchildren and is the primary care giver for her elderly mother.

Question 91: What comments do you have on the process of writing your life story?

Life's Journey of a Small-town Southern Lady

Dear Children and Grandchildren,

It is my hope that by detailing the journey I have traveled in life, it may help you gain faith and find meaning for the road you will travel. My wish is for you to examine the awesome world events in this century and become aware of the tremendous changes taking place which impacted my family's history. For you to be able to participate consciously in this cultural transformation of which we are so much a part at the end of this twentieth century, you will need to have a reasonably good idea of your own family's history.

By no means will I be able to give you much more than just what I experienced myself. Through your questioning and your curiosity to want to know more than I have included in this brief overview, I will be happy to try to fill in some of the missing pieces. You may ask or investigate other family members' stories. Each of our perceptions are based on our values and belief systems and each family member experiences differ.

During the time I made my spirituality a conscious endeavor, I learned I had acquired layers of stubborn misconceptions about myself, about parenting and about life. The problems we experienced as a family were primarily focused on the above. It has been difficult to unravel the twine that was wrapped so tightly around my heart and my mind. How I unraveled this twine—through the hard knocks of daily life, the conflicts within the family, and the hard work of self-examination—is just as much a part of my spiritual path as all the college and divinity courses I took, the in-depth study of the Bible and the other books I read, the meditations I did, or the spiritual retreats I took. I hope you will see this as you read my story.

Only a short part of my story is told in the first pages—the anxieties and fears caused by the depression years and the turbulence of the war, the specialness of being a girl and being loved by my extended family, the joys and delight of early childhood activities, the difficult times of life, the opportunities for developing skills and personal competence in high school, the struggles in marriage, and coming to grips with my fundamentalist schooling and lack of peace. All of these have laid the foundation for this work in progress of a small town southern girl.

Read my story with the love with which I offer it to you. The reason for the notebook is to allow the inclusion of each new phase of my life as it is completed. By the time I am 75 I hope to have concluded my story. When we have our time together at Christmas, I hope to be able to present to you the next phase of my life, which will describe the early years of the family and important pictures of this time. Enjoy!

"A Work in Progress"

When one reaches the seventh decade of her life, the natural response is to grow more philosophical about the future and to carefully evaluate the past. That is exactly what has happened to me. While writing the story of Mother's life in celebration of her ninetieth birthday, I was forced to reflect on my experiences as her daughter and as the middle child in our own family.

Several weeks of writing have given me a chance to be still and to integrate my thoughts and reflections on who I now am. I have had to examine my own struggle on the journey toward becoming a mature and authentic adult and how I have gone about developing my fullest potential as a human being. Now at this stage, I am still eager for continued intellectual, personal, and spiritual growth. There seems to be a drive within me to become all that I can be as I enter this new era of my life of becoming my mother's mother. I am eager to experience this period as fully and completely as possible.

Celebrating the 150th Anniversary of the Women's Rights Movement in Seneca Falls, New York, during July 16-19, 1998, was also a life-changing experience for me. The focus of Celebrate '98 was to honor the 150th birthday of the women's rights movement, to acknowledge the profound ways this has affected women today, and to chart a bright future for women and men all over the world. My impressions of this awesome event were staggering throughout this convention and especially as we signed Forum '98 Declaration of Sentiments, July 16, 1998. We pledged to shape a better world in the 21st century by upholding the principles of the Seneca Falls Declaration of Sentiments and to the Universal Declaration of Human Rights and to extend the promise of this movement to new generations.

Then as I read the First Declaration of Women's Rights and heard numerous women leaders speak, including Hillary Clinton, Betty Freidan and other famous women, I came to the realization that I had lived more than half of those 150 years and knew what it was like from my own life experiences to be denied equal rights in growing up and being female.

While at Seneca Falls I was given a document titled, "Everywoman's Story: A Memory Workbook." The contents were designed for women to write their own life story. The purpose was twofold. First, there is a tremendous need for women's experiences to be documented and archived for psychological research on women's experiences. There is a strong movement toward developing a new psychology of women since the only model for full personhood is based on the male. This model of life has been underdeveloped and distorted because it has been created by only one half of the human species.

The next purpose was to include every woman who would be willing to write about her life. I felt compelled to share my life story because of the personal and professional discriminations I have experienced in being a woman.

Another strong reason for wanting to document my life story is to share with my children, grandchildren, and other generations coming along. I think it is important to record how a woman's life was lived in the twentieth century and how each generation stands on the shoulders of those who have lived before and have paved the way for our equal rights and freedoms.

Hillary Clinton said it so well in her phenomenal keynote address to the participants, "The rights we enjoy today were not just given to us by some benevolent leaders. Women fought for these rights, were jailed for these rights, and even died for these rights. The Declaration of Sentiments—demanding that women be given the same rights as men—may have been written and adopted 150 years ago, but that shout heard 'round the world' can still be heard today as women of other nations are struggling for social, civil and political rights."

Even as I write these words, I am made conscious of all the effort, energy and struggles Elizabeth Cady Stanton, Susan B. Anthony, Lucretia Mott, Eleanor Roosevelt, and other great women have made to open the doors for us to go through.

This was the inspiration to encourage me to write my life story and how it was for a woman to grow up in the era between 1929-1999. I intend for this document to represent a critical analysis of my thoughts, experiences, activities, people, events and other factors which have been most influential in contributing to my maturity.

In writing about my life, I will also try to emphasize my personal, spiritual, intellectual and professional development along with a historical perspective of the times. I may leave out some significant events, but my plans are that this will only be a beginning story of my life and I will continue to update it as time and memory permits. ❦

Dear Reader,

It is 4 a.m In a few hours the eastern slope of Camelback Mountain will emerge from the gloom like a photograph in a darkroom. The first hikers will begin their zigzag ascent for a hawk's-eye view of the Valley of the Sun. I will assemble the final pages of this book and send them to the printer.

For now, the only light on the horizon is the glimmer of city lights draped across the floor of the Valley. Date palms, uplit in the landscaping, serve as nightlights in the boulevard out front. I sit in the glow of my computer screen and a small desk lamp.

Yesterday was Labor Day. Friends flocked to my kitchen throughout the day. The women gathered like midwives for a birth, and I found myself in the midst of a new ceremony, the delivery of a book.

Coffee brewed, the tea kettle whistled, the doorbell rang. Valerie slipped upstairs to my office to use the computer, Gerri arrived cradling a manuscript, Vangie hand-delivered her precious family photographs. The cats begged for attention, the pens hid beneath the paper, and the cream spilled. The fax beeped and last-minute changes slid into the tray from around the country. All day we worked on last-minute corrections and additions to this book, a labor of love.

When everyone had gone and Steve called from Wisconsin to ask how things were going, I told him, "Almost done." I gave myself one more morning for the book.

It feels like my last chance to speak to you. What have I forgotten? What would I most want you to remember? What are the best parting words I can offer?

In the morning light the shades of night will fall from my windows. My yellow house will shine like the sun itself. As it sweeps across our planet, sunlight will wake every woman to a different day—a day of work, of love, of joy or loss, and perhaps to a day of birth.

I remember waking one morning on Mariposa Street to a message spray-painted in big block letters on my neighbor's garage door. The message was for me. Inside her home, Charlotte Suhr was wrestling with cancer. With diet, prayer, the finest medical care available, and the devotion of her daughter, Kimberly, Charlotte was fighting for her life. She knew I had just received the news that I needed a hysterectomy to combat cervical cancer. She woke in the night and asked Kimberly to give me a message. She chose the most powerful words and the most powerful medium she could think of.

The garage door said, "Debbie, we will win! Love, Charlotte."

In the midst of her own pain, Charlotte was a ray of light in my life. In six words, she told me the story of her struggle and gave me courage.

We must make of ourselves a light. Our stories teach us to understand and to have compassion for ourselves and for one another. Our stories are our source of light. We are luminarias to those who walk beside us and those who follow in our steps. Let us tell our stories.

Love and light,

Deborah

SUGGESTED READING LIST

Aftel, Mandy. *The Story of Your Life: Becoming the Author of Your Experience.* New York: Fireside, 1996.

Brande, Dorothea. *Becoming a Writer.* 1934. Reprint. Los Angeles: Jeremy P. Tarcher, 1981.

Cameron, Julia. *The Artist's Way.* New York: Penguin Putnam Inc., 1992.

________. *The Right to Write.* New York: Penguin Putnam Inc., 1998.

________. *The Vein of Gold: A Journey to Your Creative Heart.* New York: G.P. Putnam's Sons, 1996.

Clive, John. *Not By Fact Alone: Essays on the Writing and Reading of History.* New York: Alfred A. Knopf, 1989.

Conway, Jill Ker. *In Her Own Words.* New York: Vintage Books, 1999.

_________. *True North.* New York: Alfred A. Knopf, 1994.

_________. *When Memory Speaks.* New York: Vintage Books, 1998.

_________. *Written by Herself, Autobiographies of American Women: An Anthology.* New York: Vintage Books, 1992.

Daniel, Lois. *How to Write Your Own Life Story: The Classic Guide for the Nonprofessional Writer.* Chicago: Chicago Review Press, 1997.

DeSalvo, Louise. *Writing as a Way of Healing.* New York: HarperCollins, 1999.

Evans, Sara M. *Born for Liberty: A History of Women in America.* New York: The Free Press, 1989.

Fletcher, William. *Recording Your Family History.* New York: Dodd, Mead & Company, 1983.

Flexner, Eleanor, Ellen Fitzpatrick. *Century of Struggle: The Woman's Rights Movement in the United States.* New York: Belknap Press, 1996.

Friedan, Betty. *The Fountain of Age.* New York: Simon & Schuster, 1993.

Hard, Margaret. *A Memory of Vermont.* New York: Harcourt, Brace & World, 1967.

Heilbrun, Carolyn G. *The Last Gift of Time: Life Beyond Sixty.* New York: The Dial Press, 1997.

__________. *Reinventing Womanhood.* New York: W. W Norton & Company, 1979.

__________. *Writing a Woman's Life.* New York: Ballantine Books, 1988.

Hilts, Philip J. *Memory's Ghost.* New York: Simon & Schuster, 1995.

Lerner, Gerda. *Why History Matters.* New York: Oxford University Press, 1997.

Metzger, Deena. *Writing for Your Life: A Guide and Companion to the Inner Worlds.* New York: HarperCollins Publishers, 1992.

Miedzian, Myriam and Alisa Malinovich. *Generations: A Century of Women Speak about Their Lives.* New York: The Atlantic Monthly Press, 1997.

Nelson, G. Lynn. Writing and Being: *Taking Back Our Lives Through the Power of Language.* San Diego: LuraMedia, Inc., 1994.

Neuman, Nancy M. *True to Ourselves: A Celebration of Women Making A Difference.* San Francisco: Jossey-Bass Publishers, 1998.

Oates, Stephen B. ed. *Biography as High Adventure: Life—Writers Speak on Their Art.* Amherst: The University of Massachusetts Press, 1986.

Polking, Kirk. *Writing Family Histories and Memoirs.* Cincinnati: Betterway Books, 1995.

Rainer, Tristine. *The New Diary.* Los Angeles: Jeremy T. Archer, 1978.

__________. *Your Life as Story: Writing the New Autobiography.* New York: G.P. Putnam's Sons, 1997.

Roorbach, Bill. *Writing Life Stories.* Cincinnati: Story Press, 1998.

Ross, Tom and Marilyn. *The Complete Guide to Self-Publishing.* Cincinnati: Writer's Digest Books, 1994.

Rupp, Rebecca. *Committed to Memory: How We Remember and Why We Forget.* New York: Crown Publisher, 1998.

Schacter, Daniel L. *Searching for Memory: the Brain, the Mind, the Past.* New York: BasicBooks, 1996.

Selling, Bernard. *Writing from Within: A Guide to Creativity and Life Story Writing.* Alameda: Hunter House Inc., Publishers: 1998

Steinem, Gloria. *Revolution From Within: A Book of Self-Esteem.* Boston: Little, Brown & Company, 1992.

Talese, Gay and Barbara Lounsberry. *The Literature of Reality: Writing Creative Nonfiction.* New York: HarperCollins College Publishers, 1996.

Tuchman, Barbara W. *Practicing History.* New York: Alfred A. Knopf, 1981.

Ueland, Brenda. *If You Want to Write: A Book about Art, Independence and Spirit.* Saint Paul: Graywolf Press, 1987

________. *Me.* St. Paul: North Central Publishing Company, 1083.

Underhill, Daryl Ott. *Every Woman Has a Story: Many Voice, Many Lessons, Many Lives.* New York: Warner Books, Inc., 1999.

Wakefield, Dan. *The Story of Your Life: Writing a Spiritual Autobiography.* Boston: Beacon Press, 1990.

Weatherford, Doris. *A History of the American Suffragist Movement.* Santa Barbara: ABC-CLIO, 1998.

Weingarten, Kathy. *The Mother's Voice.* New York: Harcourt Brace & Company, 1994.

Wilder, Laura Ingalls. *By the Shores of Silver Lake.* New York: HarperCollins Publishers, 1987.

Zinsser, William. *Inventing the Truth: The Art and Craft of Memoir.* Boston: Houghton Mifflin Company, 1987.

Website Addresses

International Women's Writing Guild	iwwg@iwwg.com
The STORIES Center	www.thestoriescenter.org
National Center for the Book	cfbook@loc.gov
National Museum of Women's History	www.nmwh.org
National Women's History Project	www.nwhp.org

ABOUT THE AUTHOR

Deborah was born in 1952 and raised in Sioux Falls, South Dakota. She graduated from Augustana College with a major in English and completed her graduate course work at the University of Wisconsin-Madison School of Journalism and Mass Communication.

After a 15-year career in public relations, she served as executive director of the Arizona Center for the Book, an affiliate of the National Center for the Book at the Library of Congress.

She is married to Steve Linzer and has two daughters, Maren and Jennie Swanson, and a stepson, Scott Linzer. They live in Paradise Valley, Arizona.

Deborah created the Cameo Life Stories program to accelerate the pace of progress for women through the sharing of women's histories. Response from women at the many workshops Deborah has led convinced her to write *Cameo Life Stories Writing Guide for Everywoman: Penning Your Portrait in Words.* In addition, Deborah established the nonprofit STORIES Center to carry forward the task of collecting and preserving the record of individual contributions to society.

Give the Gift of *Cameo Life Stories Writing Guide for Everywoman* to your loved ones and friends!

Check your local bookstore or order here. Call 1-800-883-2436 for more information on discounts or shipping and handling charges for 3 or more items.

Please indicate which items you wish to order and send with your check to The STORIES Center, P.O. Box 9608, Scottsdale, AZ 85252-3608.

_____ Copy(ies) of *Cameo Life Stories Writing Guide for Everywoman* at $14.95 plus $4.95 shipping for a total of $19.90 per book. My total is: $ __________

_____ Set(s) of both the *Cameo Life Stories Writing Guide for Everywoman* and the *Cameo Life Stories Workbook* for $34 (includes shipping). My total is: $ __________

_____ Gift set(s) including the *Cameo Life Stories Writing Guide for Everywoman*, the *Cameo Life Stories Workbook*, with a set of loose-leaf binder divider pages, a lovely cameo pin, and a pen to encourage your loved ones to begin recording their life stories right away. Gift wrapped with gift enclosure. $45 per set (includes shipping). My total is: $ __________

_____ Membership as a Friend of The STORIES Center, a nonprofit organization. Support Cameo Life Stories and receive a subscription to the *Story Times* newsletter at $25 per year. My total for membership is: $ __________

My check or money order for the total amount of $ __________ is enclosed.

My Name: ______________________________

Address: ______________________________

City: ____________________ State: ________ Zip: ________

Send my gift selection ☐ Book ☐ Book Set ☐ Gift Set ☐ Membership to:

Name: ______________________________

Address: ______________________________

City: ____________________ State: ________ Zip: ________

Gift card to read: ______________________________